ORIGEN

PRAYER

EXHORTATION TO MARTYRDOM

ANCIENT CHRISTIAN WRITERS

THE WORKS OF THE FATHERS IN TRANSLATION

EDITED BY

JOHANNES QUASTEN, S. T. D.
Catholic University of America
Washington, D. C.

JOSEPH C. PLUMPE, Ph. D.
Pontifical College Josephinum
Worthington, O.

No. 19

ORIGEN

PRAYER

EXHORTATION TO MARTYRDOM

TRANSLATED AND ANNOTATED

BY

JOHN J. O'MEARA

M. A., D. PHIL. (OXON)

*Professor of Latin at University College
Dublin, Ireland*

NEWMAN PRESS

New York, N.Y./Ramsey, N.J.

Nihil Obstat:

J. Quasten
Cens. Dep.

Imprimatur:

Patricius A. O'Boyle, D.D.
Archiep. Washingtonen.
die 10 Dec 1953

Library of Congress
Catalog Card Number: 78-62467

ISBN: 0-8091-0256-0

PUBLISHED BY PAULIST PRESS
Editorial Office: 1865 Broadway, New York, N.Y. 10023
Business Office: 545 Island Road, Ramsey, N.J. 07446

PRINTED AND BOUND IN THE UNITED STATES OF AMERICA

CONTENTS

ORIGEN

PRAYER

EXHORTATION TO MARTYRDOM

INTRODUCTION

1. *The Life and Work of Origen*

As neither of the works in this volume is the first or most important of the writings of Origen, a bare outline of the author's career will suffice.

He was born in Egypt, probably at Alexandria, about 185 A. D. of parents for whom the ideals and practice of Christianity were the only concern in life. Accordingly he was baptized at an early age and soon received in addition to the ordinary schooling of the time a special direction towards the study of the Bible which made an all-pervading impression on him throughout his life. When he was seventeen years of age, in 202 A. D., his father Leonidas suffered martyrdom under Septimius Severus—a fate, or rather vocation, which Origen himself did his best to achieve and for which he always thirsted. In the meantime, however, he became responsible for the support of his mother and six younger brothers. At first a wealthy woman came to their help; but shortly Origen was himself able to maintain his family with the earnings from his profession as a teacher.

About the year 203 he was invited to take charge at Alexandria of a catechetical school for elementary instruction in the rudiments of Christianity.[1] With characteristic zeal and impetuosity he not only gave up immediately his secular teaching, but also sold all his secular books and devoted himself forthwith to a most intense study of Scripture and the instruction of such as sought his aid. Since in the circumstances to become a Christian was to court death, his instruction took on the character of a preparation for martyrdom. His own life at this time was one of unremitting toil, danger, and austerity—an austerity too great (as later he was to admit), for he acted literally on the words of the Gospel: *There are eunuchs who have made themselves eunuchs for the kingdom of heaven.*[2]

His school developed to such an extent that he found it necessary about 215 A. D. to assign the elementary work to his pupil Heraclas and embark upon advanced teaching himself. This involved him in the study of pagan authors at the highest level, and soon pagans as well as Christians were flocking to him for instruction, whether in rhetoric, philosophy, or Scriptural exegesis. His presence also was in great demand everywhere, and he made numerous journeys at this period, to Rome, to visit the Governor of Arabia, and even to see the Emperor's mother, Julia Mamaea, at Antioch. He began, too, with the encouragement and generous material help of his friend and convert from Valentinianism, Ambrose,[3] to publish exegetical works—the first five books of his *Commentary on St. John*, the first eight books of his *Commentary on Genesis* (no longer extant), his *Commentary on the First Twenty-five Psalms* (of which only fragments survive), and his most important single work, the theological treatise *De Principiis*.

Suddenly all this work was rudely interrupted. Origen, a layman, had a specific function in the Church of that time—to teach. He was a *didaskalos*.[4] The office of the priest on the other hand was to administer the sacraments. A certain rivalry existed therefore between the priests and the *didaskaloi*, which disappeared only when both functions were united in the office of the priest. This kind of rivalry must have been growing between Origen and his bishop, Demetrius. It became aggravated when, in the course of a visit to Caesarea, Origen, at the express invitation of the local bishops and in full accordance with the local custom, preached to a congregation in the church. When, however, in 230 A. D. Origen accepted ordination to the priesthood in Palestine, outside his bishop's jurisdiction and without his permission, Demetrius called a synod and expelled him from the church of Alexandria. The bishops of Jerusalem and Caesarea were happy to receive him, and for the rest of his days he continued at Caesarea the work that he had begun at Alexandria.

It was during this later period of his life that he wrote both the treatise on *Prayer* and the *Exhortation to Martyrdom*. In addition he wrote, among other works, the *Hexapla*, embodying his lifelong efforts to establish a critical text of the Old Testament, and the celebrated Christian apology, the *Contra Celsum*. He was also in communication with many of the world's notabilities, including the emperor, Philip of Arabia. But his chief occupation during all this time was the almost daily exposition of Scripture in the church of Caesarea. His words were taken down and published as *Homilies*, a great number of which have come down to us in Latin translations. For him the words of Scripture were living in the fullest sense: they spoke to him who attuned himself to their message. Hence to preach was for him to pray aloud—to hold himself sensitive to the inspiration of the Word, and to pass on that inspiration to his hearers.

Origen died at Tyre in 253 A. D. shortly after the persecution of Decius who became emperor in 249 A. D. Although we do not know if his great desire to be a martyr was realized, we do know that he suffered most severely in the persecution.

He was a man of such zeal for God and His Church; so dead to the things of this world and so alive to the things of the spirit; so completely absorbed in the study of the Scriptures, that he was sometimes guilty of indiscretion; often tended to underrate the relative value of material things; and too often exaggerated the importance of the word of Scripture at the expense of reality. This is seen, for example, in the treatise on *Prayer* in his treatment of the petition: *Give us this day our supersubstantial bread.*[5] Although he does clearly say, as elsewhere, that the Eucharist is truly the Word of God and the proper nourishment for our souls, he nevertheless, again as elsewhere, seems to attach greater importance to the food for our souls which is the word of Holy Scripture. It is seen also in his insistence that the disposition of the person administering or receiving a sacrament is relatively of very great importance for the efficacy of the sacrament itself.[6] These ideas derive partly from his office of *didaskalos*, but to a great extent also from his too ardent spirit.

It must not be thought that Origen was a disloyal son of the Church. Although his errors were attacked again and again and solemnly condemned especially by the Fifth Oecumenical Council at Constantinople in 553, Origen himself was never formally declared to be a heretic. It is true that he seems sometimes to subordinate the Second to the First Person of the Trinity,[7] and gives expression to other dangerous doctrines, such as the pre-existence of the soul,[8] metempsychosis[9] (the theory of a cycle of existences) and *apocatastasis*[10] (the view that all, even Satan, will in the end be saved). It must be remembered, however, in the first place, that by intention, practice, and profession he was always a most loyal son of the Church,[11] and secondly that he lived at a time when Church doctrine was in the course of being defined: indeed he more than anyone of his time helped towards its definition. Hence there has always been sympathy for him and it has been well said that "there has been no truly great man in the Church who did not love him a little." [12] Among such men were St. Jerome, who said that Origen was "a teacher of the Church second only to the Apostle," [13] and Erasmus who declared that one page of Origen taught him more Christian philosophy than ten of Augustine.[14] In recent times there has been a notable revival of interest in this single-minded and generous man, who united in himself at once great industry, great genius, and even greater sanctity.

The question as to Origen's relations with Neo-Platonism hardly comes up for discussion in connection with the works in this volume. It will be sufficient to say here that the present writer does not accept as *proved* the thesis of R. Cadiou in his *La jeunesse d'Origène* (Paris 1935), as to the identity of our author with the Origen of the *Life of Plotinus* by Porphyry. The presence of Neo-Platonic ideas can easily be accounted for without the supposition of such an identity.[15]

Our ancient sources of information on Origen's life are the sixth book of Eusebius' *Ecclesiastical History;* the first book of Eusebius' and Pamphilus' *Apology* for Origen, known to us in Rufinus' Latin translation; and finally a tribute to his master by Gregory of Neo-Caesarea.[16] Apart from the usual reference books and encyclopedias, there is a considerable amount of modern literature dealing with Origen and his works.[17] Perhaps the most helpful is the study by J. Daniélou, *Origène* (Paris 1948).

2. *The Treatise on Prayer*

For long Origen was studied for his philosophical and theological ideas mainly. Recently, however, much work has been done to investigate his spirituality.[18] Of the treatise on *Prayer* Westcott has written: "No writing of Origen is more free from his characteristic faults, or more full of beautiful thoughts." [19] It is not merely a treatise on prayer; it is a prayer itself. For the spirit of Origen which, as Erasmus says, is everywhere aflame,[20] is burning here with such intensity as to make it impossible for the reader to remain untouched. A glance at the Table of Contents will tell him of the topics treated; but he must read the text itself to feel its power and the irresistible charm of Origen's use of Holy Writ.

The work was composed, probably about the year 233 or 234,[21] as a reply to questions raised by his friend and patron, the deacon Ambrose, to whom, with Tatiana,[22] it is dedicated.

It has, apart from introduction and epilogue, three main sections dealing with general problems in connection with prayer, a commentary on the Lord's Prayer,[23] and finally some supplementary points for the one who is to pray. The approach is, as usual in Origen, Scriptural. In the Epilogue he says that he has "examined . . . . the problem of prayer and the question of prayer *as found in the Gospels, and especially in the Gospel according to Matthew.*" [24] The reader must then be prepared to follow Origen through the closely-woven pattern of quotations from the Scriptures which largely constitutes the work.[25] This requires a prayerful disposition such as Origen himself recommends, and the minimum of distraction from outside.

The same general treatment of prayer is to be seen in the *De Oratione* of Tertullian (a work which Origen may have consulted),[26] the *De Oratione* of St. Gregory of Nyssa, and the *De Sacramentis* of St. Ambrose. Origen's treatise was but one of the first of a long series devoted to the subject of prayer in general and the Lord's Prayer in particular—but it left its mark on those that were to follow.[27]

There is one section in Origen's treatise which demands special attention. Throughout the entire tract he stresses the position of Christ as our high priest and intercessor to such a degree that several passages may be quite readily understood in a subordinationist sense. Particularly striking are chapters 14–16. In 14, taking his cue from 1 Timothy 2.1, he divides prayer into four kinds: *supplication, prayer proper, intercession,* and *thanksgiving*. All of these, save the second, he states, may be directed to Christ as well as to God the Father. But prayer proper, προσευχή, defined by him as that "offered in conjunction with praise of God by one who asks in a more solemn manner for greater things"—and worshipful prayer in the sense of divine *adoration* is evidently meant—must be addressed to the Father alone (15 f.). In support of this he says that one "may never pray to anything generated—not even to Christ, but only to God and the Father of all, to whom even Our Saviour Himself prayed . . . and teaches us to pray," and who has appointed the Saviour as our high priest and intercessor. This theory did not find adoption by any of the Fathers. In fact, the earliest ecclesiastical writers testify to private prayer directed to Jesus [28] and to hymns sung to Him.[29] Further, Origen contradicts himself, for he inserts in his homilies praises and prayers to Christ,[30] and elsewhere in his works defends the adoration of Christ against the objection of polytheism. There is the possibility, however, that Origen thinks of solemn or liturgical prayer only, especially since the treatise is addressed to a deacon. Perhaps Origen had in mind to justify the liturgical custom of praying through Christ to the Father. If this is the case, his reasoning cannot be called very fortunate or convincing, although it must be admitted that the liturgical doxology used in his time, "Glory be to the Father through the Son . . . ," pointed to Christ as the mediator of our prayer rather than as its object.[31]

3. *The Exhortation to Martyrdom*

This treatise was composed about 235 A. D. in order to provide solace for Origen's great friend and patron, Ambrose, and the presbyter, Protoctetus,[32] both of whom had been thrown into prison during the persecution of Maximin Thrax. It is, therefore, a most sincere and moving document—all the more so since Origen had neither time nor inclination to do more than put together quickly the considerations that might help his friends in their hour of trial.

The title itself, it will be well to note here, contains two words of unusual interest. As attested by the one manuscript (*Parisinus*) that bears a title, and by the thirteenth-century church historian Nicephorus Callistus, the Greek superscription reads: Εἰς μαρτύριον προτρεπτικός. Regarding the last word of the title, προτρεπτικός (supply λόγος): the "protreptic" was a tract, with a long tradition, embodying an "exhortation"—usually to philosophy—addressed nominally to some friend or acquaintance of the author, but often meant for a wider public.[33] The word μαρτύριον (μαρτυρέω, μαρτυρία, μάρτυς, etc.), adopted into Latin as *martyrium*, is originally and properly a legal term: it is "testimony," a "witnessing" to facts coming within the pale of law. In a more general sense it is testimony offered in support of any fact or truth or supposition. In earliest Christianity St. Paul calls the teaching of the Gospels "the *testimony* (μαρτύριον) of Christ." [34] The concept of μαρτύριον as bearing public "witness" to Christ and Christianity through trial and suffering, and the further concept of μαρτύριον as "witness" or "testimony" perfected and consummated by the act of dying a violent death for one's Christian convictions—in our sense of "martyrdom"—were readily suggested by the Old Testament examples of the heroic Eleazar and the Machabean brothers and adopted early in that technical meaning: see, for instance, *The Martyrdom of Polycarp*, a report of St. Polycarp's martyrdom sent by the church of Smyrna in 155 or 156 A. D. to that of Philomelium in Asia Minor. [35] In the present treatise Origen employs the word in this special Christian signification, of bearing witness to, and dying for, Christ. Returning to the title, we observe that the ancient literary testimony leaves out the genre description "protreptic" entirely and refers to the work only as Περὶ μαρτυρίου— *On Martyrdom:* thus Eusebius, Pamphilus, Jerome, and later authors. [36] For the present translation I have regarded the older manuscript tradition more reliable, and so continue also the practice of modern editors and translators of using the longer title—*Exhortation to Martyrdom*.

Apart from the fact that this treatise is of great historical value as a first-class source for the persecution of Maximin, it remains an important document of Origen's own conviction and courage, his faith and his religious loyalty. It reveals the hopes and fears of the Egyptian Christians in the first half of the third century. It is more than a private communication to his two friends, as is evident especially from sections 45 and 46 which refute certain liberal opinions regarding idolatry. Such opinions probably existed in some Christian circles. Thus the tract is intended to clarify the situation, combat confusion, and encourage depressed and wavering minds.

The work consists of seven parts. The first comprises sections 1-5 and exhorts to martyrdom; the second, sections 6-10, contains a severe warning against idolatry and apostasy; the third, sections 11-21, admonishes the Christian to bear his cross with Christ in unflinching perseverance; the fourth, sections 22-27, refers to the brilliant examples of martyrdom in the Second Book of the Machabees; the fifth, sections 28-44, deals with the necessity, essence, and different kinds of martyrdom; the sixth, sections 45-46, demonstrates by way of digression the criminal character of idolatry; and the seventh, sections 47-50, contains renewed exhortations to steadfastness in times of tribulation.

The ideas in this treatise have much in common with Tertullian's *Ad martyres* and *De fuga in persecutione*, with Cyprian's *De lapsis* and Pseudo-Cyprian's *De laude martyrii*. Many passages, too, remind one strongly of the Acts of the Martyrs, as, for instance, when Origen mentions expressly (section 36) the granting of exceptional graces to Christians who submit to suffering and torture in witness of their Faith.

* * *

The critical text followed for both works, except in the few places where I indicate disagreement, is that of Paul Koetschau, *Origenes Werke*, in Die griechischen christ-

lichen Schriftsteller (Leipzig 1899): 1.1–47 (*Exhort.*) and
2.295–403 (*De or.*), to which I refer the reader for all
questions dealing with manuscripts. I have, of course,
taken account of Koetschau's later readings as indicated by
him in his German translation, *Des Origenes ausgewählte
Schriften* I, in Bibliothek der Kirchenväter 48 (Munich
1926).[37] Apart from Koetschau's translation, I have consulted also the translations of one or both works of G.
Bardy, *Origène: De la prière; Exhortation au martyre*
(Paris 1932); H. U. Meyboom, *Origenes VI*, in Oud-
Christelijke Geschriften 38 (Leyden 1926) 1–176; and at
a stage too late to be of any help, that of E. J. Jay, *Origen's
Treatise on Prayer* (London 1954). In rendering the
texts of Scripture as given by Origen, I have always given
the Douay version, where it is a possible version; frequently, however, I have translated directly, especially as
Origen was using the Septuagint.

PRAYER
(Περὶ εὐχῆς)

INTRODUCTION

The grace of God, immense and beyond measure, showered by Him on men through Jesus Christ, the minister to us of this superabundant grace, and through the co-operation of the Spirit,[1] makes possible through His will things which are to our rational and mortal nature impossible. For they are very great, and beyond man's compass, and far transcend our mortal condition. It is impossible, for example, for human nature to acquire wisdom by which all things were made (for according to David, God *has made all things in wisdom*);[2] yet from being impossible it becomes possible through Our Lord Jesus Christ, *who of God is made unto us wisdom and justice and sanctification and redemption.*[3] *For who among men is he that can know the counsel of God? Or who can think what the will of God is? For the thoughts of mortal men are fearful, and our counsels uncertain. For the corruptible body is a load upon the soul:* and *the earthly habitation presseth down the mind that museth upon many things. And hardly do we guess aright at things that are upon the earth. But the things that are in heaven, who shall search out?*[4] And who will deny that it is impossible for men to search out *the things that are in heaven?* Yet this impossibility becomes possible through the overflowing grace of God. For he that was *caught up to the third heaven* probably did search out the things that are in the three heavens, since

15

he heard *secret words which it was not granted to man to utter.*[5] And who can say that it is possible for man *to know the mind of the Lord?*[6] Yet even this is granted by God through Christ. . . .[7]

When He makes known to them the will[8] of their lord, He no longer wishes to be their *lord*, but becomes the *friend* of those whose lord He formerly was. Just as *no man knoweth the things of a man but the spirit of a man that is in him, so the things also that are of God no man* knoweth *but the Spirit of God.*[9] And if *no man knoweth the things that are of God, but the Spirit of God*, it is impossible for man to know *the things that are of God.* But note well how this becomes possible: *Now we have received*, it is said, *not the spirit of this world, but the Spirit that is of God: that we may know the things that are given us from God. Which things also we speak: not in the learned words of human wisdom, but in the doctrine of the Spirit.*[10]

CHAPTER 2

But probably you, my most pious and industrious Ambrose,[11] and you, Tatiana,[12] most modest and valiant lady, (and I pray that as *it had ceased to be with Sara after the manner of women*,[13] so it may have ceased to be with you), are puzzled why, when we are speaking of prayer, mention has been made in the Introduction about things impossible for men becoming possible through God's grace. The reason is that I feel that to give any accurate and reverent explanation of prayer—of what it is to be about, of how one should pray, how one should speak to God in prayer, and what times are most suitable for prayer—this is one of the things that, considering our infirmity, are impossible. . . .[14]

He (St. Paul) *forbears lest, because of the greatness of the revelations, any man should think* of him *above that which he seeth in him or any thing he heareth from him,*[15] and agrees that he does not know *how he should pray.* For he says: *we know not what we should pray for as we ought.*[16] It is essential, then, not only to pray, but to pray as one ought, and to pray for what one ought. For the understanding of what we ought to pray for is ineffective unless we know also how we ought to pray. And what use is it to us to know how to pray if we do not know what to pray for?

2.   About these two points: by "what one ought to pray for," I mean the *words* of the prayer, and by "how one ought to pray" I mean the *attitude* of him who is praying.

Here, first, is an example of *what* one ought to pray for: "Ask for what is great, and what is small shall be added unto you"; [17] and "ask the things of heaven, and the things of earth shall be added unto you"; [18] and, *pray for them that calumniate you;* [19] and, *pray ye therefore the Lord of the harvest, that He send forth labourers into His harvest;* [20] and, *pray lest ye enter into temptation;* [21] and, *pray that your flight be not in the winter or on the sabbath;* [22] and, *when you are praying, speak not much,*[23] and so on.

And as for *how* one ought to pray: *I will therefore that men pray in every place, lifting up pure hands, without anger and contention. In like manner, women also in decent apparel: adorning themselves with modesty and sobriety, not with plaited hair, or gold, or pearls, or costly attire; but as it becometh women professing godliness, with good works.*[24]   And here is another lesson as to *how* one ought to pray: *If therefore thou offer thy gift at the altar, and there thou remember that thy brother hath any thing against thee; leave there thy offering before the altar and go first to be reconciled to thy brother; and then coming thou shalt offer thy gift.*[25]   Indeed, what greater gift could be offered to God by a rational being than a prayer of fragrant [26] words offered by one whose conscience is free from the stench of sin?   And a further example of *how* one ought to pray is: *Defraud not one another, except, perhaps, by consent, for a time, that you may give yourselves to prayer: and return together again, lest Satan exult over your incontinency.*[27]   Accordingly one does not pray as one ought unless one performs the duty of the ineffable mysteries of marriage also with reverence, with restraint, and without passion.   In this way the *consent* of which we speak here does away with the discord of passion, allays incontinence, and robs Satan of all joy at our expense.   In addition there is this lesson as to *how* one ought to pray: *And when you shall stand to pray, forgive, if you have aught against any man;*[28] and these words of Paul, *Every man praying or prophesying with his head covered disgraceth his head.   But every woman praying or prophesying with her head not covered disgraceth her head,*[29] are relevant on the question of *how* one ought to pray.

3.   Paul knew all this and could have multiplied such instances from the Law and the Prophets and the plentitude of the Gospel, adding variations in the exposition of

each instance. Yet seeing after all this how far off he was from knowing *what* he ought to pray for and *how* he ought to pray, from a feeling which was both modest and in no way feigned he says: *We know not what we should pray for as we ought.*[30] And to what he has said, he adds how the deficiency can be made good in the case of one who, wanting this knowledge, makes an effort to make himself worthy of having this want supplied in him. For he says that *the Spirit Himself intercedeth mightily* with God for us *with unspeakable groanings. And He that searcheth the hearts knoweth what the Spirit desireth: because He intercedeth for the saints according to God.*[31] For the Spirit that in the hearts of the blessed cries: *Abba, Father,*[32] knows well that the groans in the *earthly habitation* are likely only to *press down upon*[33] them that have fallen or strayed from the way. And in His great love and sympathy for men, hearing our sighs, He *intercedeth mightily* with God *with unspeakable groanings.* Seeing in His wisdom that our soul has been *humbled down to the dust,*[34] and imprisoned in *the body of our lowness,*[35] He does not *intercede mightily* with God with ordinary groanings, but with certain *unspeakable groanings,* that are related to those *secret words which it is not granted to man to utter.*[36] And this Spirit, not content with interceding with God, makes the intercession more urgent and *intercedeth mightily.* I believe that He does this in the case of them that "overcome gloriously," as Paul had when he says: *But in all these things we overcome gloriously.*[37] It is probable that the Spirit only "intercedes" for them that are not great enough to "overcome gloriously," nor yet such as to be beaten, but can merely "overcome."[38]

4. Akin to the text, *We know not what we should*

pray for as we ought; but the Spirit Himself intercedeth mightily with God for us with unspeakable groanings, is this other: *I will pray with the Spirit, I will pray also with the understanding. I will sing with the Spirit, I will sing also with the understanding.*[39] Our understanding cannot pray if the Spirit has not, as it were in its hearing, prayed before it. In the same way it cannot sing nor hymn the Father in Christ with due rhythm and melody, time and harmony, unless *the Spirit* that *searcheth all things, yea, the deep things of God,*[40] first has praised and hymned Him whose *deep things* He has searched and, as He is fully able, understood. It is my belief that one of the disciples of Jesus, perceiving the weakness of man, who did not know how one ought to pray, realized this especially when he heard the great and profound words spoken by the Saviour in His prayer to the Father; and so he said to the Lord when He had finished praying: *Lord, teach us to pray, as John also taught his disciples.* The full sequence of the text is as follows: *And it came to pass that as He was in a certain place praying, when He ceased, one of His disciples said to Him: Lord, teach us to pray, as John also taught his disciples. . . .*[41]

Can it be then that one who was brought up on the teachings of the Law and the utterances of the Prophets and had frequented the synagogues, had no idea whatever how to pray until he saw the Lord praying *in a certain place?* That would be a strange assertion indeed. He used to pray, obviously, after the fashion of the Jews; but he saw clearly that he needed a greater understanding of how one ought to pray. And what did John teach his disciples about prayer when they *went out to him from Jerusalem and all Judea and all the country about*[42] to be baptized? Being *more than a prophet*,[43] he must have known something about prayer which, probably, he imparted not to all that were being baptized, but only in secret to those who in addition to being baptized became his disciples.

5. Such prayers being truly spiritual—since the Spirit prays in the heart of the saints—have been written down in the Scriptures, and are full of ineffable and wonderful teaching. For example, in the First Book of Kings there is part of the prayer of Anna (for the whole prayer, *as she multiplied prayers before the Lord·*speaking *in her heart*,[44] was not written). In the Psalms, Psalm 16 is inscribed: "A Prayer of David"; Psalm 89: "A Prayer of Moses, a man of God"; and Psalm 101: "A Prayer of a poor man, when he was anxious, and poured out his supplication before the Lord." These prayers, since they are prayers truly composed and spoken by the Spirit, are full of teachings of the wisdom of God, so that one can say of what is taught in them: *Who is wise, and he shall understand these things? And prudent, and he shall know these things?* [45]

6. Since then to treat of prayer is such a great task that one needs for it the illumination of the Father, the instruction of the *first-born* [46] Word Himself, and the operation of the Spirit, in order to understand and speak as one ought of such a problem, I beseech the Spirit—imploring Him as a man (for I myself make no claim whatever of being able to pray) before I begin to speak of prayer—that we may be given to speak fully and spiritually and may explain the prayers recorded in the Gospels. So let us now begin our discussion on prayer.

PART I: PRAYER IN GENERAL

CHAPTER 3

THE TWO USES OF THE TERM "PRAYER"

As far as I can discover, I find that the first time the term "prayer" is used is when Jacob, fleeing from the wrath of his brother Esau, went to Mesopotamia, in compliance with the instructions of Isaac and Rebecca.[47] The text is as follows: *And he made a prayer saying: If God shall be with me, and shall keep me in the way by which I walk, and shall give me bread to eat, and raiment to put on, and I shall return prosperously to my father's house: the Lord shall be my God. And this stone, which I have set up for a title, shall be called the house of God: and of all things that Thou shalt give to me, I will offer tithes to Thee. . . .*[48]

2.   One should also observe that the term "prayer," which often differs in meaning from "invocation," is here employed in the case of one who promises in a vow to do certain things if God grants him certain other things.[49] But the term is also used in the ordinary way. For example, we found this to be so in Exodus after the description of the plague of the frogs, which was the second of the ten plagues . . . :[50] *But Pharao called Moses and Aaron and said to them: Pray ye to the Lord on my account to take away the frogs from me and my people; and I will let the people go to sacrifice to the Lord.*[51] If anyone finds it difficult to see that when Pharao employs the

word "prayer" the habitual meaning of "prayer" is conveyed in addition to the former meaning, he should read
what follows, namely: *And Moses said to Pharao: Set me a
time when I shall pray for thee, and for thy servants, and
for thy people, that the frogs may be driven away from
thee and from thy house and from thy people, and may
remain only in the river.*[52]

3. We noted, however, that in the case of the scin-
iphs,[53] the third plague, Pharao does not ask that prayer be
made, nor does Moses pray.   And in the case of the flies,
the fourth plague, he says: *Pray therefore for me to the
Lord.*[54] And then Moses said: *I will go out from thee, and
will pray to the Lord.   And the flies shall depart from
Pharao, and from his servants, and from his people tomorrow.*[55]   And a little further on we read: *So Moses went out
from Pharao and prayed to God.*[56]   Again in the case of
the fifth and also of the sixth plague Pharao did not ask
that prayer be made, nor did Moses pray; while in the
seventh *Pharao sent and called Moses and Aaron, saying
to them: I have sinned this time.   The Lord is just,* but *I
and my people are wicked.   Pray ye to the Lord, that the
thunderings of God and the hail and the fire may cease.*[57]
And a little further on we read: *And Moses went from
Pharao out of the city and stretched forth his hands to the
Lord; and the thunders . . . . ceased.*[58]   We shall discuss
more suitably at another time why it is not said as on the
previous occasions that *he prayed*, but rather that *he
stretched forth his hands to the Lord.*   And in the case of
the eighth plague Pharao says: *And pray to the Lord your
God, that he take away from me this death.   And Moses
going forth from the presence of Pharao, prayed to the
Lord.*[59]

4. We have said that the term "prayer" is often employed in a sense other than that which is usual, as for example in the case of Jacob.[60] And so also in Leviticus we read: *The Lord spoke to Moses, saying: Speak to the children of Israel, and thou shalt say to them: The man that shall have made a vow and promised his soul to God, shall give the price. If it be a man from twenty years old unto sixty years old, he shall give fifty sicles of silver, after the weight of the sanctuary.*[61] And in Numbers: *And the Lord spoke to Moses, saying: Speak to the children of Israel, and thou shalt say to them: When a man or woman shall make a solemn vow to consecrate themselves to the Lord, they shall abstain from wine and strong drink;*[62] and so on concerning the so-called Nazarite. And then a little farther on we find: *And he shall sanctify his head that day, and shall consecrate to the Lord the days of his vow.*[63] And again after a little we read: *This is the law of one who vows. When the days which he had determined by his vow shall be expired. . . .*[64] And again after a few verses: *And after this he that had vowed may drink wine. This is the law of one who vows, who hath vowed his oblation to the Lord in his vow—apart from those things which his hand shall find according to the force of his vow, which he vowed in accordance with the law of consecration.*[65] And towards the end of Numbers we read: *And Moses said to the princes of the tribes of the children of Israel: This is the word that the Lord hath commanded. If any man make a vow to the Lord, or make an oath or bind his soul, he shall not make his word void. He shall fulfil all that he promised. And if a woman vow any thing to the Lord and bind herself by an oath, being in her father's house and but yet a girl in age: if her father knew*

*the vows and the oaths wherewith she hath bound her soul,
and the father held his peace, she shall be bound by all her
vows, and all the oaths she swore by her soul shall bind
her.*[66]   And after this come certain legal prescriptions in
connection with such matters.   And this same point is set
down in Proverbs. . . .[67]

<It is a snare>[68] for a man to vow too quickly some-
thing belonging to him; for once he has made a vow, there
comes repentance.   And in Ecclesiastes we read: *It is better not to vow than after vowing not to perform the things
promised.*[69]   And in the Acts of the Apostles: *We have
four men who have a vow on them.*[70]

CHAPTER 4

THE TWO USES OF THE TERM "INVOCATION"

As I thought it reasonable to distinguish in the first place
the two meanings of the term "prayer" in the Scriptures,
so now I do the same for the term "invocation."[71]   For
this word too in addition to its common and customary
meaning is employed also where we would ordinarily use
the term "prayer."   As for example in what is said of
Anna in the First Book of Kings: *And Heli the priest sat
upon a stool before the door of the temple of the Lord.
As she had her heart full of grief, she "invoked" the Lord,
shedding many tears.   And she "prayed," saying: O Lord
of hosts, if Thou wilt look down on the affliction of Thy
servant, and wilt be mindful of me, and not forget Thy
handmaid, and wilt give to Thy servant a man child: I will*

give him to the Lord all the days of his life, and no razor shall come upon his head.[72]

2.   Of course one could, insisting upon the expressions *invoked the Lord* and *prayed*, say with great probability here that if Anna did both things, that is, *invoked the Lord* and *prayed*, the term "invoked" is perhaps used with the meaning which is ordinarily conveyed to us by *prayer*, and "prayed" with the meaning indicated in Leviticus and Numbers.[73]   For the words, *I will give him to the Lord all the days of his life, and no razor shall come upon his head*, are not properly an invocation but a vow such as Jephte vowed in the following: *And Jephte made a vow to the Lord saying: If Thou wilt deliver the children of Ammon into my hands, whosoever shall first come forth out of the doors of my house and shall meet me when I return in peace from the children of Ammon, the same will I offer a holocaust to the Lord.*[74]

CHAPTER 5

OBJECTIONS TO PRAYER

If next we must expound, as you have asked us, the arguments—first, of those who think that prayer effects nothing and who therefore say that it is superfluous to pray, we shall do our best to carry out your wishes.   In this connection we now use the term prayer in its most simple and ordinary meaning. . . .[75]

This view is not generally well-received and has no eminent protagonists, so much so that no one whatever who believes at all in Providence and God's supremacy in the universe can be found to reject prayer. It is a theory held either by those who are complete atheists and deny the existence of God, or by those who allow the existence of God in name but deny His Providence.[76] But indeed only the influence of the Adversary,[77] seeking to associate the most impious teachings with the name of Christ and the doctrine of the Son of God, could persuade certain men that they ought not to pray. The protagonists of this view are they who do away with all sense perception and practise neither Baptism nor the Eucharist.[78] They quibble about the Scriptures as not even recommending the prayer of which we speak, but as teaching something else quite different from it.

2. Here then, approximately, are the arguments of those who reject prayer (I deal only with those who posit a God over all and allow that there is a Providence; for it is not my purpose here to examine the arguments of those who deny God and Providence altogether): God sees all things before they come to be, and there is nothing that, when it comes to be, becomes known to Him for the first time by its coming to be, in such a way as not to have been known by Him before. What then is the use of praying to Him who knows what we need even before we pray? *For the* heavenly *Father knoweth what is needful for us, before we ask him.*[79] It is only reasonable that, being the Father and Creator of everything, *loving all things that are and hating none of the things which He has made,*[80] He should arrange—as a father would—everything in security for each one without his praying for it, watching over His children, and not waiting until they ask. Indeed, they may not even be able to ask, or through ignorance may often

wish to get something which is the opposite of what is suitable and profitable to them. And indeed we human beings share less the mind of God than little children the mind of their parents.

3. We can say not only that God foreknows what things are going to be, but also that He prearranges them, and that nothing happens contrary to His prearrangement. And so if a man prayed for the sun to rise, he would be regarded as simple in claiming that, what would happen even without his praying, happened because of it. In the same way a man who thinks that things, which would in any case happen even without his praying for them, happened because of it, has no sense. And again just as the man who, made uncomfortable and scorched by the sun at the summer solstice, thinks that by his prayer he can call the sun back to the constellations of spring and thus enjoy the balminess of the air, goes beyond all lunacy, so any man who thinks that by praying he can avoid what has been prearranged as of necessity happening to the human race, is mad beyond compare.

4. And if *sinners are alienated from the womb*,[81] and the just man *is chosen from his mother's womb*,[82] <*and*> *neither has yet been born or performed good or evil (so that the chosen design of God should depend not on deeds but upon His election)*, and it is said that *the elder shall serve the younger:*[83] in vain do we seek remission of sins or the strength of the Spirit so that we may have power *to do all things* in Christ *who strengtheneth us.*[84] For if we are *sinners*, we *are alienated from the womb.* And if we are *chosen from our mother's womb*, we shall fare excellently without ever having prayed. What prayer did Jacob make before he was born so that it is prophesied that *he*

shall overcome Esau and that his brother *shall serve* him? [85]
What impiety has Esau committed so as to be hated before
he is born?　And why does Moses pray, as we find in
Psalm 89, if God is his *refuge . . . before the mountains
were made, or the earth and the world was formed? . . . .*[86]

5.　It is in regard to all those who are to be saved that it
is written in the Epistle to the Ephesians: *The Father . . .
chose them in Him,* in Christ *before the foundation of the
world, that they should be holy and unspotted in His sight
in charity.　Who hath predestinated them unto the adoption of children through Jesus Christ unto Himself.*[87]　A
man is then either of the number of them that have been
chosen *before the foundation of the world,* and it is impossible for him to fall from the election and consequently
he has no need of prayer; or he has not been chosen nor
predestinated and he prays in vain.　Even if he pray ten
thousand times, his prayer will not be heard.　*For whom
He foreknew, He also predestinated to be made conform-
able to the image of the glory of His Son . . . . And
whom He predestinated, them He also called.　And whom
He called, them He also justified.　And whom He justified, them He also glorified.*[88]

Why does Josias [89] trouble or why is he anxious in his
prayer as to whether or no it will ever be heard?　Had he
not been prophesied by name many generations before? [90]
And as to what he should do, had he not only been
known of beforehand, but heralded in advance, in the
hearing of many men?　And why does Judas pray so that
even *his prayer becomes a sin,* seeing that from the time of
David it had been announced of him that he would lose his
office and that another would get it in his place? [91]　Obviously then, since God cannot be changed in His inten-

tion, and has anticipated all things, and abides by His prearrangement, it is absurd to pray in the belief that one can change by prayer His prearrangement, or—as though He has not prearranged all things, but awaits each one's prayer—to intercede that He may dispose things suitably for him who prays according to his prayer: in which case He would only then be disposing of things as they seemed reasonable on examination without His having previously considered them.

6. The matter can be put for the moment in the very words which you used in your letter to me: "First, if God foresees everything that will happen, and these things must happen, prayer is useless. Second, if everything happens according to the will of God, and His decisions are firm, and nothing that He wills can be changed, prayer is useless." [92]

It is well, I think, when solving the difficulties that tend to produce apathy for prayer, to treat first of the following considerations.

CHAPTER 6

OBJECTIONS ANSWERED

Of things that are moved, some have their movement from outside, as for example, (1) inanimate things and things that are kept together only by their being disposed in a certain way; and, (2) things that can move because of some natural principle or soul. These last, however, are to be considered here not as being such, but only as being on occasion like those things that are kept together merely by their being disposed in a certain way. Stones, for instance, that have been taken from a quarry and logs of wood that have ceased to grow—things which are kept together merely by their being disposed in a certain way—have their movement from outside; but the bodies of animals and plants that can be transplanted, if they are changed from one place to another by someone, are moved not as living things and plants move, but as if they were stones or logs that have ceased to grow. And even though these do move for the reason that all are perishable bodies and are in a state of flux, their movement is only a circumstance attending their decay.

In addition, there is a second class of things which are moved by an intrinsic principle or soul. They are described by those who are precise in their terminology as moving *out of* themselves.[93]

A third kind of movement is that found in animals, which is termed movement *from* themselves.[94]

I believe that the movement of rational beings is movement *by* themselves.[95]

If we take away from the animal movement *from* itself, it can no longer be considered an animal, but will be similar either to a plant which is moved by an intrinsic principle only, or to a stone which is moved by some outside agent. But if something responds to its own principle of motion, so that it will then be said to move *by* itself, this thing must be rational.

2. Those then who hold that we have no freedom of will,[96] must come to conclusions that are quite absurd: first, that we are not animals; second, that we are not rational beings: we are as it were moved by an external agent, do

not move at all of ourselves, and really do what we are
thought to do through his instrumentality.   Let a man
moreover reflect upon his own individual experience and
convince himself that he cannot without recklessness say
that it is not *he* that wills, that it is not *he* that eats, not *he*
that walks, not *he* that assents to and accepts certain views,
nor *he* that rejects others as false.   Just as it is impossible
to make a man believe certain teachings, even if you present your arguments most skilfully in ten thousand ways
and employ the most plausible reasonings, in the same way
it is impossible to make a man believe that in the matter of
human actions his will is not free.   Is there anyone who
believes that we can understand nothing?   Is there anyone
who lives on the basis of suspending judgment on everything? [97]   Does a man not punish his servant when he
catches sight of him doing some wrong?   And who does
not find fault with a son who does not pay proper respect
to his parents, or does not blame and condemn a woman
who has committed adultery as having done a shameful
act?   Truth compels and forces us, no matter how many
and ingenious the arguments to the contrary, to act, to
commend, and to condemn.   We believe that our wills are
free and consequently subject to commendation or condemnation.

   3.   If we are satisfied about our freedom of will, which
manifests innumerable tendencies to virtue or vice, or again
to one's duty or the opposite of one's duty, it follows that
God necessarily knew what form it would take before it
took that form along with all the other things that were to
be *from the creation and foundation of the world*.[98]   And
in all the things which God prearranges according as He
has foreseen each of our free actions, He prearranged
according to the requirements of each of our free actions

both that which was to happen as a result of His Providence and that which was to happen in the sequence of events that were to be. Yet the foreknowledge of God is not a *cause* of everything that is to be and of the effects of our free actions resulting from our own impulses. For even if we suppose that God did not know what was to be, we could for all that still choose and do this or that. But as a result of His foreknowledge the free actions of every man *fit in* with that disposition of the whole which is necessary for the existence of the universe.[99]

4. If then God knows the free will of every man, therefore, since He foresees it, He arranges by His Providence what is fair according to the deserts of each, and provides what he may pray for, the disposition of such and such thus showing his faith and the object of his desire. Providing for this, and following some such line in His disposition, He will have made arrangements somewhat in this way: "I will give ear to this man who prays with understanding on account of the prayer itself which he will utter; but this other man I will not hear, because he will be unworthy to be heard, or because he asks for things as would be neither good for him to receive nor fitting for me to give. If the prayer of such and such is like the latter case, for example, I shall not hear him; but if like the former, I shall." (And if someone is disturbed that, because God's foreknowledge of what is to be is infallible, everything happens of necessity, we must say to him that God has a firm knowledge on this point precisely that such and such a man does not firmly and fixedly will what is good, or will so desire what is bad that it will be impossible to convert him to what is good.) And again: "I will do such and such a thing for this man who prays, for it is fitting for me to do this since both his prayer will be beyond re-

proach and his address without blame. And to this other
man, when he shall pray for a certain thing, I will give this
and that *more abundantly than he desires or understands.*[100]
For it is fitting that I should overcome such a one in doing
good, and that I should give him more than he could ask
for. To this other man who will be of such and such a
character, I will send a particular guardian angel [101] to work
with him at his salvation from such and such a time, and
to remain with him up to a certain time. And to another I
will send another angel, one, for example, of higher rank,
because this man will be better than the former. And in
the case of another, who, having devoted himself to lofty
teachings, becomes weak and returns to material things, I
will deprive him of his more powerful helper; and when
he departs, a certain evil power—as he deserves—will seize
the opportunity of profiting by his weakness, and will
seduce him, now that he has shown his readiness to sin, to
commit such and such sins."

5. Thus, as it were, will He speak who prearranges all
things: "Amon will beget Josias, who will not emulate his
father's failings but, taking the way that leads to virtue,
because of those that will be with him, he will be an upright man and good, and will raze the altar iniquitously
built by Jeroboam.[102] And I know that when my Son will
live among men, Judas, who will be upright and good at
first, will change later and fall into human sins. And for
these it will be right that he should suffer certain punishments."[103] (Perhaps this foreknowledge of all things was
possessed also by the Son of God, as it certainly was with
regard to Judas and other mysteries.[104] In His observation
of the unfolding of things to come, He saw Judas and the
sins that he would commit. Thus, even before Judas was
born, He could say with full knowledge by the mouth of

David: *O God, be not thou silent in my praise,*[105] and so on.)

"And since I foreknow the future and what great religious zeal Paul will have, I shall choose him in myself [106] before the founding of the universe and as I set about the beginning of its creation, and shall give him at his birth in charge to these powers—his co-workers in the salvation of men—*separating him from his mother's womb.*[107] I shall allow him in the beginning of his youthful zeal to persecute in ignorance and under the pretext of religion those who believe in Christ, and to keep the garments of them that stone my servant and martyr Stephen,[108] so that when he has put his hot-headed youth behind him, he may later start anew, and turning to what is best, may *not glory in my sight* [109] but say: *I am not worthy to be called an apostle, because I persecuted the church of God.*[110] Seeing all the goodness that I shall show him after the aberrations of his youth made under the pretext of religion, he will say, *But by the grace of God I am what I am;* [111] and, prevented by his consciousness of what in his youth he had done against Christ, he will not be *exalted by the greatness of the revelations* [112] which in my goodness will be manifested to him."

CHAPTER 7

Further, regarding the objection to prayer which asks for the sun to rise,[113] this much must be said. The sun has a certain freedom of will too, inasmuch as it and the moon praise God. *Praise ye Him, O sun and moon*, says Scripture. And it is clear that this holds also for the moon and consequently for all the stars: *Praise Him, all ye stars and light*.[114] Just as we have said that God makes use of the free will of every man on earth and arranges it for some purpose, fitting in with the requirements of what is on the earth, so we must suppose that through the freedom of will of the sun and moon and stars, being harmonious and firm, fixed, and wise, He has arranged *the whole order of heaven*[115] and the march and movement of the stars that fits in with all the universe. And if my prayer be not amiss when offered on behalf of what depends on the free will of another man, so much more likely am I to succeed when my prayer is offered for what depends on the free will of the stars that dance in the heavens for the good of the universe. And further, regarding the inhabitants of the earth one must say that various kinds of impressions which have their source in what surrounds us, induce our weakness or our inclination towards the good either to do or to say this or that. But where the heavenly bodies are concerned, what impression can arise to divert or move each of them from its course, so beneficial to the universe, possessing as they do a soul strengthened by reason and removed from the influence of these impressions, and moreover using a body that is so ethereal and purified?[116]

CHAPTER 8

ADVANTAGES OF PRAYER

Neither is it irrelevant to use some such example as the following to induce men to pray and turn them from the neglect of prayer. Just as it is impossible to beget children without a woman and the act which results in the begetting of children, so it is impossible to obtain such and such requests if one does not likewise pray with certain dispositions and with a certain kind of faith, and a record of life lived in such and such a way. One must not merely babble in words, or ask for trifling things, or pray for the things of the earth, or come to prayer *in anger and* distracting *contentions.*[117] Nor can one think of devoting time to prayer unless one is purified. For he who prays will not obtain remission of his sins unless he forgive from his heart his brother who has offended him and asked his pardon.[118]

2. I think that he profits in many ways from his prayer who prays in the proper way or as well as he can. In the first place he certainly benefits somewhat who disposes his mind to pray, because by the very attitude with which he prays he shows that he is placing himself before God and speaking to Him as present, convinced that He is present and looking at him. For as certain mental images and remembrances of things which are recalled, defile the minds occupied by these same images, we must hold in the same way that we profit by the recollection of the God in whom we believe and who sees the most secret movements of the soul. The soul is disposing itself to please Him as being

37

present and looking on and anticipating every thought, *the searcher of hearts and reins.*[119] Even if we suppose that no other advantage comes to the man who prepares his mind to pray, we must not think that he who thus carefully disposes himself in the time of prayer receives a benefit that is negligible. Those who give themselves continually to prayer know by experience that through this frequent practice they avoid innumerable sins and are led to perform many good deeds. For if the remembrance and recollection of some illustrious man confirmed in wisdom induces us to emulate him and often restrains our impulses towards what is evil, how much more does the remembrance of God, the Father of all, and prayer to Him benefit those who are convinced that they are present with and speaking to God who is there and listens to them!

CHAPTER 9

And now we must prove from Sacred Scripture what we have said, as follows. The man who prays should *lift up pure hands* by *forgiving* every man *his offences against himself,* banishing the passion of anger from his soul and being wroth with no man.[120] Again, in order that one's mind may not be troubled by thinking on other things, one must, while praying, forget everything outside of the soul. And is not this in itself a most happy state? Paul teaches this in his First Epistle to Timothy when he says: *I will therefore that men pray in every place, lifting up pure hands, without anger and contentions.*[121]

Moreover a woman, especially when she prays, must be modest and decorous in soul and body, being most particularly careful when she is praying of her respect towards God so as to banish from her mind every unbridled and womanish recollection and to adorn herself not *with plaited hair, or gold, or pearls, or costly attire, but as it becometh a woman* to be adorned who is *professing godliness.*[122] I wonder that anyone should doubt that when she so prepares herself for prayer she is happy in the very preparation itself. Paul teaches the same lesson in the same Epistle: *In like manner women also in decent apparel: adorning themselves with modesty and sobriety, not with plaited hair, or gold, or pearls, or costly attire; but, as it becometh women professing godliness, with good works.*[123]

2. And the prophet David says that the saint who prays enjoys many other benefits. It will be quite expedient to mention them now so that we may see clearly the very great advantages which, even if considered by themselves, the disposition and preparation for prayer confer upon him who has dedicated himself to God. He says: *To thee have I lifted up my eyes, who dwellest in heaven;*[124] and: *To thee, O God, have I lifted up my soul.*[125] The eyes of the spirit are lifted up when they cease to truck with things of the earth and to be filled with the images of things material, and are so elevated that they contemn the things that are made and think only of God who listens to them and with whom they converse respectfully and in a fitting manner. Truly do those eyes already profit in the greatest measure, *beholding* as they do *the glory of the Lord with open face and being transformed into the same image from glory to glory.*[126] Then do they partake of the effect of some intellectual principle

that is divine, as is made clear from the text: *The light of Thy countenance, O Lord, is signed upon us.*[127] And the soul which is lifted up and follows the Spirit, which is separated from the body and not only follows the Spirit but lives in Him—as is made clear from the text: *To thee have I lifted up my soul* [128]—surely it has ceased to be soul and becomes spiritual.[129]

3. If the greatest of perfections is forgiveness—according to the Prophet Jeremias, who sums up all the Law in the words: *For I commanded not your fathers these things in the day that I brought them out of the land of Egypt, but this I commanded them,* that *each should forgive* his neighbour *in his heart,*[130]—then, putting remembrance of evil behind us, when we come to pray we observe the command of the Saviour who says: *When you shall stand to pray, forgive if you have aught against any man.*[131] Clearly, if we dispose ourselves to pray in this way, we have already gained most excellent benefits.

CHAPTER 10

All this has been said on the supposition, that even though we should gain nothing else by our prayer, we gain the most excellent benefits in understanding how to pray and disposing ourselves accordingly. It is evident that the man who prays thus, even while he is still speaking and contemplating the power of Him who is listening to him, will hear the words, *Behold, I am here.*[132] He will have cast off any dissatisfaction about Providence [133] before he prays. This is clear from the text: *If thou wilt take away*

*the chain out of the midst of thee and cease to stretch out
the finger and to speak the word of murmuring.*[134]　For he
who is well satisfied with whatever happens, is free from
every chain, and does not stretch out his finger to God
who arranges what He wills for our training; nor does he
even murmur his difficulties in secret, not being heard by
men.　For like the murmuring of evil servants who criti-
cize, but not openly, the commands of their masters, is the
murmuring of those who do not dare with their voice and
whole soul to speak ill of Providence because of what
happens.　They act as if they hoped that their complaints
would not be known to the Lord of all.　I think this is
what is meant in Job: *In all these things that happened to
him Job did not sin "with his lips" against God;*[135] whereas
it was written of the previous trial: *In all these things that
happened to him Job sinned not before God.*[136]　And the
word which enjoins that this murmuring should not take
place is also to be found in Deuteronomy: *Beware lest perhaps a hidden word steal into thy heart, something forbidden,* and thou say: *The seventh year draweth nigh* and so
on.[137]

CHRIST PRAYS WITH US

2.　The man who prays in this way and who has already received such benefits, becomes more fitted to be
united with the Spirit of the Lord who fills the whole
world and with Him who fills the whole earth and heavens
and who speaks thus by the mouth of the prophet: *Do not
I fill heaven and earth? saith the Lord.*[138]　Moreover, because of the purification already mentioned, he shares in
the prayer of the Word of God, who stands in the midst
even of those who are not aware of it,[139] who is not want-

ing to the prayer of anyone and prays to the Father with him whose mediator He is. For the Son of God is the High Priest [140] of our offerings and our advocate with the Father,[141] praying for those who pray and pleading with those who plead. He will not pray for us as His friends if we do not pray constantly through His intercession. Nor will He be an advocate with God for His followers if we do not obey His teaching that we ought always to pray and not to faint. *For He spoke*, it is said in the Gospel, *a parable, that we ought always to pray and not to faint. There was a judge in a certain city*, and so on.[142] And before that: *And He said to them: Which of you shall have a friend and shall go to him at midnight and shall say to him: Friend, lend me three loaves, because a friend of mine is come off his journey to me, and I have not what to set before him.*[143] And a little later: *I say to you, although he will not rise and give him because he is his friend; yet, because of his importunity, he will rise and give him as many as he needeth.*[144] And what man who believes in the infallible word of Jesus who says: *Ask, and it shall be given you; . . . for every one that asketh receiveth*[145] —will not turn to prayer without hesitation? The good Father gives to us, if we ask Him for it, *the living bread* (and not the *stone* proffered as nourishment by the Adversary to Jesus and His disciples)[146]—to us who *have received* from the Father *the spirit of adoption of sons.*[147] *The Father gives the good gift, raining from the heaven on them that ask Him.*[148]

CHAPTER 11

THE ANGELS AND SAINTS PRAY WITH US

It is not only the High Priest who prays with those who truly pray, but also the angels who *have joy in heaven upon one sinner that doth penance, more than upon ninety-nine just who need not penance,*[149] and also the souls of the saints who have passed away. This is clear from the case of Raphael offering a rational sacrifice to God for Tobias and Sara.[150] For the Scripture says that after they had prayed, *the prayers of them both were heard in the sight of the glory of the great Raphael, and he was sent to heal them both.*[151] And Raphael himself, in revealing to them his mission to them both, enjoined upon him as an angel by God, says: *When thou didst pray now, thou and thy daughter-in-law Sara, I offered the memory of your prayer before the holy one;*[152] and a little further on: *I am Raphael, one of the seven angels who bear up <the prayers of the saints> and enter before the glory of the holy one.*[153] And so, according to the word of Raphael, *prayer is good with fasting and alms and justice.*[154] And in the case of Jeremias, who appears in the Machabees as *admirable for age and glory*[155] so that *an extraordinary dignity and greatness* was about him, and who *stretched forth his right hand and gave to Judas a sword of gold*[156] —to him another holy man[157] who had died bore witness saying: *This is he that prayeth much for the people and for all the holy city, Jeremias the prophet of God.*[158]

43

2. And as knowledge is revealed to the saints *now through a glass in a dark manner, but then face to face,*[159] so it would be unreasonable not to employ the analogy for all the other virtues also, which if prepared already in this life will be perfected in the next. Now the one great virtue according to the Word of God is love of one's neighbour.[160] We must believe that the saints who have died have this love in a far greater degree towards them that are engaged in the combat of life, than those who are still subject to human weakness and are engaged in the combat along with their weaker brethren. The saying: *If one member suffer any thing, all the members suffer with it; or if one member glory, all the members rejoice with it,*[161] does not apply only to those who here on earth love their brethren. For one can quite properly say also of the love of those who have quit this present life: . . . *the solicitude for all the churches. Who is weak, and I am not weak? Who is scandalized, and I am not on fire?*[162] And Christ Himself agrees with this, saying that with each of the saints that are sick, He also is sick, and in prison, and naked and a stranger and hungry and thirsty.[163] Who is there that takes up the Gospel that does not know that Christ, by referring to Himself whatever befalls those who believe in Him, regards their sufferings as His own?

3. If the angels of God *came* to Jesus *and ministered to Him,*[164] and if it is not right for us to believe that this ministry of the angels to Jesus was for a short time only during His bodily sojourn among men, when He was still *in the midst* of those who believed, not as *he that sitteth at table* but as *he that serveth,*[165] how many angels, do you think, minister to Jesus who wishes to *gather together the sons of Israel one by one* and assemble those of the dispersion and

saves them that are in fear and *call upon Him?* [166]   And do they not contribute more than the apostles to the growth and increase of the Church, so that John says in the Apocalypse that certain angels stand over the churches? [167]   Nor is it in vain that *the angels of God ascend and descend upon the Son of man*, and are seen by eyes *illumined by the light of knowledge.*[168]

4.   At the time of prayer itself the angels are reminded by him who is praying of the things which he needs, and they do what they can for him acting according to the general injunction which they have received.   To make sure that what we have in mind is understood, we may use some such examples as the following.   Suppose a certain physician, an eminently just man, is in attendance on one who is sick and prays for a return of his health.   The physician knows well the treatment necessary to cure the disease of which the man in question prays to be cured.   It is clear that he will be moved to cure the man who thus prays; for he assumes, probably with good reason, that this is God's will, who hears the prayer of him who asked that his disease be taken away from him.

Or again take the case of a man who is of the number of those who have acquired more than sufficient of the needs of life and charitably hears the request of a poor man who petitions God for his wants.   It is clear that this man too will accede to the petition of the poor man.   For he obeys the will of the Father who brings together at the time of prayer the one who prays and the other who can grant the prayer and cannot, because of God's kindly provision, ignore the needs of the former.

5.   We must not, therefore, think that when these things happen they happen by chance.   For He who *has*

numbered all the hairs on the head [169] of the saints brings
together in harmony at the time of prayer both him who
can do a service, giving ear to him who is in need of His
benevolence, and the one who devoutly prays. In the
same way we must suppose that the angels who are the
overseers and ministers of God are present to one who is
praying in order to ask with him for what he petitions.
The angel, indeed, of each one, even of the *little ones* in
the Church, always *seeing the face of the Father who is in
heaven* [170] and beholding the divinity of our Creator, prays
with us and co-operates with us, as far as is possible, in
what we seek.

CHAPTER 12

Moreover, I believe that the words of saints when praying are charged with great power, especially when they
pray with the spirit and the understanding. [171] This is like
a light issuing from the mind of him who is praying; and,
proceeding from his mouth, it frees him through the
power of God from the intellectual venom injected by
the adverse powers in the minds of those who neglect
prayer and ignore the *pray without ceasing* [172] which
Paul prescribes following the exhortations of Jesus. For
it issues from the soul of the holy man who prays, like a
dart <sharpened> by knowledge and reason and faith,
wounding to subjugation and destruction the spirits that
are hostile to God and wish to ensnare us in the toils of
sin. [173]

2. He *prays without ceasing* who joins prayer to works

that are of obligation, and good works to his prayer. For virtuous works, or the carrying out of what is enjoined, form part of prayer. It is only in this way that we can understand the injunction, *pray without ceasing,* as something that we can carry out; that is to say, if we regard the whole life of the saint as one great continuous prayer. What is usually termed "prayer" is but a part of this prayer, and it should be performed not less than three times each day. This is clear from what we hear of Daniel, who prayed three times each day as long as great danger threatened him.[174] And Peter—*going up to the higher parts of the house to pray about the sixth hour,* . . . when *he saw* . . . *a vessel descending* from heaven, . . . *let down by the four corners* . . .[175]—indicates the second of the three prayers, that which is spoken of also by David before him: *In the morning Thou shalt hear my prayer. In the morning I will stand before Thee, and will see.*[176] And the third is indicated by: *the lifting up of my hands as evening sacrifice.*[177] Nor can we without this prayer spend the nighttime as we ought, as David says: *I rose at midnight to give praise to Thee for the judgments of Thy justice.*[178] And Paul, as is told in the Acts of the Apostles, at Philippi *at midnight praying with Silas praised God* so that *they that were in prison heard them.*[179]

CHAPTER 13

EXAMPLES OF PRAYERS THAT WERE HEARD

And if Jesus prays and does not pray in vain since He obtains His requests through prayer, and perhaps would not obtain them without prayer,[180] which of us should be indifferent to prayer? For Mark says: *And rising very early, going out, He went into a desert place; and there He prayed.*[181] And Luke: *And it came to pass that as He was in a certain place praying, when He ceased, one of His disciples said to Him. . . .*[182] And in another place: *. . . and He passed the whole night in the prayer of God.*[183] And John records a prayer of His, saying: *These things Jesus spoke; and lifting up His eyes to heaven, He said: Father, the hour is come. Glorify Thy Son, that Thy Son may glorify Thee.*[184] So, too, the following, *I knew that Thou hearest me always,*[185] which is reported by the same as said by the Lord, makes clear that he who prays *always* is *always* heard.

2. But what use is there to recall all the examples of those who, because they prayed as they ought, received great favours from God? Everyone can choose for himself many examples from the Scriptures. Anna obtained the birth of Samuel, who was reckoned with Moses,[186] because when she was barren she prayed to the Lord with faith.[187] And Ezechias, being still childless and having learned from Isaias that he was about to die, prayed and was included in the genealogy of the Saviour.[188] Again,

when, as a result of a single order arising from the intrigues
of Aman, the people were about to be destroyed, the
prayer and fasting of Mardochai and Esther were heard,
and hence there arose, in addition to the feasts ordained
by Moses, the festival of Mardochai for the people.[189]   And
Judith, too, having offered holy prayer, overcame Holofernes with the help of God, and so a single woman of the
Hebrews brought shame to the house of Nabuchodonosor.[190]   Further, Ananias and Azarias and Misael became
worthy to be heard and to be protected by *the blowing of
a wind bringing dew*, which prevented the flame of the
fire from being effective.[191]   And the lions in the den of
the Babylonians were muzzled through the prayers of
Daniel.[192]   And Jonas, too, not having despaired of being
heard from out of *the belly of the whale* that had swallowed him, escaped from the belly of the whale and thus
fulfilled the remainder of his prophetical mission to the
men of Ninive.[193]

3.   And if we wish to remember with gratitude the
benefits done to us and praise God for them, how many
will not each one of us have to count!   Souls without issue
for so long, having perceived the sterility of their private
reasonings and the barrenness of their own understanding,
have conceived of the Holy Spirit through constant
prayer and have begotten words of salvation filled with
true knowledge.   And,—since we have often to encounter
myriads of the Adversary's host who wish to rob us of our
divine faith—how many of our enemies have been beaten!
We took courage from the thought that while *some trust
in chariots, and some in horses, we call upon the name of
the Lord*,[194] and see that in truth *vain is the horse for
safety*.[195]   What is more, the man who trusts in the praise

of God often routs even the supreme commander of the Adversary, that deceitful and plausible reasoning which causes many even of those who are reckoned as believing to be fainthearted: for "Judith" translated signifies "praise." [196] And need I say how many, having stumbled often on overpowering temptations, more burning than any flame, have yet suffered nothing from them? They have come through them entirely unscathed, without being harmed by as much as *the smell of the fire* of the enemy! [197] And how many savage beasts infuriated against us—wicked spirits and evil men—have we encountered and often through our prayers muzzled so that they were unable to fix their teeth in those among us who had become *the members of Christ!* [198] For often in the case of each one of the saints *has the Lord broken the grinders of the lions and they came to nothing like water running down.* [199] We know, too, that in many instances men who had fled from the precepts of God and had been given over to death which was strengthening its grip on them, were saved from such a terrible fate through repentance: they did not despair that they could be saved even when subdued in the belly of death. [200] For *death in his strength swallowed them down, but God wiped away every tear from every face.* [201]

4. Having enumerated those who have benefited from prayer, I think it was quite necessary that these things should be stated. For it is my endeavour to turn those who desire a life of the spirit and in Christ [202] away from praying for insignificant and earthly things, and to invite the readers of this book to mystical things of which I have given models for their imitation. Every prayer for the spiritual and mystical favours adduced by us above is in

every instance offered by one who *does not war according to the flesh*,[203] but who *by the Spirit mortifies the deeds of the body*.[204] For the benefits that derive from a spiritual understanding [205] are superior to any benefit that may appear to be granted to those who pray according to the literal sense. In order, then, to avoid being barren and sterile we, too, must exercise ourselves, and being spiritual give ear to the law of the spirit. We shall then be heard and delivered from our barrenness and sterility, as were Anna and Ezechias.[206] We shall be saved from the wickedness of spiritual enemies that attack us, as were Mardochai and Esther and Judith.[207] And since Egypt—that is, symbolically, every terrestrial place—is an iron furnace,[208] everyone that escapes from the wickedness of human life and is not burned by sin and whose heart is not full of fire like an oven, should give thanks no less than those who were tried in the fire of dew.[209]

But he, too, who prays and says: *Deliver not up to beasts the soul that confesses to Thee*,[210] and is heard and suffers nothing from the asp or basilisk—because he has been enabled through Christ to walk upon and has *trampled underfoot the lion and the dragon*,[211] availing himself of *the* glorious *power* given by Jesus *to tread upon serpents and scorpions and upon all the power of the enemy*,[212] and suffers no injury from such things—should give thanks even more than Daniel; for he has been delivered from beasts that are more fearful and harmful.[213] Again, the man who knows what beast is symbolized by the whale that swallowed Jonas, and has grasped that it is that spoken of by Job: *Let him curse it who curses the day, who is ready to subdue the great leviathan:*[214] if ever through some disobedience *he be in the belly of the fish*,[215] let him repent and pray, and he will be delivered from it. And when he has been delivered and remains obedient to the commandments of God, he will be able through the goodness of the Spirit [216] to prophesy even now to men of Ninive who are doomed to destruction, and to become to them a cause of salvation [217]—if he does not suffer annoyance at God's goodness and demand that He should continue in His severity towards such as have repented.[218]

5. The great miracle which Samuel is said to have accomplished through prayer is spiritually possible of accomplishment even now for anyone who is truly faithful to God and worthy to be heard. For it is written: *Now then stand <and see> this great thing which the Lord doth in your sight. Is it not wheat harvest to-day? I will call upon the Lord, and He shall send thunder and rain.*[219] And the text a little later says: *And Samuel cried unto the Lord, and the Lord sent thunder and rain that day.*[220] Indeed to every saint and true disciple of Jesus the Lord says: *Lift up your eyes and see the countries; for they are white already to harvest. And he that reapeth receiveth wages and gathereth fruit unto life everlasting.*[221] In this time of harvest *the Lord doth a great thing in the sight* of those who hear His prophets. When one who has been adorned by the Holy Spirit *calls upon the Lord*, God gives from heaven *thunder and rain* that waters the soul. Thus he who before was in wickedness fears exceedingly the Lord and the minister of God's goodness, who appears as worthy of reverence and veneration on account of the favours granted to him. Again, Elias, when the heavens had been closed to the impious for three years and six months, later opened them by the word of God.[222] This can always be brought about by anyone who receives rain upon his soul through prayer, whereas formerly because of sin he was deprived of it.

CHAPTER 14

WHAT WE SHOULD PRAY FOR

Now that we have gone through the benefits which have come to the saints through prayer, let us meditate on the words: "Ask for what is great, and what is small shall be added unto you," and "ask the things of heaven, and the things of earth shall be added unto you." [223] Every symbolical and figurative good is small and of earth when compared with true and spiritual good. And thus the Word of God in inviting us to imitate the prayers of the saints in order that we may ask for the real favours which they obtained in a figurative manner, aptly tells us that the things of heaven and what is great are signified by the things of earth and what is small. This is said: "You who wish to be spiritual, ask in your prayers for <the things of heaven and what is great.> Thus, having received them as being of heaven, you will inherit the kingdom of heaven, and as being great, you will enjoy the greatest blessings. And the Father will supply you in due measure with what is required of the things of earth and what is small, because your bodies need them." [224]

THE FOUR KINDS OF PRAYER

2. And since the Apostle in the First Epistle to Timothy uses four words for four things that have close relevance to the question of prayer, it will be useful to take his text and see if we properly understand, in its precise

meaning, each of the four. This is what he says: *I desire, therefore, first of all, that* SUPPLICATIONS, PRAYERS, INTERCESSIONS, *and* THANKSGIVINGS *be made for all men,* and so on.²²⁵ I believe, then, that SUPPLICATION is offered by one who needs something, beseeching that he receive that thing; PRAYER is offered in conjunction with praise of God by one who asks in a more solemn manner for greater things; INTERCESSION is the request to God for certain things made by one who has greater confidence; and THANKSGIVING is the prayer with acknowledgment to God for the favours received from God: either the one who acknowledges, understands the greatness of the favour done him, or he who has received it attaches such greatness to it.

SUPPLICATION

3. Examples of the first kind are: Gabriel, speaking to Zachary, who doubtless was praying for the birth of John, says the following: *Fear not, Zachary, for thy* SUPPLICATION *is heard; and thy wife Elizabeth shall bear thee a son, and thou shalt call his name John.*²²⁶ And there is written in Exodus regarding the golden calf: *But Moses* BESOUGHT *the Lord his God, saying: Why, O Lord, is Thy indignation enkindled against Thy people whom Thou hast brought out of the land of Egypt, with great power?* ²²⁷ And in Deuteronomy: *And I made* SUPPLICATION *before the Lord as before, forty days and forty nights (I neither ate bread, nor drank water), for all the sins you committed.*²²⁸ And in Esther: *Mardochai* BESOUGHT *God, remembering all the works of the Lord and said: O Lord, Lord, Almighty King. . . .*²²⁹ And Esther herself BE-

SOUGHT *the Lord the God of Israel, and said: O my Lord, who art our king. . . .*[230]

PRAYER

4. Regarding the second kind, see Daniel: *And Azarias standing up* PRAYED *in this manner, and opening his mouth in the midst of the fire he said. . . .*[231] And Tobias: *And I began to* PRAY *with tears, saying: Thou art just, O Lord, and all Thy works are just, and all Thy ways mercy and truth. And Thy judgments are true and just forever.*[232] And since the passage in Daniel has been obelized on the ground that it is not found in the Hebrew text, and those of the circumcision reject the Book of Tobias as not being canonical, I shall quote the words of Anna from the First Book of Kings: *And she* PRAYED *to the Lord, shedding many tears. And she made a vow, saying: O Lord of Hosts, if Thou wilt look down on the affliction of Thy servant,* and so on.[233] And in Habacuc: *A* PRAYER *of Habacuc the prophet with song. O Lord, I have heard Thy voice and was afraid. O Lord, I reflected on Thy works and I was astonished. In the midst of two animals Thou wilt be known; in the approach of the years Thou wilt be recognized.*[234] The example just given illustrates very well the definition of *prayer* inasmuch as he who offers it unites it with praise of God. And again, in the book of Jonas: *Jonas* PRAYED *to the Lord his God out of the belly of the fish. And he said: I cried out of my affliction to the Lord my God, and He heard me. Out of the belly of hell Thou didst hear the screams of my voice. And Thou hast cast me forth into the deep in the heart of the sea, and a flood hath compassed me.*[235]

INTERCESSION

5. Concerning the third kind: the Apostle rightly assigns *prayer* to us, but *intercession* to the Spirit as being superior and having confidence in Him to whom He addresses Himself. *For,* he says, *we know not what we should pray for as we ought; but the Spirit Himself* INTERCEDETH MIGHTILY *for us with unspeakable groanings. And He that searcheth the hearts knoweth what the Spirit desireth: because he* INTERCEDETH *for the saints according to God.*[236] The Spirit, therefore, *asks* and *intercedes,* but we *pray.* And Josue's words commanding the sun to stand over Gabaoth seem to me to be an intercession also: *Then Josue spoke to the Lord in the day that God delivered the Amorrhite into the hands of Israel, when He broke them at Gabaoth, and they were broken in the sight of the children of Israel. And Josue said: Let the sun stand over Gabaoth and the moon over the valley of Elom.*[237] And in Judges, Samson in my opinion said in intercession: *Let me die with the foreigners—when he bent in his strength and the house fell upon the princes and all the people that were there.*[238] Even though it is not written that Josue and Samson *interceded* but that they *said,* nevertheless their words seem to be an *intercession,* which we must judge to be different from a *prayer,* if we are to give words their proper meaning.

THANKSGIVING

An example of *thanksgiving* is the utterance of Our Lord, saying: *I confess to Thee, O Father, Lord of heaven and earth, because Thou hast hid these things from the wise and prudent and hast revealed them to little ones.*[239] For the term *confess* comes to the same as *give thanks.*

6. Now, it is not out of place to address supplication, intercession, and thanksgiving to <saintly> men also. The two latter (intercession and thanksgiving) may be addressed not only to saintly men but even to <other men>. But supplication may be addressed only to saints, should another Paul or Peter be found, in order that they may help us to become worthy of receiving the power, granted to them, of removing sin.[240]   But, perhaps, if we have done injustice to any man—even if he be not a saint—and we become aware of the injury done to him, we may supplicate even him so that he may pardon us our injustice. And if we address ourselves thus to saintly men, how much more should we thank Christ [241] who has conferred so many benefits on us through the will of the Father! We should also intercede with Him as Stephen did, saying: *Lord, lay not this sin to their charge;* [242] and, following the example of the father of the lunatic, we shall say: *Lord, I supplicate Thee, have pity on my son* [243]—or on myself or on anyone else.

CHAPTER 15

ONE MAY PRAY TO THE FATHER ALONE

If we understand what prayer really is, we shall know that we may never pray to anything generated—not even to Christ [244]—but only to God and the Father of all, to whom even Our Saviour Himself prayed, as we have already said, and teaches us to pray. For when He is asked, *Teach us to pray,* [245] He does not teach how to pray to Himself, but to the Father, and to say: *Our Father, who art in heaven,*[246] and so on. For if the Son, as is shown elsewhere,[247] is distinct from the Father in nature and person,[248] then we must pray either to the Son and not to the Father, or to both, or to the Father only. Everyone will agree that to pray to the Son and not to the Father would be very strange, and maintained against the clearest evidence; and if to both, then we must obviously pray and make our requests in the plural saying, "Grant ye," "favour ye," "provide ye," "save ye," and everything similar in the same way. But this is clearly incongruous, nor can anyone point out where anyone has used it in Scripture. There remains, then, to pray to God alone, the Father of all, but not apart from the High Priest who was appointed with an oath by the Father,[249] according to the words: *He hath sworn and he will not repent: Thou art a priest for ever according to the order of Melchisedech.*[250]

ONE MUST PRAY THROUGH CHRIST

2. The saints, then, in their prayers of thanks to God acknowledge their thanks to Him through Christ Jesus. And as, if one is to pray correctly, one does not pray to Him who prays Himself, but rather to the Father whom Our Lord Jesus taught us to call upon in our prayers, in the same way one must not offer a prayer to the Father apart from Him.[251] He Himself makes this clear when He says: *Amen, amen, I say to you: if you ask my Father anything, He will give it to you in my name. Hitherto you have not asked anything in my name. Ask, and you shall receive, that your joy may be full.*[252] He did not say simply, *ask me,* or *ask the Father;* but rather, *If you ask the Father anything, He will give it to you in my name.* Until Jesus taught this, no one had asked the Father in the

name of the Son; and what Jesus said was true—*Hitherto
you have not asked anything in my name;* and true too—
Ask, and you shall receive, that your joy may be full.

3. But suppose someone, believing through confusion
about the meaning of the term "worship"²⁵³ that we
should pray to Christ Himself, brings against us the text,
Let all the angels of God worship Him—which is admit-
tedly said of Christ in Deuteronomy: ²⁵⁴ we should reply
that the Church, too, called by the prophet "Jerusalem," is
said in the following text to be "worshipped" by kings and
queens, that nurse her and provide for her: *Behold I will
lift up my hand to the Gentiles and will set up my standard
to the islands. And they shall bring thy sons in their arms
and carry thy daughters upon their shoulders. And kings
shall be thy nursing fathers, and queens thy nurses. They
shall worship thee with their face toward the earth, and
they shall lick up the dust of thy feet. And thou shalt
know that I am the Lord and thou shalt not be confounded.*²⁵⁵

4. And as He has said: *Why callest thou me good?
None is good but one, that is God* ²⁵⁶ the Father, so He
might equally say: "Why prayest thou to me? One
should pray to the Father alone, to whom I also pray.
Learn this from the Scriptures. You should not pray to
Him who has been set over you as High Priest ²⁵⁷ by the
Father, nor to the Advocate who has this office from the
Father; ²⁵⁸ but you should pray through your High Priest
and Advocate who *can have compassion on your infirmi-
ties, being tempted in all things like as you are,* but,
through the gift of my Father, *tempted without sin.*²⁵⁹
Learn, then, what great gift you have received from my
Father, through having received *the spirit of adoption of*

sons in your rebirth in me, so that you may be called *sons of God* and my brothers.[260] Surely you have read the words said by me, in the person of David, to the Father about you: *I will declare Thy name to my brethren; in the midst of the church will I praise Thee.*[261] It is not right that they who have been held worthy to have the same Father with Him, should pray to their Brother. You should pray with me and through me to the Father alone."

CHAPTER 16

Giving heed then to Jesus when He says these things, let us pray through Him to God; let us all say the same thing and not be divided in the method of our prayer.[262] Are we not divided when we pray, some to the Father, and some to the Son? Men commit a sin of ignorance [263] when in all sincerity, but without due investigation and inquiry, they pray to the Son, either with the Father or without Him. Let our prayer, then, come to Him as God; let us appeal to Him as Father; let us supplicate Him as Lord; let us thank Him as God and Father and Lord. He is not Lord of a mere slave. For the Father can rightly be regarded also as the Lord of His Son, and Lord also of those who have through Him become sons. And just as *He is not the God of the dead, but of the living,*[264] so neither is He Lord of slaves of no birth, but of slaves who were well-born, but were, through infancy, at first in fear; [265] later, however, their serfdom became more happy through love than it had been when they were in fear.[266] For there are also in the soul marks—visible to Him alone that searcheth the hearts [267]—by which the slaves of God are distinguished from His sons.

SPIRITUAL AND MATERIAL FAVOURS

2. Everyone, then, that asks God for the things of the earth and what is small disobeys Him who bids us ask from God for the things of heaven and what is great, and who does not grant favours that are of the earth and small.[268] And if someone objects that material favours have been bestowed on the saints because of their prayers, and brings forward the words of the Gospel itself which teach us that what is of the earth and small is added unto us, we reply to him as follows: If a man gives us some material object, we must not say that such and such a person gave us the shadow of a material object. He did not purport to give two favours, the thing and its shadow. He gave an object, and his intention was to give an object. But consequent on his giving the object is our receiving its shadow also. In the same way, if we lift up our thoughts and consider the principal gifts made by God to us, we shall rightly say that the material favours given to each of the saints *unto profit* or *according to the rule of faith* or *according to the will* of the Giver,[269] are but accompaniments of the great and heavenly spiritual gifts. For He wills wisely, even though we may be unable to give for each gift a cause and reason worthy of the Giver.

3. And so it was more the soul of Anna that was cured of barrenness and bore fruit than her body when she conceived Samuel.[270] Ezechias begot divine children of the mind rather than such as are born of the body from the seed of the body.[271] Esther and Mardochai and the people were delivered even more from spiritual attacks than from

Aman and the conspirators.[272]   <Judith> cut off the power of the prince who wanted to destroy her soul rather than <the head> of Holofernes.[273]   And who will not admit that on Ananias and his companions descended the spiritual benediction that is granted to all the saints and is spoken of by Isaac when he says to Jacob, *God give thee the dew of heaven,*[274] rather than the physical dew which quenched the flame of Nabuchodonosor? [275]   And they were invisible lions that were muzzled for the prophet Daniel so that they could do no hurt to his soul, rather than the lions that were seen and to whom we all referred the passage when we met it in the Scriptures.[276]   And who has escaped from the belly of that beast subdued by Jesus Our Saviour and that swallows down everyone that flies from God, as had Jonas, who as a holy man was receptive of the Holy Spirit? [277]

CHAPTER 17

And it is not to be wondered at if while all receive equally the same bodies that, so to speak, produce such shadows, they yet do not receive equal shadows, and some do not receive any shadow at all.[278]   Those who study problems dealing with sun-dials, and the relationship between shadows and the body that supplies the light, clearly understand that this is the case with regard even to material bodies.   At some moments they perceive that the indicators leave no shadow; and at other times, so to speak, they leave a short shadow; and at still other times, by contrast, they leave a long shadow. We should not be greatly surprised, therefore, if in accordance with the disposition of Him who grants us what is essential—a disposition which takes account of certain ineffable and mystical analogies adapted to those who are to receive and the times of reception—when He gives us what is essential, sometimes no shadows whatsoever follow for those who receive; sometimes there are shadows for a few things, but not for all; and sometimes they are smaller by comparison with those granted to others. As he, then, who seeks the rays of the sun neither rejoices nor grieves whether the shadow of bodies be present or absent, seeing that he has what is most necessary as long as he receives the light, whether there is no shadow or more or less of it, so if we be given the spiritual gifts and receive illumination from God in the full possession of the things that are truly good,[279] we shall not waste words over such an insignificant thing as a shadow. For all material and corporeal things, whatever they be, have no more value than a feeble and fleeting shadow. They can in no way stand comparison with the saving and holy gifts of the God of all. What comparison can there be between material wealth and wealth *in all utterance and in all knowledge?* [280] And who but a madman would compare health of the flesh and bones with health of mind, strength of soul, and balanced reasoning? All this, when regulated by God's Word, makes of the sufferings of the body but a tiny scratch, or even something less than a scratch.

2.   He that has understood what is meant by the beauty of the bride whom the Bridegroom, the Word of God, loves, that is to say, of the soul blooming with beauty supercelestial and supramundane, will be ashamed to

honour with the same term "beauty" the bodily beauty of woman or child or man. The flesh is incapable of real beauty, since it is all ugliness.[281] *For all flesh is as grass; and the glory thereof,*[282] as seen in the reputed beauty of women and children, is compared by the prophet to a flower: *All flesh is as grass, and all the glory thereof as the flower of the field. . . . The grass is withered and the flower is fallen; but the word of the Lord endureth forever.*[283] In like manner, who that has reflected on the nobility of the sons of God [284] will rightly term nobility that which is commonly so named among men? How can the spirit that has considered the *immovable kingdom* [285] of Christ, do otherwise than contemn as utterly worthless every earthly kingdom? And when a human spirit has plainly seen, so far as a human spirit that is still bound in the body can, the army [286] of angels and the commanders-in-chief among them of the forces of the Lord—the archangels, thrones, dominations, principalities and super-celestial powers [287]—and understands that it can be equally honoured by the Father as they are, how will it not, even if it be weaker than a shadow, despise as utterly void and, in comparison, of no account at all, these things that are wondered at by fools? And even if it is given all these things, still it will contemn them, rather than fail to gain the true principality and divine power.[288]

We must pray, then, we must pray for the essentially and truly great and heavenly things, and leave to God what is concerned with the shadows that accompany the essential gifts. He understands *what is needful for us,* because of our mortal body, *before we ask Him.*[289]

PART II: THE LORD'S PRAYER

CHAPTER 18

Having sufficiently, according to the grace given to us by God through His Christ [290] (and I hope in the Holy Spirit—which you readers of this treatise will judge), spoken so far of the problem of prayer in general, we shall now proceed to the next task, and consider the prayer dictated by the Lord and the efficacy which fills it.

2. And first of all we must notice that Matthew and Luke may seem to most to have written the same form of prayer according to which we should pray. The words given by Matthew are as follows:

Our Father, who art in heaven, hallowed be Thy name. Thy kingdom come. Thy will be done on earth as it is in heaven. Give us this day our supersubstantial bread. And forgive us our debts, as we also forgive our debtors. And lead us not into temptation, but deliver us from evil.[291]

But Luke reads thus:

Father, hallowed be Thy name. Thy kingdom come. Give us each day our supersubstantial bread. And forgive us our sins, for we also forgive everyone that is indebted to us. And lead us not into temptation.[292]

3. Against those who hold this opinion we must say, first, that the words, even if they approximate to one another in some points, appear to differ in others, as we shall

make clear in our examination of them. In the second place, there is the prayer spoken on the mountain whither, *seeing the multitudes, He went up;* then *when He was set down, His disciples came unto Him; and opening His mouth, He taught them*[293]—for it is in connection with the account of the beatitudes and the precepts which follow that this prayer is found reported in Matthew.[294] It is impossible that this is the same prayer as that spoken to *one of His disciples, as He was in a certain place praying, when He ceased,* and he requested that he be taught *to pray, as John also taught his disciples.*[295] How can we admit that the very same words were spoken on one occasion without any previous request and in a fixed arrangement, and on another in answer to a request from a disciple? But perhaps one might urge in reply to this that the prayers in question are really one and the same prayer: on one occasion it was given at length; and on another to one of the disciples who had requested it—probably because he was not present when it was spoken as given in Matthew, or because he could not recall the words after the passage of time. All the same, it is perhaps better to regard them as two different prayers with certain parts in common. We have also searched Mark for some such similar prayer that might have escaped our notice, but we have found no trace of one.

CHAPTER 19

DISPOSITION FOR THE PRAYER

We have said above [296] that the man who is about to pray should prepare and dispose himself and only then proceed to pray. Let us see now Our Saviour's words on this point as set down by Matthew before the actual prayer itself. They are as follows: *When ye pray, ye shall not be as hypocrites that love to stand and pray in the synagogues and corners of the streets, that they may be seen by men: amen I say to you, they have received their reward. But thou when thou shalt pray, enter into thy chamber and, having shut the door, pray to thy Father in secret: and thy Father who seeth thee in secret will repay thee. And when you are praying, do not babble, as the heathens. For they think that in their much speaking they may be heard. Be not you therefore like them, for your Father knoweth what is needful for you, before you ask Him. Thus therefore shall you pray. . . .*[297]

2. Our Saviour, then, appears in many places to attack the love of glory as a deadly malady. Such is the case here where He forbids hypocrisy at the time of prayer. For it is typical of the hypocritical to wish to take pride in the eyes of men for his piety or generosity. We should remember the words: *How can you believe, who receive glory from men, and the glory which is from God alone, you do not seek?*[298] We should despise all human glory, even if we think it is merited, and seek the real and true glory that is given by Him alone who in a manner worthy

of Himself glorifies him that is worthy of glory as befits Himself and above the deserts of the one who is glorified. And that very thing which might otherwise be judged worthy of commendation and praise becomes sullied when, thinking that these will follow, we do it *that we may be honoured by men,* or *that we may be seen by men.*[299] As a result we receive no reward whatever for this from God. For although every word of Jesus is true, even more true, if we may do some violence to language, is every word of His which is accompanied by His usual oath. He says of those who because of the glory that comes from men appear to do good to their neighbour, or who *pray in the synagogues and corners of the streets that they may be seen by men,* these very words: *Amen, I say to you, they have received their reward.*[300] In the same way the rich man of whom Luke speaks, because *he had received good things in his lifetime,*[301] was no longer able to receive them after the present life. And he who *receives his reward*[302] for giving someone something, or for his prayers, since he has not *sown in the spirit* but *in the flesh,* will *reap indeed corruption, but* will not *reap life everlasting.*[303] For he *sows in the flesh* who *does an alms-deed* to *the sound of a trumpet before him in the synagogues and in the streets, that he may be honoured by men,* or *who loves to stand and pray in the synagogues and corners of the streets, that he may be seen by men,*[304] and be regarded as pious and holy by them that see him.

3. The man who follows the *wide* and *broad way that leadeth to destruction*[305] and which is in no way straight and direct, but is everywhere tortuous and winding (for the straight line is broken most of the way), follows it in the same way as does he who *prays in the corners of the*

streets.[306]   In his love of pleasure he finds himself not in
one street but in *many*.   In these streets others, who *are
dying like men* [307] because they have separated themselves
from what is divine, are to be found to glorify and exalt
them that in their eyes practise piety in the streets.   As a
matter of fact, there are always those who appear in their
prayers to be *lovers of pleasure more than of God*,[307a]
when in the midst of feastings and drunkenness they in-
dulge in drunken prayer.   Such truly *stand and pray in
the corners of the streets!*   For every man that lives the
life of pleasure loves the broad way and strays from the
narrow and strait way [308] of Jesus Christ, that has no occa-
sional bend nor any angle whatsoever.

CHAPTER 20

If there is a difference between Church and Synagogue
(for the true Church *has no spot or wrinkle or any such
thing, but is holy and without blemish*,[309] and neither *the
son of the prostitute may enter* it nor *an eunuch* nor *one
castrated*, nor the Egyptian or Idumean—but only their
sons in the third generation, because of the difficulty of
their being assimilated to the Church—nor the Moabite nor
the Ammonite until the tenth generation is completed and
the time set for them is run; [310] whereas the Synagogue is
built by a centurion before the coming of Jesus, and he
does this before receiving testimony that he has *such faith*
as the Son of God *has not found even in Israel*); [311] it is
this, that the man who likes *to pray in the synagogues* is not
far from *the corners of the streets*, whereas the saint is not

such: he not merely *likes* to pray, but *loves* to do so; and that not *in the synagogues*, but in the churches; and not *in the corners of the streets*, but in the straightness of the *narrow and strait way;* and not that he *may be seen by men*, but that he may be seen *in the sight of the Lord his God*.[312]   For he is *a male* who observes *the acceptable year of the Lord*,[313] and obeys His commandment that says: *Three times in a year shall all the males appear before the Lord God*.[314]

2.   But we should pay particular attention to the words: *that they may be seen*.[315]   Nothing that merely "appears to be" is good.   It only seems to be and does not truly exist. It leads the imagination astray and does not give an accurate and true representation.   Actors in certain theatrical plays are not what they profess to be, nor are they what they seem to be in the role they play.   In the same way all who simulate the appearance of goodness are not just, but act as if they were just.   They act in a theatre of their own —*in the synagogues and the corners of the streets*.   But the man who is no mere actor, but has rid himself of everything that is not his very own, and sets out to make himself accepted in a theatre incomparably greater than any mentioned, *enters into his chamber* [316] to his stored-up wealth where he has shut away for himself *the treasure of wisdom and knowledge*.[317]   He pays no attention to nor does he desire anything outside, but closes all doors of sensation so that he may not be drawn away by the senses, nor any sensory image come into his mind.   He prays to the Father who does not shun nor abandon such *secrecy*, but abides there, and with Him, His Only-Begotten Son.[318]   For *I*, He says, *and the Father will come to him and will make our abode with him*.[319]   It is clear that when we pray in

this way, we shall be conversing with God who is just but also a Father, who does not abandon His sons, but who is present to our secrecy [320] and guards it, and increases the wealth in our treasury—if only we close the door.

CHAPTER 21

When praying let us *not babble*,[321] but let us speak to God. We *babble* when we do not scrutinize ourselves and the words in which we offer our prayer, but speak of perishable works or words or thoughts, which are base and reprehensible and foreign to the incorruption of the Lord. The man who *babbles* at prayer is actually in a worse state than those *in the synagogues* mentioned above, and on a way more dangerous than those *at the corners of the streets*, without a claim to a trace of even the appearance of good. For according to the words of the Gospel only the pagans *babble:* they do not have even a notion of what great or heavenly petitions are, but every prayer they offer has to do with their physical and external needs. The man, then, who petitions the Lord who dwells in heaven and above the heights of heaven [322] for earthly things, is like a pagan who *babbles*.

2. It appears, indeed, that the man who speaks much is a babbler, and the babbler is one who speaks much.[323] For no material or corporeal thing can be one, but everything that is regarded as one is separated, broken up, and divided into many parts and so loses its unity. Obviously, the good is one, but base things are manifold. Truth is one, but falsehoods are many. True justice is one, but it has

many counterfeits. The wisdom of God is one, but many are *the wisdoms of this world and the princes of this world that come to naught*.[324] The word of God is one, but many are the words that are foreign to God. No man, then, will escape from the sin of speaking much, nor can anyone, *thinking that in his much speaking he may be heard*, be heard.[325]

Accordingly, our prayers should not resemble the babbling or speaking much of the pagans, or what they may be doing in imitation of the serpent.[326] *For the* God of the saints, being a *Father, knoweth what is needful for* His sons, since their needs are worthy of their Father's knowledge. But if a man knows not God, and knows not the things of God, neither will he know of what he is in need. The things which he thinks he needs are tainted with sin; whereas he who has considered the better and divine favours of which he is in need, will receive those favours known to God and which he has considered. The Father was aware of them even before they were asked for.

And now that we have said this about what precedes the Prayer in Matthew's version, let us consider the teaching of the Prayer itself.

CHAPTER 22

OUR FATHER WHO ART IN HEAVEN

Our Father who art in heaven.[327] It is worthwhile to examine carefully the so-called Old Testament to see if we can find anywhere in it a prayer by someone who calls

God "Father." For the moment, although we have exam-
ined it as carefully as we can, we have not found such.
We do not say, of course, that God is not spoken of as
"Father," or that those who were regarded as believing in
God were not called "sons of God"; but that we have not
yet found in a prayer that confidence in calling God
"Father" which was proclaimed by the Saviour.[328] That
God is called "Father," and those who have recourse to the
Word of God were called "sons," is to be seen in many
places, as for example in Deuteronomy: *Thou hast for-
saken the God that begot thee, and hast forgotten the God
that nourished thee.*[329] And again: *Is not He thy father
that hath possessed thee, and made thee, and created
thee?*[330] And again: . . . *sons that are unfaithful.*[331]
And in Isaias: *I have brought up children and exalted
them; but they have despised me.*[332] And in Malachias:
*The son shall honour the father and the servant his master.
If, then, I be a father, where is my honour? And if I be a
master, where is my fear?*[333]

2. Therefore, even though God is called "Father," and
those who are begotten by the word of faith in Him are
called "sons," yet one cannot find among the ancients the
concept of positive and unalterable sonship. At all events
the texts quoted demonstrate that those who were styled
sons were in fact subjects. For according to the Apostle,
*as long as the heir is a child, he differeth nothing from a
servant, though he be lord of all; but is under tutors and
governors until the time appointed by the father.*[334] But
the *fulness of the time*[335] consists in the coming amongst
us of Our Lord Jesus Christ, when those who wish it receive adoption as sons, as Paul says in these words: *For
you have not received the spirit of bondage in fear; but*

you have received the spirit of adoption of sons, whereby we cry: Abba, Father.[336] And in the Gospel according to John we read: *But as many as received Him, He gave them power to be made the sons of God, to them that believe in His name.*[337] And in the Catholic Epistle of John we have learned about those who have been born of God that, because of this *spirit of adoption, whosoever is born of God committeth not sin, for His seed abideth in him; and he cannot sin, because he is born of God.*[338]

3. If we were to understand what is implied by: *When you pray, say, Father*—which is what is written in Luke—we would, if we were not true sons, shrink from addressing Him by that name, lest to our other sins we should add the charge of impiety. What I mean is something like what Paul says in the First Epistle to the Corinthians: *No man can say "Lord Jesus" but by the Holy Spirit, and no man speaking by the Spirit of God, saith "Anathema" to Jesus.*[339] He uses "Holy *Spirit*" and "Spirit of God" to mean the same. It is not altogether clear what is meant by *to say "Lord Jesus" by the Holy Spirit,* for innumerable hypocrites and many of the heterodox and sometimes even evil spirits that are vanquished by the power of the name, use these words. No man will venture to contend that any of these say *"The Lord Jesus" by the Holy Spirit.* Consequently they cannot be shown to say "Lord Jesus." Only those who are the servants of the Word of God and in whatever they do call no man Lord but Him, can by their very state say "Lord Jesus." If these are they who say "Lord Jesus," then it is likely that everyone that sins anathematizes the Word of God in his sinning, and through his evil deeds cries out "Anathema to Jesus." And since one kind of man says: "Lord Jesus," and his opposite

says: "Anathema to Jesus," so *whosoever is born of God* [340] and does not sin, shares in the seed of God which keeps him from all sin and says through his actions: *Our Father who art in heaven.* And *the Spirit Himself giveth testimony to their spirit* that they are *the children of God, His heirs, and joint heirs with Christ* [341]—because, suffering with Him, they may also truly hope to be glorified with Him. But that such men may not say *Our Father* half-heartedly, besides their works, their heart also, which is the fount and origin of good works, *believes unto justice*, while *their mouth makes confession* in harmony *unto salvation.* [342]

4. Further, every thought, word, and deed of theirs, formed by the Only-Begotten Word after Himself, [343] reproduces *the image of the invisible God* [344] and conforms *to the image of Him that created* [345] them—*who maketh His sun to rise upon the good and bad and raineth upon the just and the unjust.* [346] Thus there is in them *the image of the Heavenly One,* [347] who Himself is the image of God. The saints, being the image of an image, and that image the Son, take the impression of sonship, not only becoming of the same form as *the body of the glory* [348] of Christ, but also like unto Him who is in the body. They become conformed to Him who is *in the body of His glory*, being *reformed in the newness of their mind.* [349] And if these say in all things: *Our Father who art in heaven*, then it is clear that *he that committeth sin*, as John says in his Catholic Epistle, *is of the devil; for the devil sinneth from the beginning.* [350] And as *the seed of God*, which *abideth in him* who *is born of God*, makes it impossible for him who is formed according to the Only-Begotten Word [351] to sin, so in every man that commits sin the seed of the devil is present, and as long as it remains in his soul, it makes it

impossible for the soul so afflicted to reform. But since *for this purpose the Son of God appeared, that He might destroy the works of the devil,*[352] it is possible through the indwelling of the Word of God in our soul *to destroy the works of the devil,* to root out the evil seed placed in us, and to become *children of God.*

5. So, let us not think that we are taught to say words which are to be used only at a certain time appointed for prayer. If what we have said[353] on prayer *without ceasing*[354] is understood, then all our life must be a prayer *without ceasing* in which we say: *Our Father who art in heaven.* Let us in no way have *our citizenship* upon earth,[355] but in every way *in the heavens* which are God's thrones; for God's kingdom is built on all those who bear *the image of the Heavenly One*[356] and so have become heavenly themselves.

CHAPTER 23

When it is said that the Father of the saints is in heaven, it must not be understood that He is circumscribed by a bodily form and has a habitation in heaven. For if He were so contained, God would be less than the heavens, since the heavens would be enclosing Him. Rather must we believe that by the ineffable power of His divinity all things are contained and maintained by Him. In general, too, the passages which taken literally might be understood by the uninitiated to mean that God is in a place, must be taken properly as conveying great spiritual concepts about God. Such passages are the following found in the Gospel according to John: *Before the festival day of the pasch, Jesus knowing that His hour was come, that He should pass out of this world to the Father: having loved His own who were in the world, He loved them unto the end.*[357]   And a little farther on: *Knowing that the Father had given Him all things into His hands and that He came from God and goeth to God.*   And later on: *You have heard that I said to you: I go away, and I come unto you. If you loved me, you would indeed be glad because I go to the Father.*[358]   And again farther on: *And now I go to Him that sent me, and none of you asketh me: Whither goest Thou?*[359]   If these passages are to be taken in a local sense, it is clear that the following must be taken in the same way: *Jesus answered and said to them: If any man love me, he will keep my word. And my Father will love him, and we will come to him and will make our abode with him.*[360]

2.   But these words about the coming of the Father and the Son to him who loves the word of Jesus do not mean a coming to a place, nor should they be taken as referring to a place. The Word of God in coming down to dwell with us and, considering His own proper dignity, humbling Himself while He is among men,[361] is said to *pass out of this world to the Father,*[362] so that we too may contemplate Him there in His perfection, when He returns from the emptiness wherewith *He emptied Himself* among us to His own *fulness.*[363]   And we too, if we follow Him as guide, will there receive fulness and be delivered from all our emptiness. Let the Word of God go, then, *to Him that sent him.*[364] Let Him *pass out of the world.* Let Him *go to the Father.* At the end of the Gospel according to John we find the words: *Do not touch me, for I am not*

yet ascended to my Father.[365] Let us try to understand
these words also in a mystical sense: we shall understand
the ascent of the Son *to the Father* in a manner more becoming to God if we consider it with pious understanding
as being more an ascent of the mind than of the body.[366]

3. It was necessary, I think, to go into these points in
connection with the words, *Our Father who art in heaven,*
to settle once and for all the degrading notion of people
holding God to be in heaven in a local sense, and not to
permit anyone to say that God is in a physical place. This
is tantamount to saying that He has a body, from which
follow the most impious conclusions, namely that He is
divisible, material, and perishable. For every body is divisible, and material, and perishable. Or else, if they are
not deluding themselves and claim to have clear discern-
ment in the matter, let them tell us how in that case He
could possibly have a nature other than material.

Since many texts in Scripture, written before the coming of Christ in the body, seem to say that God is in a
physical place, it will not be irrelevant, it seems to me, to
cite some of those texts in order to remove all doubt from
those who through narrowness of outlook are disposed to
believe that the God of all is confined in a small and circumscribed place.

First, then, in Genesis: Adam and Eve, it is said, *heard
the voice of the Lord God walking in paradise at the after-
noon air; and Adam and his wife hid themselves from the
face of the Lord God, amidst the trees of paradise.*[367] We
shall ask them that do not wish to go to the treasures of
Scripture, that do not even begin to knock at its door: [368]
can they understand how the Lord God, *who fills heaven
and earth,*[369] who, as they understand it, uses the heaven

physically as His throne and the earth as a footstool under His feet,[370] can be contained by a place so small in comparison with the whole heaven and earth, that not only is the physical paradise of which they speak not filled completely by God, but is so much greater than He that it can hold Him as He walks around in it and the sound of His footsteps can be heard? And still more absurd in their interpretation would be the fact that Adam and Eve, fearing God because of their transgression, *hid themselves from the face of God amidst the trees of paradise.* For it is not said that they wished to hide themselves in this way, but that they actually hid. And how could God, as they understood it, search for Adam saying: *Where art thou?* [371]

4. We have treated of these questions at considerable length when we were examining Genesis.[372] However, not now to pass over in complete silence a problem of such importance, we shall content ourselves by recalling the words, *I will dwell in them and walk among them,* spoken by God in Deuteronomy.[373] As is His walking in the midst of His saints, so is His walking in paradise. All sinners hide before Him, avoiding His glance and losing their confidence. So too *Cain went out from the face of God and dwelt in the land of Naid over against Eden.*[374] Hence, as is God's living in the saints, so is His living in heaven, whether "heaven" refers to every saint that bears the *image of the Heavenly One,*[375] or to Christ, in whom are all the lights and stars of heaven that are saved.[376] Or, again, He dwells <there> through the saints that are in heaven <according> to the words, *To Thee have I lifted up my eyes, who dwellest in heaven.*[377] And the passage in Ecclesiastes, *Be not hasty to utter a word before the face of God; for God is in heaven above, and thou upon earth*

below,[378] is intended to make clear the distance between those who are in *the body of lowness,*[379] and him who is with the angels, elevated by the help of the Word,[380] and with the holy powers, or with Christ Himself. It is not absurd that He, allegorically termed "heaven," should properly be the "throne of the Father," and that His Church, termed "earth," should be the footstool for His feet.[381]

5. We have added these few passages also from the Old Testament which are thought to represent God in a local sense. It was our purpose to encourage, as we were able, the reader in every way to interpret Sacred Scripture in a more elevated and spiritual sense, whenever it seems to teach that God is in a place. It was proper to go into this matter in connection with the words, *Our Father who art in heaven,* words which remove, so to speak, the substance of God from that of all created things. With them He has no part, but to them has been given a certain power and glory of God,[382] and, so to speak, an effluence of His divinity.[383]

CHAPTER 24

HALLOWED BE THY NAME

Hallowed be Thy name: Whether this signifies that what is prayed for has not yet happened, or, if it has happened, implies that it does not persist and asks that it should be preserved, it is clear from the text itself that the name of the Father is not yet hallowed and that we are bidden to

say in Matthew and Luke: *Hallowed be Thy Name.*[384]
And how is it, one may object, that a man can ask that the
name of God may be hallowed, as though it were not hallowed? Let us see what is meant by the "name" of the
Father, and the words "be hallowed."

2. A name is a term which summarizes and manifests
the personal character of him who is named.[385] For example, there is the personal character of the apostle Paul,
partly in his soul, which consequently is of a particular
kind, partly in his mind, as a result of which he contem-
plates certain things, and partly in his body, which consequently is of such and such a kind. This character,
personal and incommunicable—for there is no man living
who is identical with Paul—is made manifest in his being
called "Paul." [386] But as among men their personal charac-
ters change, so quite properly do their names, as we find in
Scripture. Thus when the personal character of Abram
changed, he was called Abraham; [387] and when that of
Simon, he was called Peter; [388] and when that of him who
pursued Jesus—Saul—he was called Paul.[389] But in the case
of God, who is always the same, unchangeable, and persists
forever immutable, there is but one name reserved, as it
were, for Him forever—HE WHO IS. So in Exodus [390]
and in any later designation of the same kind. Since then
we all, although making a variety of suppositions about
Him, know something of God, but do not all know what
He is—for few indeed, and fewer—if I may say so—than
few are they who grasp His holiness in all things—rightly
are we taught to pray that our concept of God may be
hallowed amongst us. Thus we shall see His holiness in
creating, in providing, in judging, in choosing and aban-

doning, in accepting and rejecting, in rewarding and punishing each one according to his merits.

3.   In these activities and others like them is found, so I
may say, the stamp of the personal character of God, that
which in my opinion is called in Scripture the "name of
God." So in Exodus: *Thou shalt not take the name of the
Lord thy God in vain.*[391]   In Deuteronomy: *Let my voice
be awaited as the rain; let my speech distil as the dew, as a
shower upon the herb, and as rain upon the grass; because
I will invoke the name of the Lord.*[392]   And in the Psalms:
*They shall remember Thy name throughout all genera-
tions.*[393]   The man who brings into his concept of God
ideas which have no place there *takes the name of the Lord
God in vain.*   But the man who is able to use his *voice as
the rain* that helps the souls of his listeners to bear fruit,
who uses *speech* that consoles *as the dew*, and brings a most
helpful *shower* and efficacious *rain* of words by way of
effectual edification for them that hear him, achieves all
this through this name.   Realizing that he needs God to
accomplish all these things, he calls to his aid Him who in
fact provides what we have been describing.   Anyone that
clarifies the things that pertain to God recalls these things
rather than learns them, even though he seems to hear from
someone, or thinks that he discovers, the mysteries of worship.[394]

4.   As he who is praying ought to be aware of these
considerations <that> he may <with reason> ask that
the name of God be hallowed, so we read in the Psalms:
Let us extol His name together.[395]   Here the prophet enjoins on us to hasten in full harmony, *in the same mind,
and in the same judgment*, to attain to the true and lofty
knowledge of the personal character of God.   For one

extols the name of God "together" when, sharing in the effluence of divinity in being upheld by God and over-coming one's enemies who cannot joy over one's fall, one extols that same power of God, in which one shares. This is shown in the twenty-ninth Psalm in the words: *I will extol Thee, O Lord, for Thou hast upheld me and hast not made my enemies to rejoice over me.*[396] We extol God when we dedicate within ourselves a house to God; for the title of the Psalm is: A PSALM OF A CANTICLE, AT THE DEDI-CATION OF DAVID'S HOUSE.

5. Still speaking of the words, *Hallowed be Thy name*, and the other words set forth in the imperative mood, we must point out that quite frequently too the translators use the imperative instead of the optative; for instance, in the Psalms we have: *Let deceitful lips be made dumb, which speak iniquity against the just,*[397] instead of "may they be made dumb," and in the one hundred and eighth Psalm, which refers to Judas: *Let the usurer search all his sub-stance,* and, *Let there be none to help him.*[398] The whole Psalm is a prayer concerning Judas, that things such as these may befall him.

On the other hand, Tatian,[399] because he did not under-stand that the form "let it be" does not always stand for the optative, but in some places has the force of the im-perative, came to most impious conclusions about God when He said, *Let there be light,*[400] implying that He wished, rather than commanded the light to be. Tatian impiously maintains that God was in darkness. In reply we ask him how he understands the text: *Let the earth bring forth the green herb;* and, *Let the waters that are under the heaven be gathered together into one place;* and, *Let the waters bring forth the creeping creatures having life*, and, *Let the earth bring forth the living creature.*[401] Was it in order to be able to stand on a firm place that He prays that *the waters which are under the heaven be gathered together into one place,* or in order that He might partake of the fruits of the earth that He prays that *the earth bring forth?* And, as with light, is it the same kind of need He has for the animals of the sea, land, and air, so that He prays for them also? If it is absurd, as Tatian himself says, that God should be praying for these, especially as He uses the imperative mood, why should we not understand the sentence, *Let there be light,* in the same way, that is to say, that it is an order, and not a wish? Since the prayer is cast in the form of the imperative, I thought it necessary to make mention of Tatian's false interpretations, because of those who have been deceived and have followed his impious teaching. We ourselves have had experience of such people.

CHAPTER 25

THY KINGDOM COME

Thy kingdom come. If *the kingdom of God,* according to the word of Our Lord and Saviour, *cometh not with observation;* and *neither shall they say: Behold here, or behold there*—but *the kingdom of God is within* us [402] (for *the word is very nigh unto* us, *in* our *mouth and in* our *heart*): [403] then it is clear that he who prays for the coming of the kingdom of God rightly prays that the kingdom of God might be established, and bear fruit and be perfected in himself.[404] Every saint, being ruled by God as his king and obedient to the spiritual laws of God, as it were, dwells within himself as in a well-ordered city. The Father is present to him, and Christ reigns with the Father in the soul that is perfect according to the words mentioned by me a little earlier: *We will come to him and will make our abode with him.*[405] And by the kingdom of God, I believe, is meant the happy enthronement of reason and the rule of wise counsels; and by the "kingdom" of Christ, the saving words that reach those who hear, and the accomplished works of justice and the other virtues. For the Son of God is Word and Justice.[406] On the other hand, every sinner is subject to tyranny under *the prince of this world,*[407] since every sinner is a slave to *this present wicked world* in not giving himself over to Him *who gave Himself for our sins, that He might deliver us from this present wicked world,* and might deliver us *according to the will of God and Our Father*[408]—as is said in the Epistle to the Galatians. He who is subject to the tyranny of *the prince of this world* is also under the reign of sin because he has sinned voluntarily. Hence Paul bids us not to submit to sin that would rule over us; and we are told this as follows: *Let not sin therefore reign in your mortal body, so as to obey the lusts thereof.*[409]

2. But someone may say regarding both petitions— *Hallowed be Thy name,* and *Thy kingdom come,* that if a man prays so as to be heard, and is sometimes heard, then, it is clear, there is that person for whom at some time the name of God will be hallowed as we have described, and for him the kingdom of God will come. And if these things will be accomplished for him, how can he with propriety continue to pray for what is already present, saying,

as though they were not, *Hallowed be Thy name, Thy kingdom come?* In this case, there will be a time when it will be proper to refrain from praying, *Hallowed be Thy name, Thy kingdom come.*

To reply: He who prays for *the word of knowledge* and *the word of wisdom,*[410] will always with propriety pray for them since through being heard he will always be receiving greater visions of wisdom and knowledge— though he *knows in part* only what he may be able to comprehend in the present time, while *that which is perfect,* which will *do away with that which is in part,* will then be revealed when the mind will contemplate the spiritual *face to face* [411] without the aid of any sensation. So also *that which is perfect* in the hallowing by each one of us of the name of God and the coming of His kingdom is not possible, unless the *perfection* of *knowledge* and *wisdom* and perhaps, too, of the remaining virtues *is come.* And we journey towards perfection if, *forgetting the things that are behind, we stretch forth ourselves to those that are before.*[412] The kingdom of God will be fully established in us if we advance with ceaseless effort, when the word of the Apostle will be fulfilled, namely that Christ, when *all* enemies *shall be subdued unto Him, shall deliver up the kingdom to God and the Father, so that God may be all in all.*[413] Therefore, *praying without ceasing* [414] with a disposition made divine by the Word, let us say to our Father in heaven: *Hallowed be Thy name. Thy kingdom come.*

3. Further, in regard to the kingdom of God we must also consider this, that just as *justice has no participation with injustice,*[415] and *light has no fellowship with darkness,* and *Christ has no concord with Beliar,*[416] so the kingdom

of sin cannot be reconciled with the kingdom of God. If, therefore, we wish to be under the kingship of God, *let not sin reign in our mortal body*,[417] nor let us obey sin's injunctions when she invites our soul to *the works of the flesh* [418] and acts in which God has no part. But rather let us *mortify our members which are upon the earth*,[419] and *bring forth* the *fruit of the Spirit*,[420] so that the Lord may walk in us as in a spiritual paradise,[421] ruling alone as king over us with His Christ, who *sits* in us *on the right of the spiritual power* [422] which we pray to receive, and who will continue to sit there *until* all *His enemies* within us *become His footstool*,[423] and *all principality and power and virtue be brought to naught* in us.[424]

It is possible that all this should happen to each one of us and that even the last enemy, death, should be destroyed,[425] so that Christ may say in us: *O death, where is thy sting? O Hades, where is thy victory?* [426] Let then *what is corruptible* in us *put on* holiness and *incorruption* in chastity and all purity, and *what is mortal*, having conquered death, *put on the immortality* of the Father.[427] Thus God will be reigning in us, and we shall already enjoy the benefits of regeneration and resurrection.[428]

CHAPTER 26

THY WILL BE DONE ON EARTH AS IT IS IN HEAVEN

Thy will be done on earth as it is in heaven. Luke after *Thy kingdom come* has omitted this and has *Give us each day our supersubstantial bread*.[429] Let us then study the words which we have cited as found in Matthew alone and which come next in order. Let us who pray while still "on earth" and understanding that the will of God is done in heaven by all the denizens of the heavens, pray that His will be done in all things by us "on earth," as it is by them. This will happen, if we do nothing contrary to His will. And when this will of God is done by us on earth as it is in heaven, then we shall be like them that are in heaven, inasmuch as we shall *bear* as they do *the image of the Heavenly One*,[430] and we shall inherit the kingdom of heaven,[431] and those that come after us on earth will pray to be like unto us, when we are in heaven.

2. But one could apply the clause *on earth as it is in heaven* which we have in Matthew only, to the other requests also so that we would be commanded to say something like this in our prayer: *Hallowed be Thy name on earth as it is in heaven. Thy kingdom come on earth as it is in heaven. Thy will be done on earth as it is in heaven.*[432] For the name of God is hallowed by those in heaven, and the kingdom of God has come to them, and the will of God is done in them. All these things are wanting to us "on earth," though they can be achieved by us if we show ourselves worthy to be heard by God in all these matters.

3. Further, noting the words, *Thy will be done on earth as it is in heaven*, one might ask: How is the will of God done in heaven where there are *the spirits of wickedness*[433] through whom *the sword* of God *will be inebriated even in heaven?*[434] If then we pray that the will of God be done on earth as it is in heaven, may we not inadvisedly be praying that there also remain on earth adverse spirits whither they also come from heaven? For many on earth

become wicked because they are conquered by the *spirits of wickedness that are in the heavenly places.*

But if one understands "heaven" allegorically and maintains that it stands for Christ, and "earth" for the Church (for who is as worthy to be the throne of the Father as Christ?   And what can be compared to the Church as a footstool for the feet of God?),[435] he will easily solve the difficulties raised.   We say that each member of the Church must pray that he may accomplish the will of the Father as Christ did, who came to do the will of the Father and accomplished it perfectly.[436]   For in being *joined to Him* we can become *one spirit* with Him,[437] and consequently accomplish the will of God so that it will be fulfilled on earth as it is in heaven.   *He who is joined to the Lord,* according to Paul, *is one spirit.*   I believe that this interpretation if considered carefully, is not lightly to be put aside.

4.   He, however, who contradicts this will quote the words of Our Lord at the end of the Gospel according to Matthew when, after His resurrection, He declared to the eleven disciples: *All power is given to me in heaven and in earth.*[438]   Having power over those in heaven, He says that He has received power also over those on earth. Those in heaven were first enlightened by the Word,[439] and *at the end of the world*[440] those of the earth will in their turn, through the power given to the Son of God, imitate them, over whom Our Saviour has power and who are perfect in heaven.   Thus it is as if He wished to make His disciples by their prayers co-workers with Himself for the Father, so that as those in heaven are subject to truth and the Word,[441] those on earth may likewise be set right through the power which has been given to Him in heaven

and earth, and may be brought by Him to the happy end destined for those who are in His power. And he who says that "heaven" means the Saviour, and "earth" the Church, holding that *the first-born of every creature*,[442] on whom the Father rests as on a throne, is "heaven," may notice that the "man" whom He put on [443] in intimate union with that power, in that *He humbled Himself* and *became obedient unto death*,[444] said after His resurrection: *All power is given to me in heaven and in earth.* The "man" in the Saviour received power over those in heaven as those contained in the Only-Begotten,[445] so that he might share it with Him, joined to His divinity and made one with Him.

5.   But since he who would offer this alternative interpretation still leaves unsolved the difficulty of how the will of God is done in heaven, seeing that *the spirits of wickedness in the heavenly places* enter into combat with *those on earth*, this can be solved if we consider the following.

It is not because of the place where he dwells, but because of his dispositions, that he who is still on earth has his *citizenship in heaven* and *lays up treasures in heaven*.[446] Having his heart in heaven and *bearing the image of the Heavenly One*,[447] he is no longer of the earth nor of the lower world,[448] but of heaven and the heavenly world that is better than this. So, conversely, *the spirits of wickedness* who still dwell *in the heavenly places* [449] have their *citizenship* on earth. They plot against men and enter into combat with them. They lay up treasures on earth and bear *the image* of *the earthly*,[450] which is *the beginning of God's fashioning, made to be the sport of the angels*.[451] They are not of the heavens, nor do they have their home in the heavens—because of their evil disposition. When, therefore, one prays, *Thy will be done on earth as it is in heaven*, there should be no thought at all of them in heaven, but that because of their arrogance they have fallen with him who *fell from heaven like lightning*.[452]

6. And perhaps when our Saviour says that we should pray that the will of the Father be done on earth as it is in heaven, He is not commanding absolutely that we pray for those physically on the earth that they may become like those who are in the heavenly place; but rather, in enjoining the prayer, He wills that all beings that are on the earth, that is to say, the lower kind and those identified with the earthy, should become like to the better, to them whose *citizenship is in heaven*, and have become all heaven. For the sinner, wherever he may be, is earth,[453] and if he does not repent, he will pass somehow to that to which he is akin. But he who does the will of God and does not disobey His saving and spiritual laws, is heaven.

If, then, we are still earth on account of sin, let us pray that the will of God encompass us for our correction, as it has done those who before us have become heaven or are heaven. And if in the eyes of God we are not regarded as earth, but already as heaven, let us ask that on earth, that is to say, among those who are of the lower kind, as in heaven, the will of God may be accomplished, in order that the earth may, so to speak, be made into heaven, and thus one day there will be no more earth but everything will have become heaven.[454] Then if, according to this explanation, *the will* of God *is done on earth as it is in heaven*, the earth will remain earth no longer. If I may employ perhaps a clearer example—if the will of God is done in those who are intemperate, as it is in those who are temperate, the intemperate will be temperate; or if the will of God is done in the unjust, as it is in the just, the unjust will be just. In the same way, if *the will* of God *is done on earth as it is done in heaven,* we shall all be heaven. *Flesh* which *profiteth nothing,* and *blood* which is akin to flesh, *cannot possess the kingdom of God.*[455] But if they be changed from flesh and earth and dust and blood to heavenly substance, it may perhaps be said that they will inherit it.

CHAPTER 27

GIVE US THIS DAY OUR SUPERSUBSTANTIAL BREAD

Give us this day our supersubstantial bread—or as Luke has it: *Give us each day our supersubstantial bread.*[456] Since some understand from this that we are commanded to pray for material bread, it will be well to refute their error here, and to establish the truth about the supersubstantial bread. We must ask them how it could be that He who enjoined upon us to ask for great and heavenly favours,[457] should command us to intercede with the Father for what is small and of the earth, as if He had forgotten—so they would have it—what He had taught. For the bread that is given to our flesh is neither heavenly, nor is the request for it a great request.

THE TRUE BREAD

2. We, on our part, following the Master Himself who teaches us about the bread, shall treat of the matter at

some length.   In the Gospel according to John He says to
those who had come to Capharnaum seeking for Him:
*Amen, amen, I say to you, you seek <me>, not because
you have seen miracles, but because you did eat of the
loaves and were filled.*[458]   He who has eaten of the bread
blessed by Jesus and is filled with it, tries all the more to
understand the Son of God more perfectly, and hastens to
Him.   Hence His admirable command: *Labour not for
the meat which perisheth, but for that which endureth
unto life everlasting, which the Son of man will give
you.*[459]   And when those who were listening to this asked
Him, saying: *What shall we do that we may work the
works of God? Jesus answered and said to them: This is
the work of God, that you believe in Him whom He hath
sent.*[460]   Now God *hath sent His Word, and healed them—*
obviously the sick—as it is written in the Psalms.[461]   Those
who believe in the Word do the works of God which are
meat that endureth unto life everlasting.   And *my Father,*
He says, *giveth you the true bread from heaven.   For the
bread of God is that which cometh down from heaven and
giveth life to the world.*[462]   The "true bread" is that which
nourishes the true man, the *man created* after *the image of
God,*[463] and through which he who is nourished by it is
made *to the image of Him that created him.*   What is
more nourishing for the soul than the Word? [464]   And
what is more precious for the mind of him that understands it than the wisdom of God?   And what is in better
accord with rational nature than truth?

3.   If someone objects at this point, saying that He
would not have taught us to ask for the supersubstantial
bread while leaving it possible that another kind of bread
be understood, let him observe that in the Gospel accord-

ing to John also He sometimes speaks of bread as being something other than Himself, and sometimes as being Himself. An instance of the former is this: *Moses gave you bread from heaven, not the true bread, but my Father giveth you the true bread from heaven.*[465] But to those who say to Him: *Give us always this bread,* He says regarding Himself: *I am the bread of life. He that cometh to me shall not hunger; and he that believeth in me shall never thirst;*[466] and shortly afterwards: *I am the <living> bread which came down from heaven. If any man eat of this bread, he shall live for ever; and the bread that I will give is my flesh which I will give for the life of the world.*[467]

4. Further, since every form of nourishment is called "bread" in the Scriptures, as is clear from what is written concerning Moses, that for forty days he neither ate "bread" nor drank water;[468] and since the word that nourishes is manifold and varied, for not everyone can receive the solid and strong nourishment of God's teachings: therefore, wishing to give an athlete's nourishment suitable to the more perfect, He says: *The bread that I will give is my flesh, which I will give for the life of the world.*[469] And a little later: *Except you eat the flesh of the Son of man and drink His blood, you shall not have life in you. He that eateth my flesh and drinketh my blood hath everlasting life, and I will raise him up in the last day. For my flesh is meat indeed, and my blood is drink indeed. He that eateth my flesh and drinketh my blood abideth in me, and I in him. As the living Father hath sent me and I live by the Father, so he that eateth me, the same also shall live by me.*[470] This is the *true meat,* the flesh of Christ, which, being Word became flesh according to what is written:

And the Word was made flesh. When we <eat and>
drink Him, then He *dwells among us.* When He is dis-
tributed, then is the text fulfilled, *We saw His glory.*[471]
*This is the bread that came down from heaven. Not as
your fathers did eat and are dead. He that eateth this
bread shall live forever.*[472]

5. Paul, speaking to the Corinthians as *unto little ones*
and such as *walked according to man,* says: *I gave you
milk to drink, not meat; for you were not able as yet. But
neither indeed are you now able; for you are yet carnal.*[473]
And in the Epistle to the Hebrews: *And you are become
such as have need of milk, and not of strong meat. For
everyone that is a partaker of milk is unskilful in the word
of justice; for he is a little child. But strong meat is for
the perfect, for them who by custom have their senses ex-
ercised to the discerning of good and evil.*[474] It is my
opinion that the words: *One believeth that he may eat all
things, but he that is weak eats herbs,*[475] are not primarily
spoken of bodily nourishment, but rather of the words of
God which nourish the soul.[476] The true believer and the
truly perfect can eat everything, as is shown in the passage,
One believeth that he may eat all things. But he that is
weak and imperfect contents himself with teachings that
are simple and not strong enough to make him full of
vigour. Paul has him in mind when he says, *But he that is
weak eats herbs.*

6. Then, too, what Solomon says in Proverbs teaches,
in my opinion, that the man who does not because of his
simplicity—and without having erroneous ideas—grasp the
more forceful and important doctrines, is in a better position than another who is more apt, quicker, and better at
understanding things, but who does not see clearly the

pattern of peace and unity in the universe. Here is the text: *It is better to be invited to herbs with love and grace, than to a fatted calf with hatred.*[477] Often we enjoy more a simple and frugal hospitality offered with good conscience by hosts who receive us but cannot offer us more, than a sublime discourse which, however, is raised *against the knowledge of God* with much persuasion, and teaching another doctrine than that of the Father of Our Lord Jesus, who gave us the Law and the Prophets.[478] In order, then, that our soul may not become ill through want of nourishment and that we may not die to God through hunger for the Word of the Lord,[479] let us, while leading in obedience to the teaching of Our Saviour a better life and with greater faith, ask the Father for the living bread which is the same as the supersubstantial bread.

SUPERSUBSTANTIAL

7. We must now examine the meaning of the word "supersubstantial." First we must note that the term *epiousios* (supersubstantial) is not used by the Greeks: neither does it occur with the scholars, nor does it have a place in the language of the people. It seems to have been invented by the Evangelists.[480] At least, Matthew and Luke, when they introduce it, are in complete agreement in their use of it. The translators of the Hebrew texts have done this same kind of thing with regard to other words also. Thus, what Greek has ever used the terms *enotizou* or *akoutistheti* to signify "receive in your ear" and "make yourself to hear"? [481] A term very similar to *epiousios* is found in the Books of Moses, and is there put in the mouth of God: *You shall be to me a periousios people.*[482] I be-

lieve that both words derive from the word *ousia* (substance). The first indicates the bread uniting with our *ousia*. The second describes the people as abiding with the *ousia* of God and partaking in it.

8. *Ousia*, properly understood, is regarded as incorporeal by the philosophers who insist that the pre-eminent reality is incorporeal.[483] It has, then, for them an unchanging existence which admits neither increase nor decrease. To admit either increase or decrease is the property of corporeal things which, because they are subject to change, need something to sustain and nourish them. If within a given time they acquire more than they lose, they increase; if less, they decrease. Again, it may happen that they receive nothing from outside, in which case they are, so to speak, in a state of pure decrease.

But for those who believe that incorporeal reality is secondary and that corporeal reality is primary, *ousia* can be described as follows.[484] It is the prime matter of all existing things, that from which the things that exist come into being; it is the matter of corporeal things, from which corporeal things come into being; it is the matter of things that have a name, from which these things come into being. It is the first undetermined principle; it is that which is presupposed to things that are; it is that which receives all changes and transformations, while being itself from its very concept unchangeable; it is that which persists through all change and transformation. According to these, *ousia* is from its very concept undetermined and without form. It has no fixed size, and is open to any determination as something made ready. In their terminology they call "determinations" those operations and actions generally, in which movements and dispositions are associated. They hold that *ousia* does not in its own proper concept share in any of these things, but that just the same because of its passivity it is always inseparable from one of them, and prepared to receive all the operations of an agent however that may act on it and transform it. For the force [485] that goes with *ousia* and pervades all things is the cause both of every determination and the operations that concern it. They say that *ousia* is entirely changeable and divisible and that every *ousia* can be fused with any other, but so as to be united with it into one.

9. In conducting our investigation into the meaning of *ousia*, because of the texts speaking of *epiousios* bread and *periousios* people, we have given this explanation of the various significations of the term *ousia*. In what went before we had shown that the bread which we have to ask for is of the spirit. We must therefore think here of *ousia* as being of the same nature as the bread. And just as material bread which is used for the body of him who is being nourished, enters into his substance, so *the living bread* and that *which came down from heaven*,[486] offered to the mind and the soul, gives a share of its own proper power to him who presents himself to be nourished by it. And so this will be the supersubstantial bread which we ask for. And again, as according to the quality of the food it is strong and suitable for athletes, or, on the other hand, is of milk and vegetables,[487] so he who takes food is of varying strength. In the same way it follows that when the Word of God is given as milk to infants, as herbs adapted to the weak, and as meat proper for those engaged in combat, each of those who are nourished will, according as he gives himself up to the Word, be able to do this or that, or become a man of such or such character. One must remem-

ber that some so-called food is actually noxious, some is disease-bearing, and some even impossible to take.[488] All this should be taken into account in the analogy with reference to the differences between doctrines that are thought to be nourishing. The supersubstantial bread, then, is that which is most adapted to the rational nature and is akin to its very substance, bringing to the soul health and well-being and strength, and giving to him that eats of it a share of its own immortality. For the Word of God is immortal.

10. This supersubstantial bread, so it seems to me, has another name in Scripture, namely *tree of life*. If a man stretches out his hand and takes of it, he lives forever.[489] This tree is also given a third name, *wisdom of God*, by Solomon when he says: *She is a tree of life to them that lay hold on her, and safe to them that lean on her as on the Lord.*[490] Since the angels also are nourished on the wisdom of God and receive strength to accomplish their own proper works from the contemplation of truth and wisdom, so in the Psalms we find it written that the angels also take food, the men of God, who are called Hebrews, sharing with the angels and, so to speak, becoming table-companions with them. As much is said in the passage, *Man ate the bread of angels.*[491] Our mind must not be so beggarly as to think that the angels forever partake of and nourish themselves on some kind of material bread which, as is told, came down from heaven upon those who went out of Egypt,[492] and that it was this same bread which the Hebrews shared with the angels, the spirits dedicated to the service of God.[493]

11. In our inquiry into the meaning of the supersubstantial bread, and the tree of life, and the wisdom of God,

and the nourishment shared by angels and men, it will not be out of place to establish here whether what Genesis tells about the three men who were received by Abraham and who partook of *the three measures of flour which were kneaded into cakes baked upon the hearth*,[494] is merely a figurative account. The saints can sometimes share spiritual and rational food not only with men, but also with the more divine powers. They do so either to help them, or to show what excellent nourishment they have been able to prepare for themselves. The angels rejoice and nourish themselves on such a demonstration, and become the more ready to co-operate in every way and for the future to join their efforts towards a more comprehensive and more profound understanding for him who, provided only with the nourishing doctrines that earlier were his, has brought joy to them and, to put it thus, nourished them. Nor must we wonder that man should give nourishment to the angels. Christ Himself confesses that He *stands at the door and knocks*, that He *may come in to him* who *opens the door to Him, and sup with him*.[495] And then He gives of His own to him who first nourished, as well as he could, the Son of God.

12.   He that receives the supersubstantial bread is made strong in his heart and becomes a son of God.[496] But he that shares of the dragon is nothing but a spiritual Ethiopian [497] changing himself into a serpent through the snares of the dragon. Thus, even if he says that he wishes to be baptized, he hears himself reproved by the Word: *Serpents, ye brood of vipers, who hath showed you to flee from the wrath to come?* [498] And David, speaking of the body of the dragon which is eaten by the Ethiopians, says: *Thou didst crush the heads of the dragons in the water.*

<Thou hast broken the head of the dragon:> Thou hast given him to be meat for the people of the Ethiopians.[499] But if, inasmuch as the Son of God exists substantially, as does the Adversary also,[500] there is nothing incongruous in either of them becoming the food of this person or that, why do we hesitate to admit that in the matter of all powers, good and evil, and men, each of us can be nourished by them all? Thus, when Peter was about to join company with the centurion, Cornelius, and those who were with him at Caesarea, and then to share the words of God with the Gentiles also, he saw *a vessel let down by the four corners from heaven wherein were all manner of four-footed creatures and creeping things and beasts of the earth.*[501] And when he was commanded *to rise, to kill and eat,* he declined at first, saying: Thou knowest that *I never eat anything that is common or unclean.*[502] He was then told *to call no man common or unclean;* for that which was cleansed by God must not be called common by Peter. The text says: *That which God hath cleansed, do not thou call common.*[503] Thus the distinction made by the law of Moses in the terminology applied to numerous animals as being clean and unclean food,[504] and that with reference to the varying dispositions of rational beings, teaches us a lesson: namely, that some such beings can serve us as nourishing food, while of others quite the opposite is true, until God purifies them and makes them all nourishing—even those *of every kind.*[505]

13. Since this is the case, and the difference between nourishments is as we have said, the supersubstantial bread is unique—above all those that are mentioned. We must pray to be made worthy of it, and to be nourished by *the*

Word of God, which was *in the beginning with God,*[506] so that we may be made divine.

THIS DAY

Someone will say that the term *epiousios* is formed from the verb *epienai:* [507] that is to say, that we are bidden to ask for the bread that properly belongs to the age that is to come. Thus God by anticipation gives it to us now, and in this way what should be given as it were tomorrow is given to us "this day." Here "this day" means the present age and "tomorrow" the age that is to come. But, at least in my opinion, the first meaning given is better, as will become clear if we examine what is meant by the term *semeron* ("this day") which is added by Matthew, and the phrase, *kath hemeran* ("each day"), as is written in Luke.[508]

In many places in Scripture it is customary to use the term "this day" (= "to-day") for the entire (present) age;[509] as for example in the text: *He is the father of the Moabites unto this day;* [510] and, *He is the father of the Ammonites unto this day;* [511] and, *This word was spread abroad among the Jews even unto this day;* [512] and in the Psalms, *To-day if you shall hear His voice, harden not your hearts.*[513] And in Josue this is brought out very clearly as follows: *Depart not from the Lord in the days of this day.*[514] And if "this day" stands for the whole of the present age, "yesterday" may stand for the age that is past. I believe that this is so in the Psalms and in Paul's Epistle to the Hebrews. In the Psalms we find: *For a thousand years in Thy sight are as yesterday which is past.*[515] Here, I presume, the famous millennium is in question: it is compared to "yesterday" as distinct from "to-day." And the Apostle writes: *Jesus Christ, yesterday, and to-day, and the same for ever.*[516] It is not surprising at all that all time has the same meaning for God as the interval of one day for us. Indeed I believe that it has less.

14. We must also examine the question as to whether or no the meaning of the feasts and festal assemblies determined by "days" or "months" or "seasons" or "years" is to be explained in terms of *ages.* If the *Law has a shadow of the things to come,*[517] it must be that the many sabbaths are the "shadow" of a great many days, and the new moons will be realized at definite intervals of time. That will come about when the path of a certain moon (I do not know which) will meet with that of a certain sun. And if the first month, and the tenth day until the fourteenth, and the fourteenth to the twenty-first of the feast of Azymes[518] all *have a shadow of the things to come—who is wise*[519] and so much *the friend of God*[520] as to discern the first of many months, its tenth day, and so on? And what need I say of the feast of the seven weeks of days,[521] and the seventh month, of which the first day is called the day of trumpets, and the tenth, the day of atonement?[522] Only God who ordained them knows what they mean. Who is there who has grasped the mind of Christ so well that he knows the meaning of the seventh year of freedom of Hebrew slaves,[523] and the remission of debts, and the intermission of the cultivation of the holy land?[524] Over and above the feast of every seventh year is the feast called the Jubilee.[525] No one can ever come near divining its precise meaning or the true import of the prescriptions enjoined by it, except Him who knows the Father's will

and His disposition for every age according to *His incom-*
prehensible judgments and unsearchable ways.[526]

15.　I have often been puzzled when I put side by side
two texts of the Apostle as to how there can be an *end of*
ages, in which once and for all *Jesus hath appeared for the*
destruction of sin,[527] if after the present age there are to be
other succeeding ages.　The texts are as follows: in the
Epistle to the Hebrews—*But now once at the end of ages*
He hath appeared for the destruction of sin by the sacrifice
of Himself; and in the Epistle to the Ephesians, . . . *that*
He might show in the ages to come the abundant riches of
His grace, in His bounty towards us.[528]

My opinion in face of this difficulty, in which great
issues are involved, is that as the completion of the year is
achieved in its last month, after which another month be-
gins again, so perhaps many ages, as it were a year of ages,
have been completed in the present age, after which certain
ages to come will begin and the next age will be their first.
It is in these future ages that God will *show the riches of*
His grace in His bounty.　The man plunged deepest in sin,
who has *blasphemed against the Holy Spirit,*[529] will be
under the domination of sin during the whole of the present age, and from the beginning to the end of the age to
come; after that he will achieve salvation in a way I cannot
account for.

16.　The man who has grasped these things and consid-
ers in his mind a *week* of ages, so that he may have the
vision of some holy Sabbath; who has pondered on a
month of ages, so that he may see God's holy new moon;
and a *year* of ages, that he may contemplate the feasts of
the year, when *all the males shall appear before the Lord*
God;[530] and the *years* corresponding to these great ages,

that he may comprehend the seventh holy year; and the *seven weeks of years* of ages, that he may praise Him who disposed these things so wonderfully: how can he trifle over even the smallest part of an *hour* of a *day* of an age so great? Will he not rather do all he can that by making himself worthy through his preparation in this life to partake of the supersubstantial bread "this day," he may receive it "each day"? The term "each day" has been made clear in what was said above. He who "to-day" prays to God, who is from infinity to infinity, not only for "this day" but also for "each day," will be prepared to receive from Him, who is able to give *more abundantly than we desire or understand*,[531] things greater even—if I may use hyperbole—than the things that *eye hath not seen, greater than ear hath not heard, greater than that hath not entered into the heart of man*.[532]

17. I have considered it very necessary to raise all these questions in order that the terms "to-day" and "each day" may be understood in our prayer to His Father to give us the supersubstantial bread. Finally, if we consider the term "our" and prefer to consider it as used in the latter Gospel, where there is written not: *Give us this day our supersubstantial bread*, but *Give us each day our supersubstantial bread*,—nevertheless the question arises as to how this bread is "ours." But as the Apostle says that *all things* belong to the saints *whether it be life, or death, or things present, or things to come*,[533] it will not be necessary to say anything about the matter here.

CHAPTER 28

AND FORGIVE US OUR DEBTS, AS WE ALSO FORGIVE OUR DEBTORS

And forgive us our debts, as we also forgive our debtors; or as Luke has it: *And forgive us our sins, for we also forgive every one that is indebted to us.* On the question of debts the Apostle also says: *Render therefore to all men their dues: tribute, to whom tribute is due; fear to whom fear; custom, to whom custom; honour to whom honour. Owe no man any thing, but to love one another.*[534] We owe debts, therefore, in that we have certain duties not only of giving, but also of speaking as is right, and doing certain things, but over and above this we are under an obligation of having a certain disposition towards others. Either, then, we discharge these debts by carrying out the injunctions of God's law, or, if we despise sane reason and do not discharge them, we continue to remain in debt.

OUR DEBTS

2. As to what we owe our brothers, we must consider that it is quite the same whether we owe it to those regenerated with us in Christ[535] by reason of religion, or those born of the same fathers or mothers as ourselves. Further, we have a certain debt to our fellow citizens; and another, common to us all, towards all men; and a particular debt to strangers and to those who are old enough to be our fathers; and another to those whom it is proper for us to

honour as sons or brothers. He who refuses to discharge
these debts to his brethren still remains debtor of what he
has not paid. In the same way if we fail towards men in
our obligations to them, contracted through the spirit of
wisdom which issues in charity, our debt becomes the
greater.

But towards ourselves also we have debts: we must use
our body in such a way as not to waste its substance in our
love of pleasure; and we owe it to our soul to look after it
carefully, to provide that the mind retain its keenness, and
that our speech may never be barbed, but always helpful,
and never given to vain talk. And again, if we do not
discharge our debts towards ourselves, our debt becomes
all the heavier.

3. In addition to all this and above all else we are the
work and image of God[536] and consequently are under
debt to preserve a certain disposition towards Him and *to
love* Him *with our whole heart, and with our whole
strength, and with our whole mind.*[537] If we do not honour
these obligations, we continue to be debtors to God and
sin against the Lord. And who will then pray for us?
For *if one man sinning shall sin against another, they shall
pray for him . . .; but if he shall sin against the Lord, who
shall pray for him?*[538] So speaks Heli in the First Book of
Kings. Moreover, we are debtors to Christ who *hath
purchased* us *with His own blood,*[539] just as every slave is
in debt to him who purchased him for the sum of money
he gave for him. And, again, we are in debt to the Holy
Spirit, and this we discharge when we *grieve not* Him *in
whom we are sealed unto the day of redemption.*[540] And
if we do not grieve Him, we *bring forth the fruit*[541] which

is demanded of us, for He is present to us and quickens our soul.[542]

And if we do not know exactly the angel in heaven who for each one of us *sees the face of the Father*,[543] nevertheless, if we but reflect, it will become clear to each of us that in some things we are in debt to him too. Since *we are made a spectacle to the world and to angels and to men*,[544] we must realize that just as the actor in the theatre is under obligation to say certain things and do certain things in the sight of the spectators and if he fails to carry out this obligation is punished as having insulted the whole audience, so we, too, have obligations to the whole world and all the angels and the whole human race. Wisdom will instruct us about these obligations—if we are willing to learn.

4. Apart from these more general obligations there is the debt of the widow, who is provided for by the Church; the debt of the deacon; that of the priest; and the heaviest of all, that of the bishop exacted from him under penalty of punishment by the Saviour of the whole Church.[545] Then the Apostle has mentioned a mutual debt of husband and wife, saying: *Let the husband render the debt to his wife, and the wife also in like manner to the husband;* and he adds, *Defraud not one another.*[546]

What need is there for me to say more? Those who come upon this book can read through it and see from what has been said what their own debts are. If we do not discharge these debts, we shall remain bound by them; if we do discharge them, we shall be free. This only I add: while a man is alive, there is not a single hour, day or night, in which he is not a debtor.

5. When a man owes a debt, he either pays it or defaults. In our life it is the same—we can pay our debts, we

can default. There are those who owe nothing to any-
body. Some pay most of what they owe and <remain in
debt for a little. Others> pay a little and remain in debt
for most of what they owe. And some may pay nothing
and owe all. He who pays all and owes nothing may discharge his obligation within a certain time and requires a
remission of debts incurred before that time. Such a remission can reasonably be obtained by one who does his
best by a certain time to discharge all obligations as yet
unpaid.

All our transgressions are engraved on our reason and
become the *handwriting of the decree against us*[547] by
which we shall be judged. They are as debt accounts, to
express it thus, written in our own hand by us all, and
presented before the tribunal, *when we shall all stand before the judgment seat of Christ, that every one may receive the proper things of the body, according as he hath
done, whether it be good or evil.*[548] It is of these debts that
it is written also in Proverbs: *Do not give thyself as a
surety, because you stand in awe of a person. For if he
have not wherewith to restore, they shall take the covering
from thy side.*[549]

OUR DEBTORS

6. But if we are in debt to so many, it is also true that
there are some who are in debt to us. Some have obligations towards us as their fellow men; others as to their fellow citizens; some as to fathers; others as to sons; and in
addition, some as wives to their husbands, and as friends to
friends. Therefore when some of our many debtors to us
may prove rather tardy in the matter of discharging their
obligations towards us, we shall act with humanity, not

remembering their debts to us, but rather those that we owe ourselves in which we have often failed—not only our debts to men, but those also to God Himself. When we but recall the debts which we have not discharged but have refused to pay: debts incurred when the time went by in which we ought to have done certain things for our neighbour, we shall be more sympathetic to those who are debtors to ourselves and who have not discharged their debt; [550] and especially so if we do not allow ourselves to forget our transgressions of God's law, and our *iniquity spoken on high* [551]—spoken either through ignorance of the truth or because of dissatisfaction with circumstances that overtook us.

7. If we do not wish to act indulgently towards our debtors, we shall suffer what he suffered who did not remit a hundred pence to his companion in slavery,[552] although he had obtained a remission of his own debt. As we are told in the parable in the Gospel, his master had him bound and exacted from him all that he had remitted, saying to him: *Wicked and slothful servant, shouldst not thou have had compassion on thy fellow servant, even as I had compassion on thee? Cast him into prison till he pay all the debt.* And the Lord adds: *So also shall my heavenly Father do to you, if you forgive not, every one his brother, from your hearts.* We must indeed pardon those who state that they repent of the faults which they have committed against us, even if they repeat the performance over and over again: *If thy brother,* He says, *sin against thee seven times a day, and seven times in a day be converted unto thee, saying, "I repent," forgive him.* [553] It is not we that will be hard towards those who do not repent: such men themselves do harm to themselves; *for he that reject-*

eth instruction hateth himself.[554]   But even in such cases we must do our best to heal a man who is so completely perverted that he is not even aware of his evil plight and is *drunk, not with wine,*[555] but—and this is more ruinous— drunk with the darkness of evil-doing.

THE REMISSION OF SINS

8.   When Luke writes: *Forgive us our sins*—since *sins* are incurred when we do not discharge the *debts* we owe— he says the same thing as Matthew, who does not seem to take account of the man who wishes to forgive only those of his debtors who repent.   And Luke says that the Saviour ordained that we should add in our prayer, *for we also forgive "everyone" that is indebted to us.*[556]   All of us indeed can forgive sins committed against us, as is evident from the words, *as we also forgive our debtors,*[557] and, *for we also forgive everyone that is indebted to us.*[558]   He, how- ever, who is inspired by Jesus as were the Apostles, and who can be *known by his fruits*[559]—because having re- ceived the Holy Spirit and become spiritual, he obeys the impulse of the Spirit[560] as a son of God and conducts him- self according to reason in all things—he forgives what God forgives and retains the sins that cannot be healed.   In this he resembles the prophets who do not speak their own thoughts, but those rather of the will of God; and so in this too he serves God, who alone has the power to forgive.

9.   The actual terms describing the power of the Apostles to remit are found in the Gospel according to John as follows: *Receive ye the Holy Spirit.   Whose sins you shall forgive, they are forgiven them; and whose sins you shall retain, they are retained.*[561]

If a man does not weigh these words carefully, he might blame the Apostles for not forgiving everyone his sins so that they might be forgiven by God also: that they retain the sins of some, so that because of them they are retained also by Him. Here it will be good to take an example from the Law to help us to understand how God forgives men's sins through the ministry of men. Those who are priests in the Law are prohibited from offering sacrifice in case of certain sins that the trespasses may be forgiven to them on whose behalf the sacrifices are offered. And the priest who has power to offer sacrifice for certain voluntary and involuntary transgressions does not offer a holocaust [562] for sin in the case of adultery, deliberate murder, and other serious sins. In the same way the Apostles also and their successors, priests according to the *great High Priest*,[563] having received the science of divine therapy, know from their instruction by the Spirit for what sins, when, and how they must offer sacrifice. They know also the sins for which they must not do so. So the priest Heli,[564] knowing that his sons Ophni and Phinees had sinned, could not help them in any way toward the forgiveness of their sin and he confesses his helplessness when he says: *If one man sinning shall sin against another, they shall pray for him; but if a man sin against the Lord, who shall pray for him?* [565]

10. I fail to understand how some men, arrogating to themselves a power greater than the sacerdotal dignity and perhaps not having an accurate grasp of the knowledge proper to a priest, boast that they can forgive idolatry and remit adultery and fornication. They comport themselves as if through their prayer for such as have dared to commit these crimes, even *the sin unto death* were for-

given. They do not read the text: *There is a sin unto death; for that I say not that any man ask.*[566]   And we must not forbear to mention that the valiant Job in offering sacrifice for his sons said: *Lest perhaps my sons have thought evil in their mind against God.*[567]   Note that it is for sins that were in doubt, and that, moreover, sins which had not reached even the lips, he offers sacrifice.[568]

CHAPTER 29

AND LEAD US NOT INTO TEMPTATION. BUT DELIVER US FROM EVIL

And lead us not into temptation. But deliver us from evil. Luke does not have the words: *But deliver us from evil.*[569]   As the Saviour does not bid us to ask what is impossible, I think it well to examine how it is that we are commanded, in spite of the fact that the whole life of man upon earth is a *temptation*, to pray that we do not enter *into temptation*. For since on earth we are encompassed by the flesh that *wars against the spirit*[570] and whose *thought is enmity to God*[571] and cannot in any way be brought into *subjection to the law of God*, we are in temptation.

TEMPTATION

2.   That the whole life of man upon the earth is a temptation we have learned from Job, as follows: *Is not the life of men upon the earth temptation?*[572]   The same is made

clear by the passage in the seventeenth Psalm: *In Thee I shall be delivered from temptation.*[573] And Paul, writing to the Corinthians, says that God does not grant us the grace not to be tempted, but rather not to be tempted above our strength: *No temptation has taken hold on you but such as is human. And God is faithful, who will not suffer you to be tempted above that which you are able; but will make also with temptation issue, that you may be able to bear it.*[574] Whether *our wrestling be against the flesh that lusts* and wars *against the spirit,*[575] or against *the soul of all flesh*[576] (an expression used to designate the guiding principle which dwells in the body, and is called "heart"[577]), and this wrestling is by those who are tried by human temptations; or whether, as trained and perfect athletes, who no longer struggle *against flesh and blood* and are not tested by temptations that are human (which they have already trampled under their feet[578]), *our wrestling is against principalities and powers and the rulers of the world of this darkness and the spirits of wickedness*[579]—in either case we are not free from temptation.

3. How is it, then, that the Saviour orders us to pray not to enter into temptation, when God tempts all men in some way? *Remember*, as Judith[580] says not only to the governors of her time, but also to all those who read her book, *what things He did to Abraham and how He tempted Isaac and what happened to Jacob in Mesopotamia of Syria while he was shepherding his uncle Laban's sheep. For not as He tested them to discover their hearts, doth the Lord punish us who chastises for their amendment, those who draw near Him.*[581] David shows that this is universally true of all the just, saying: *Many are the afflictions of the just.*[582] And the Apostle says in the Acts *that through*

many tribulations we must enter into the kingdom of God.[583]

4.   But if we do not understand the petition not to enter into temptation—and most people do not understand it— we must add that the Apostles were not heard when they made the same petition.   For they endured thousands of afflictions during their whole lives—*in many more labours, in stripes more frequently, in prisons above measure, in deaths often.*   Paul in particular received *of the Jews five times forty stripes save one.   Thrice was he beaten with rods, once he was stoned, thrice he suffered shipwreck.   A night and a day he was in the depth of the sea.*[584]   He was a man who *suffered tribulation in all things . . . ; was straitened; suffered persecution; was cast down;*[585] and admitted: *Even unto this hour we both hunger and thirst and are naked and are buffeted and have no fixed abode. And we labour, working with our own hands.   We are reviled, and we bless.   We are persecuted, and we suffer it.   We are blasphemed, and we entreat.*[586]   If the prayers of the Apostles were not heard, what hope has one who is inferior to them of being heard by God?

5.   A man who does not examine closely the intent of the Saviour in His command would, quite likely, take it that the words of the twenty-fifth Psalm: *Prove me, O Lord, and try me; burn my reins and my heart,*[587] contra- dicted what Our Lord taught us about prayer.   Has any- one ever thought man to be beyond temptations of which he was aware from the day he attained to reason?   Is there any time when a man is sure that he has not to struggle against sinning?   Is a man poor?   Let him fear lest he *should* ever *steal and forswear* the *name of God.*[588]   Is he rich?   Let him not be too confident: he may *become full*

of lies and in his pride say, *Who sees me?* Paul himself, *rich* as he is in *all utterance and in all knowledge*,[589] has not because of this been exempted from the danger of sinning through exalting himself. He has need of *a sting of Satan to buffet him*,[590] *lest he be exalted*. And if a man is conscious of his perfections and rises above all evil, let him read what is written in the Second Book of Paralipomenon on the subject of Ezechias who is said to have fallen because *his heart was lifted up*.[591]

6. But if anyone because we have not spoken much about the poor man, is at his ease as though poverty were not subject to temptation, let him know that the tempter does his best *to cast down the poor and needy*,[592] especially as, according to Solomon, *he that is poor beareth not reprehension*.[593] What is the use of counting the number of men who, because of their earthly riches which they did not use properly, have received the same punishment as the rich man in the Gospel?[594] Or the number of the poor who have endured their poverty ignobly and conducted themselves in a lowly and servile manner—not *as becometh saints*[595]—and who consequently have forfeited *the hope laid up for them in heaven?*[596] And those who occupy a middle station between riches and poverty, are not because of their moderate estate entirely removed from sinning.

7. A strong man in good physical health imagines that he is above temptation because of his health and good physical condition: but I ask who but those in their health and strength *violate the temple of God?*[597] No one will venture a reply, for the facts are evident to all. And what man that is sick has escaped the solicitations to *violate the temple of God* when he happened to be idle and quite susceptible to thoughts about impure actions? Need I men-

tion the other solicitations that harass him if *with all watchfulness* he does not *keep his heart?* [598] Many who succumbed to toil and could not endure sickness manfully, have shown that they were more grievously ill in their soul than in their body. And many because they wished to escape obscurity, being ashamed to bear nobly the name of Christ, have fallen into everlasting shame. [599]

8. There is the man who thinks he can be at ease, as though he were not tempted when he is honoured among men. Are these not hard words, *They have received their reward* [600] from men—words addressed to men elated over the acclaim of the multitude, as though it were for good? And is there no rebuke for them in this: *How can you believe, who receive glory from another, and the glory which is from God alone, you do not seek?* [601] Need I recount the sins of pride of those who are regarded as well-born, and the fawning servility, due to ignorance, of the so-called low-born toward their supposed superiors? Such servility separates entirely from God those who bear no real friendship, but only simulate what is noblest in man—love.

9. The whole *life of man on earth* is, then, as has been said, *temptation.* [602] Accordingly, let us pray to be delivered from temptation, not that we should not be tempted—which is impossible, especially for those *on earth*—but that we may not yield when we are tempted. He who yields to temptation enters, I believe, into temptation because he is entangled in its nets. Our Saviour, going into these nets on behalf of those who had been caught in them before, and *looking through the nets*, as is said in the Canticle of Canticles, [603] speaks to those who have been previously caught by them and have entered into temptation, saying

to them as to His bride: *Arise, come, my neighbour, my beautiful one, my dove.*[604]

To show that any time is a time of temptation for men, I add this thought that not even he who *meditates day and night on the law of God* [605] and tries to put into practice the words, *the mouth of the just shall bring forth wisdom,*[606] is free from temptation.

10.   Need I speak of all those also who have dedicated themselves to the study of the Holy Scriptures and have wrongly understood the messages given in the Law and the Prophets, and have embraced impious and atheistic doctrines or doctrines that are foolish and ridiculous? Those who fall into such errors, while apparently not deserving the charge of negligence in their studies, are legion. The same misfortune has befallen many students of the writings of the Apostles and Evangelists, men who, because of their own stupidity, have invented a Son or Father foreign to the true thinking and theology of the saints.[607] He who does not think in accordance with truth about God or His Christ has apostatized from the true God and His Only-Begotten Son.[608] His foolishness has invented a god whom he thinks to be the Father and the Son, and his worship is no worship. This happens to him because he has no understanding of the temptation present in the reading of the holy books and does not hold himself armed for the combat that is even then upon him.

GOD PERMITS TEMPTATION

11.   We should pray, then, not that we may not be tempted—which is impossible—but that we may not be brought under the power of temptation, which happens to them that are caught and conquered by it. Since it is

written elsewhere than in the Lord's Prayer not to *enter into temptation* [609] (the meaning of which ought to be fairly clear from what has been said) and in the Lord's Prayer we must say to God the Father: *Lead us not into temptation*, it is well to see how we are to understand God's leading into temptation the man who does not pray or whose prayer is not heard. For when a man enters into temptation and is conquered by it, it is absurd to think that God leads a man into temptation, in the sense of handing him over to defeat. And no matter how we explain it, the same incongruity remains in the text, *Pray lest ye enter into temptation.* [610] If it is evil to fall into temptation—and we pray that this may not befall us—is it not preposterous to suppose that the good God, who *cannot bring forth evil fruit,* [611] should encompass a man with evil?

12. It will be well, therefore, to compare with these texts the words of Paul in his Epistle to the Romans: *Professing themselves to be wise, they became fools. And they changed the glory of the incorruptible God into the likeness of the image of a corruptible man, and of birds and of fourfooted beasts and of creeping things. Wherefore, God gave them up to the desires of their heart, unto uncleanness, to dishonour their own bodies among themselves;* [612] and a little farther on: *For this cause God delivered them up to shameful affections. For their women have changed their natural use into that use which is against nature. And, in like manner, the men also, leaving the natural use of the women, have burned in their lusts,* and so on; and again a little later: *And as they liked not to have God in their knowledge, God delivered them up to a reprobate sense, to do those things which are disgraceful.* [613]

It has been necessary to quote all these texts for the

benefit of those who would divide the deity into two.
One must say to those who would distinguish between the
"good" Father of Our Lord and the God of the Law,[614]
that if the "good" God leads him whose prayer is not
heard, into temptation; and if the Father of the Lord *gives
up* those who have committed some sin *to the desires of
their heart unto uncleanness to dishonour their own bodies
among themselves;* and if He who, as they maintain, keeps
aloof from judging and punishing, *delivers them up to
shameful affections* and to *a reprobate sense, to do those
things which are disgraceful:* they would not have become
subject *to the desires of their heart,* if God had not *given
them up* to them; they would not have fallen into *shameful
affections,* if God had not *given them up* to them; and
they would not have come to *a reprobate sense,* if God had
not so judged them and *given them up* to it.

13. I know well that these thoughts will greatly
trouble them, and for this reason they have conceived another god in addition to the God who created heaven and
earth. Because they have found many similar texts in the
Law and the Prophets, they have taken offence at Him
who makes such pronouncements as being not good. In
face of the difficulties raised by the words, *Lead us not into
temptation,* in connection with which we have quoted the
texts from the Apostle, we must see if we can find satisfac-
tory solutions of these incongruities.

I believe that God in dealing with every rational soul has
regard always to its eternal life. It always is in possession
of freedom of choice,[615] and it is by its own responsibility
that it either finds itself in a better state on ascending to
the summit of all good, or, on the contrary, descends
through carelessness to such or such great depth of evil.

And as a quick and accelerated recovery induces some to make little of the illnesses into which they have fallen as being readily curable, so that in fact they suffer a relapse after having recovered, so God will be acting reasonably in such cases if He bears with their wickedness however it grows, and even overlooks its aggravation to where it becomes incurable. For through long continuance in evil and by having their fill of the sin they lust after, they by their satiety are to perceive the harm they have suffered and to hate what formerly they cherished. In this way they can be healed and enjoy with greater security the health of soul restored to them. An example is the *multitude mixed* with the children of Israel: *They burned with desire, and sitting they wept, and with them the children of Israel, and said: Who shall give us flesh to eat? We remember the fish that we ate in Egypt free cost. The cucumbers come into our mind, and the melons and the leeks, and the onions and the garlic. Now our soul is dry, our eyes behold nothing else but manna.* Again a little further on it is said: *Now Moses heard the people weeping by their families every one at the door of his tent.* And, again a little further on the Lord says to Moses: *And thou shalt say to the people: Be ye sanctified tomorrow, and you shall eat flesh. For you have wept before the Lord saying: Who will give us flesh to eat? It was well with us in Egypt. And the Lord will give you flesh to eat, and flesh you shall eat. Not for one day shall you eat it, nor two, nor five days, nor ten days, no nor for twenty days. But even for a month of days you shall eat it, till it come out at your nostrils and become loathsome to you; because you have cast off the Lord, who is in the midst of you, and have wept before Him saying: Why came we out of Egypt?* [616]

14. Let us look into this story, then, and see whether our bringing it serves to remove for you the seeming contradiction between the text, *Lead us not into temptation,* and the words of the Apostle. *A multitude mixed* with the children of Israel *burned with desire and wept, and with them the children of Israel.* Clearly, as long as they did not have what they craved, they could not sense satiety nor cease to feel the pangs of desire. But God who loves men and is good, in giving to them what they desired did not wish to give it to them in such a way as to leave in them the desire. Therefore God says not that they were to eat meat for one day only—their passion for meat would have remained in their inflamed and burning soul, if they had had the meat for a short time only. Neither does God give them what they desire for two days. But purposing to cause surfeit in them, He in a way does not make promises to them, but for one who understands His words, He is actually threatening them in apparently granting them their wishes, saying: "You shall eat meat *not for five days* only, nor for twice five days, nor twice that again, but you shall eat it for so long, *for a* whole *month, till* what you had thought to be beautiful *come out at your nostrils and become loathsome to you.* And with it will disappear your blameworthy and shameful desire. I purpose to take you away from life when you are free from desire and that once you have passed away in this state, you may be able, purged from desire and remembering with what pains you were liberated from it, never again to relapse into it; or, if this should ever happen again, it will be only at long intervals that you fall again into evil, when you will have for-

gotten the sufferings caused by desire [617] and fail to guard yourselves and to take to yourselves reason which delivers you entirely from all passion; and so when in your lust of created things, you will again seek to obtain a second time what you desire, you will again hate the object of your desires, and <be able> to hasten back to the good things and that heavenly good in contempt of which you craved for what was inferior."

15. Similar to this is what they also shall suffer who have *changed the glory of the incorruptible God into the likeness of the image of a corruptible man, and of birds and of fourfooted beasts and of creeping things,* because they shall be abandoned and *given up to the desires of their heart unto uncleanness, to dishonour their own bodies.*[618] For they have given to an inanimate and insensible body the name of Him who has given to all beings endowed with sensation and reason not only the power of perception, but rational perception as well, and to some even the power of perfect and virtuous perception and understanding. It is but right that such men should be abandoned by God who was abandoned by them, and should be *delivered up to shameful affections.* Thus *they receive the recompense due to their error* [619] through which they were brought to love unclean pleasure. This *recompense of error* weighs more heavily on them in their being *delivered up to shameful affections* than if they were purified in the fire of wisdom [620] and *in prison were forced to pay to the last farthing* [621] everything that they owed. For when they are *delivered up to shameful affections,* not only to those according to nature, but also to many which are against nature, they defile themselves and become so gross [622] through the flesh as though they no longer had a

soul or intelligence, but had become wholly flesh. But in
the *fire* and the *prison* they do not so much receive the
recompense of their error, as a help towards the purification of the evils of their error, bestowed on them along
with the saving trials that come upon the lovers of pleasure.
They are delivered from all *filth* and *blood* with which
they were so besmirched and defiled that they could not
even think of saving themselves from perdition.   God,
then, *shall wash away the filth of the sons and daughters of*
Sion and shall wash away the blood out of their midst by
the spirit of judgment and the spirit of burning.[623]   For *He*
cometh like a refining fire and like the fuller's herb,[624]
cleansing and purifying them that have need of such remedies for *not liking to have God in their knowledge.*[625]
Submitting themselves to these remedies, they will readily
hate *the reprobate sense.*   For God does not wish that good
be done to any one against his own will, but that he accept
it voluntarily; and there are perhaps some who have been
so long habituated to wickedness that they are slow to
discern its shame and turn away from what they had falsely
mistaken for what is good.

16.   See whether it is for this reason that God hardens
the heart of Pharao so that at a moment when he was not
hardened he could say: *The Lord is just: I and my people*
are wicked.[626]   His heart has to be hardened further and
he has to suffer more, that he may not, because he has been
freed of his hardheartedness too quickly, think too lightly
of that hardheartedness and so may have to have his heart
hardened over and over again.   If, then, *not unjustly are*
nets spread for birds, as is said in Proverbs,[627] and it is just
that God should lead men *into the net*, as is said, *Thou hast*
brought us into the net;[628] and if not even the sparrow,

the most insignificant of birds, falls *into the net without the will of the Father* [629] (for what falls into the net falls into it for the simple reason that it fails to use properly the power of its wings given it to bear it aloft): then let us pray not to do anything which would demand that in God's just judgment we be led into temptation. Such is the fate of the man who is *given up by God to the desires of his heart unto uncleanness;* and of him who *is delivered up to shameful affections;* and of him who, *as he liked not to have God in his knowledge, is delivered up to a reprobate sense, to do those things which are disgraceful.* [630]

USEFULNESS OF TEMPTATION

17. Temptation fulfills approximately the following purpose. The gifts which our soul has received are unknown to everyone except God. They are unknown even to ourselves. Through temptations they become known. Thereafter we can no longer be ignorant of what we are: we know ourselves and can be aware, if we but co-operate, of our wrongdoings. We can also give thanks for the benefits conferred upon us and made manifest by temptations. Temptations that come upon us serve the purpose of showing us who we really are and to make manifest *the things that are in our heart.* [631] This is made clear by what the Lord says in the book of Job and what is written in Deuteronomy, as follows: *Do you think I should have treated you otherwise but to make you appear just?* [632] And in Deuteronomy: *He afflicted thee with want, and gave thee manna for thy food,* and *brought thee through the desert wherein there was the serpent that bit, and the scorpion, and thirst, that the things that were in thy heart might be made known.* [633]

18. And if we wish to recall an instance from history, we must know that Eve was not a prey to deception and weak in judgment only when she began to disobey God and listen to the serpent. No, her condition was present even before it became manifest. The serpent with its own cunning had perceived her weakness and so approached her.[634] In the same way the wickedness of Cain did not begin to be when he killed his brother: [635] God, *who knoweth the hearts*,[636] had previously *had no respect* for him *and his offerings*.[637] But this wickedness was made manifest only when he slew Abel. And again, if Noe had not drunk the wine which he had himself produced and had not, as a result, been inebriated and uncovered, neither Cham's precipitance and want of respect for his father, nor his brothers' reverence and respect for their parent would have appeared.[638] And it might seem that Esau plotted against Jacob because the latter had stolen the blessing; [639] but his soul had in it even before this the roots of his being *a fornicator* and *profane person*.[640] So, too, the magnificent continence of Joseph, whereby he was prepared to resist every desire, would not have become known to us if his mistress had not conceived a passion for him.[641]

19. And therefore in the intervals separating temptations we shall look to the future and prepare ourselves against whatever may befall us. Whatever may come, we must not be taken by surprise but show ourselves well-disciplined. What is wanting to us because of human weakness will, provided we have done what is in our power, be made up by God who co-operates *unto good in all things* with them *that love Him*,[642] with them of whom in His infallible foreknowledge He foresees what by their own efforts they will one day be.[643]

CHAPTER 30

DELIVER US FROM EVIL

In the words, *Lead us not into temptation,* Luke seems to me to have implied also the idea, *Deliver us from evil.*[644] And surely it is likely that the Lord spoke pithily to the disciple, who was already rather advanced in knowledge, but more explicitly to the multitude who had need of more detailed instruction. Now, God *delivers us from evil,* not when the Adversary does not attack us at all with his own devices, whatever they may be, and the ministers of his will, but rather when we overcome him through taking a courageous stand in face of whatever befalls us. This is also our interpretation of the words: *Many are the afflictions of the just; but out of them all doth He deliver them.*[645] God delivers us from afflictions, not when afflictions no longer beset us—as Paul says, *In all things we are afflicted,*[646] as much as to say that at no time are we without affliction—but rather, when *we are afflicted, we are* through God's help *not distressed.* To be "afflicted" indicates, according to a certain Hebraic idiom, a critical situation that arises against one's will. To be "distressed," however, indicates a state arising from one's will, inasmuch as one is overcome by, and yields to, affliction. And so Paul quite rightly says: *In all things we are afflicted, but are not distressed.* We have the same idea, I think, in the Psalms: *When I was in affliction, Thou hast enlarged me.*[647] For through the co-operation and presence of the Word of God encouraging and saving us, our mind through

God's help is made joyful and courageous in the time of trial; and this experience is called "enlargement."

2.   The same is to be understood when we speak of a person being *delivered from evil*. God delivered <Job>, not because <the devil> did not receive the power to heap upon him all sorts of temptations—he did receive it—but because no matter what befell him, Job did not sin before the Lord, and showed himself to be just. He who said: *Doth Job fear the Lord in vain? Hast not Thou made a fence for everything inside and outside of his house and all his substance round about, blessed the works of his hands, and multiplied his possessions upon the earth? But put forth Thy hand a little and touch all that he hath: indeed, he will curse Thee to Thy face,*[648] was put to shame, because he had then, too, maligned Job. Though he had endured so many misfortunes, Job does not curse God *to His face*, as the Adversary suggested, but, even when he was given up to the Tempter, continues to bless the Lord and reproves his wife when she said to him: *Speak a word against God and die*. He rebuked her, saying: *Thou hast spoken like one of the foolish women. If we have received good things at the hand of God, why should we not receive evil?* [649]   And a second time *the devil spoke to the Lord* concerning Job: *Skin for skin, and all that a man hath he will give for his life. But put forth Thy hand, and touch his bone and his flesh: and then Thou shalt see that he will curse Thee to Thy face.*[650] But defeated by the champion of virtue, he is exposed as a liar; for, although he had endured the most severe trials, Job continued *not to sin with his lips* before God.[651] Having endured two such trials and triumphed in both, Job did not have to face a third. The combat of three trials was to be reserved for

the Saviour, as is reported in the three Gospels. In it our Saviour, considered in His manhood, overcame the Enemy in all three trials.[652]

3. Having carefully examined and meditated upon these words, we can now pray with a full understanding *not to enter into temptation* and *to be delivered from evil*, and we deserve, for having heard God, to be heard by Him. Therefore let us pray that when tempted, we may not suffer death, and when assailed by the *fiery darts of the Evil One*,[653] not be set on fire by them. Now all those are set on fire whose hearts, according to one of the twelve Prophets, have become *like an oven*.[654] But they are not set on fire who, thanks to the *shield of faith*, . . . *extinguish all the fiery darts* hurled against them by the Evil One.[655] They have within them *fountains of water springing up into life everlasting*,[656] which prevent the fire of the Evil One from growing strong and easily extinguish it with the flood of inspired and salutary thoughts engraved through the contemplation of truth upon the soul of him who tries to be spiritual.[657]

PART III: SUPPLEMENTARY POINTS

CHAPTER 31

To complete this discussion on the theoretical aspects of prayer, it seems to me proper to treat briefly of the disposition and deportment which one should have in prayer; of the place where one should pray; of the direction in which one should face, circumstances permitting; of the time most suitable and desirable for prayer; and of all such matters. Disposition refers to the soul; deportment to the body. Paul, indicating—as we have stated earlier [658]—what disposition means, says that we should *pray . . . without anger and contention;* [659] and of deportment, that we should *pray . . . lifting up pure hands.* [660] This last point seems to me to have been taken from the Psalms where we read: *. . . the lifting up of my hands, as evening sacrifice.* [661] On the question of place (Paul says), *I will therefore that men pray in every place.* [662] As regards direction, we read in the Wisdom of Solomon: *That it might be known that we ought to prevent the sun to bless Thee and to converse with Thee at the dawning of the light.* [663]

DISPOSITION FOR PRAYER

2. In my opinion, the man who is about to pray and who first pauses and prepares himself for prayer, will be more attentive and in the proper mood throughout the whole of his prayer. He should banish all temptation and distractions and remind himself as well as he can of the

sublimity of Him whom he is approaching, and that it is impious to draw nigh to Him in a spirit of frivolity and carelessness—with contempt, as it were. He should put away from his mind all outside thoughts, and so come to prayer: he should, so to speak, lift up his soul before lifting up his hands; lift up his mind to God before lifting his eyes; and, before standing to pray, lift up his spirit from the things of earth and direct it to the Lord of all. He should banish all remembrance of wrongs which others may seem to have done him,[664] in the same way as he wishes God to forgive him for the many times he has sinned against and wronged his neighbours, or if he is conscious of having acted against right reason.

DEPORTMENT IN PRAYER

Further, while there are many ways of bodily deportment, there can be no doubt that the position of extending one's hands[665] and elevating the eyes is to be preferred above all others; for the position taken by the body is thus symbolic of the qualities proper to the soul in the act of praying. This we say should be, except under particular circumstances, the normal position taken. Circumstances can permit us to pray with propriety while sitting—for example because of some serious foot ailment; or even while lying down—because of fever or similar illnesses. We can even, depending on circumstances, if, for instance, we are on a voyage or if our business does not allow us to withdraw to pray as we should, pray without appearing to do so.

3. As for bending one's knees, this is required when a man is going to confess his sins before God and beseech

Him for the healing of His forgiveness. One ought to know that this is the attitude proper to one who humbles and submits himself, as Paul says: *For this cause I bow my knees to the Father, of whom all paternity in heaven and earth is named.*[666] Spiritual genuflection, so called because all beings submit to God *in the name of Jesus* and humble themselves before Him, is, I think, signified by the Apostle in the words: *In the name of Jesus every knee should bend of those that are in heaven, on earth, and under the earth.*[667] One must not suppose that the heavenly bodies are so formed as to have physical knees. Indeed they who have studied the matter carefully have shown that their bodies are spherical.[668] If a man will not admit this, he will yet have to admit, unless he chooses to scorn common sense, that every bodily member has its proper function, if it is to be true that God has made nothing without reason. He is mistaken in either case—whether he says that bodily members were given them by God to no purpose and without their proper functions, or says that the intestines and colon serve their proper functions in the heavenly bodies also.[669] And a man will arrive at a most absurd conclusion if he believes that the heavenly bodies, like statues, resemble men outwardly only and not also within. These are my comments on the question of genuflection and on the text: *In the name of Jesus every knee should bend of those that are in heaven, on earth, and under the earth.*[670] So, too, the word of the Prophet, *Every knee shall bow to me*, means the same.[671]

THE PLACE OF PRAYER

4. On the question of place it is to be observed that every place is suitable for prayer for him who prays well:

In every place offer incense to me . . ., says the Lord, and, *I will, therefore, that men pray in every place.*[672] It is enjoined that every man, in order to pray in peace and without disturbance, should choose a special place in his own house, if there is room for it—his sanctuary, so to speak, and there he should pray.[673] When deciding upon this place one should also make sure to investigate if in the place of one's prayer anything has ever been done against the law or right reason. For in that case he would as it were make both himself and the place of his prayer such that God's attention would shun it.

And as I reflect further on this matter of place, I must also make mention of a consideration that may appear somewhat offensive, but careful reflection makes it a matter that can scarcely be disregarded. The point is whether or not it is holy and pure to address oneself to God in a place where the marriage act is performed. There is question here of intercourse—not that which is forbidden, but which is allowed by the Apostle when he speaks—*by indulgence, not by commandment.*[674] If a man cannot *give himself to prayer* as he should, but only *by consent, for a time*, one should probably also give thought to the suitability of the place for it.

5. But as a place for prayer, the place where the faithful congregate is especially conducive to prayer and makes it more effectual. This is but natural as it is here that the angelic powers join the assemblies of the faithful, whither comes the power of Our Lord and Saviour Himself, where the spirit of the saints gather, both those—so I believe—of the departed who have gone before and, evidently, of those who are still among the living; though to explain this is not an easy matter.

On the question of the angels the following is a necessary conclusion: If *the angel of the Lord shall encamp round about them that fear Him, and shall deliver them;* [675] and if what Jacob says is true not only in his own case but also in the case of all those who are dedicated to the omniscient God, when he speaks of *the angel that delivereth me from all evils:* [676] then it is probable that, when many are assembled legitimately for the glory of Christ, *the angel* of each *encamps* round each of *them that fear God*, and that he stands at the side of the man whose protection and guidance has been entrusted to him. Thus, when the saints are assembled together, there is a twofold church present, that of men and that of angels. [677]

And if Raphael says of the one man Tobias that *he offered as a memorial his prayer* and that of Sara, [678] who later became his daughter-in-law when she married (the young) Tobias, what are we to say when many assemble *in the same mind and in the same judgment*, and together form one body in Christ? Paul says of *the power of the Lord* that is present in the Church—*you being gathered together and my spirit, with the power of the Lord Jesus* [679] —as much as to say that *the power of the Lord* abided not only with the Ephesians but also with the Corinthians. If Paul, who was still clothed in the body, could think of himself as conveyed in his own spirit to Corinth, we should feel confident that the blessed ones who have departed from the body are present in spirit in the churches, and that perhaps even earlier than those who are still in the body. Therefore we should have great regard for prayers made there, because they are of special value to him who participates as he should.

6. But as the *power of Jesus*, the *spirit* of Paul and

others like him,[680] and the angels of the Lord that surround
each one of the saints, assemble and join those who gather
together legitimately, so one must suppose that if a man
becomes unworthy of a holy angel, he may even give himself up to an angel of the devil because of the sins he commits and his disobedience wherewith he contemns God.
Such a man, as long as there are not many like him, will
not for long be without the providence of the angels who,
in obedience to the will of God that watches over the
Church, will bring the failings of such a man to the notice
of the many. But when such men become very numerous,
and assemble like ordinary associations of men concerned
with purely temporal affairs, they will no longer receive
providential attention. This is seen in Isaias where the
Lord says: . . . *not even if you came to appear before
me;* for, He says, *I will turn away my eyes from you; and
when you multiply prayer, I will not hear.*[681] Perhaps,
instead of the double assembly of holy men and blessed
angels of which we spoke, another double assembly meets
there,—one of impious men and wicked angels; and of this
assembly the holy angels and pious men might say: *I have
not sat with the council of vanity, neither will I go in with
the doers of unjust things. I have hated the assembly of
the malignant, and with the wicked I will not sit.*[682]

7. That is why, I believe, those who in Jerusalem and
throughout the whole of Judea committed so many sins,
were made subject to their enemies. For the peoples who
abandoned the Law were abandoned by God and by their
angel guardians and the holy men who could have saved
them. In this way whole assemblies are sometimes left to
themselves, to succumb to temptations, so that even *what
they think to have is taken away from them;*[683] and as the

fig tree was cursed and torn up from the roots for not having given fruit to Jesus when He was hungry,[684] they too will be withered and deprived of what little vivifying power they may still have from the faith that remains in them.

I think it was necessary to say these things when speaking of the place of prayer and of the extraordinary blessings realized—in point of place—from uniting with the godfearing faithful assembled for one and the same purpose.

CHAPTER 32

ORIENTATION

And now we must add a few remarks on the direction in which we should face while praying.[685] There are four cardinal points—north, south, east, and west. It should be immediately clear that the direction of the rising sun obviously indicates that we ought to pray inclining in that direction, an act which symbolizes the soul looking towards where *the true light* rises.[686] But a man may prefer to offer his petitions while facing in the direction in which his house faces, whichever way the doors of the house open. He argues that where the house does not happen to have an opening to the east, the view to the sky is something far more inviting to prayer than to see blank walls. We reply that the direction in which men's houses face is a matter of convention, while it is by nature that the east takes precedence over the other cardinal points, and that one should choose nature before convention. Moreover, following this argument, why should a man who wishes to pray in the open face the east rather than the west? And if in that case it is in accord with reason to prefer the east, should we not do so everywhere? So much, then, for this subject.[687]

CHAPTER 33

THE FOUR PARTS OF PRAYER

I think that I should bring this treatise to a close by going through the essential parts of prayer. There are, as I have found scattered in the Scriptures, four such parts that need to be outlined, and each one should organize his prayer according to these.[688] Here are the component parts: at the beginning, in the prologue of one's prayer, one should with all one's strength *glorify* God through Christ, who is glorified with Him, in the Holy Spirit, who is praised with Him. Next each one should *thank* God for all His benefits, recalling both those bestowed upon men in general and upon himself in particular. This thanksgiving should, I think, be followed by a sorrowful *confession* of one's sins and we should ask of God first to heal us and so deliver us from the habit which leads us into sin, and then remit our past sins. After the confession comes the fourth point, which in my view is that we should *petition* God for great and heavenly gifts, for oneself and for all, for one's relatives and friends; and, finally, the prayer should end with a glorification of God through Christ in the Holy Spirit.

2. These component parts, as I have said before, I have found here and there in the Scriptures; the *glorification* of God, for example, in Psalm 103 in the following words: *O Lord, my God, how exceedingly great art Thou! Thou hast put on praise and beauty, Thou art clothed with light as with a garment. Who stretchest out the heaven like a cloak, who coverest the higher rooms thereof with water. Who makest the clouds Thy steps, who walkest upon the wings of the winds. Who makest Thy angels into winds, and Thy ministers a burning flame. Who hast founded the earth upon its own bases: it shall not be moved for ever and ever. The deep like a garment is its clothing, above the mountains shall the waters stand. At Thy rebuke they shall flee, at the voice of Thy thunder they shall fear.*[689] The greater part of this Psalm is taken up with a glorification of the Father. Each one will see for himself, as he collects further examples, how the component of glorification is to be found in many places.

3. On the point of giving *thanks*, we may quote the instance from the Second Book of Kings. Nathan has conveyed certain promises to David, and David, who is speaking, is astonished at the gifts of God and returns Him thanks for them in these terms: *Who am I, O Lord, my Lord, and what is my house that Thou hast shown Thy love for me thus far? And I was so very little in Thy sight, my Lord, and Thou didst speak of the house of Thy servant for a long time to come; but this is the law of man, O Lord, my Lord. And what can David say more unto Thee? For Thou knowest Thy servant, O Lord. Because of Thy servant and according to Thy own heart*

*Thou hast done it, and Thou didst do all these great things,
so that Thou wouldst make it known to Thy servant that
Thou mightest be magnified, O Lord, my Lord.*[690]

4.   And an instance of *confession* of sin: *Deliver Thou
me from all my iniquities.*[691]   And again: *My sores are
putrefied and corrupted because of my foolishness. I am
become miserable, and am bowed down even to the end.
I walked sorrowful all the day long.*[692]

5.   Here is an instance of *petition* from the twenty-
seventh Psalm: *Draw me not away together with the
wicked; and with the workers of iniquity destroy me
not;* [693] and other texts like this.

6.   Lastly, it is good to end prayer as it was begun—
with a doxology, hymning and glorifying the Father of all
things through Jesus Christ in the Holy Spirit *to whom be
glory for ever and ever.*[694]

CHAPTER 34

EPILOGUE

These, my dear Ambrose and Tatiana, brother and sister
in the diligent and sincere service of God, are the results of
my best efforts on the subject of prayer and the prayer
found in the Gospels, and what is said by way of introduction to it in the Gospel according to Matthew.   I have no
doubt that, if you *forget the things that are behind and
stretch forth* yourselves *to those that are before* [695] and
meanwhile pray for me, I shall be able to receive from God

—who is their donor—more and more inspired thoughts in addition to the present, so as to treat the subject again and do better justice to its grandeur and sublimity, and with greater clarity. But for now do read this with your kindly indulgence.

EXHORTATION TO MARTYRDOM
(Εἰς μαρτύριον προτρεπτικός)[1]

PART I: INTRODUCTION—EXHORTATION TO
MARTYRDOM

Weaned from milk, drawn away from the breast—accept tribulation upon tribulation, accept hope upon hope—after a little, after a little—through contempt of lips, through another tongue.[2]

You, too, my most pious friends in God, Ambrose and Protoctetus,[3] according to Isaias are no longer *carnal*, nor *infants in Christ*, but rather have *advanced in the age* of intelligence.[4] *You* no longer *have need of milk, but of solid food.*[5] Hear then how, since *you have been weaned from milk* and *drawn away from the breast*, not a simple tribulation, but tribulation upon tribulation is prophesied for you as for athletes [6] that have indeed been weaned. He who does not refuse *tribulation upon tribulation*, but promptly *accepts* it as a valiant athlete would, *accepts* also *hope upon hope* which he will enjoy shortly after the *tribulation upon tribulation*. This is the meaning of: *after a little, after a little*.

2. Even if men who are ignorant of the language of Sacred Scripture contemn, despise, and treat us as mad or impious, we should remind ourselves that the *hope upon hope* which will be given us *after a little* will be given us *through contempt of lips, through another tongue*. Who would not *accept tribulation upon tribulation* in order

forthwith to *accept hope upon hope?* With Paul he thinks
that *the sufferings of this time*, by means of which we, so
to speak, purchase a blessed life hereafter, *are not worthy
to be compared with the glory to come that shall be revealed in us* by God; [7] and that especially as *this light and
momentary affliction*—called light, and in fact light for
such as are not overwhelmed by circumstances—the more
it exceeds all bounds, the greater and richer *the weight of
eternal glory* it *works for us.*[8] This will be so if to the
discomfiture of those who would afflict and, as it were,
stifle our souls, we refuse to let our minds dwell upon our
troubles and consider not these present evils, but rather the
good which will accrue to us from endurance of them and
is reserved for them that by the grace of God have *struggled lawfully* in Christ.[9] For God multiplies His benefits
and grants favours which outweigh what is merited by the
toils of combat. And these are such as could not be given
by a parsimonious God, but a generous giver who in His
wisdom multiplies His graces towards those who through
their contempt of this *earthen vessel* show with all their
might that they love Him with their *whole soul.*[10]

3. I believe that they love God with their *whole* soul
who, because of their great desire to be united with Him,
separate and cut off their soul not only from the earthly
body but from every kind of body. Without distraction
or disturbance they undergo separation from *the body of
their lowliness* [11] when through death, as it is held to be,
the opportunity offers of putting away *the body of this
death,*[12] and of being heard when praying with the
Apostle: *Unhappy man that I am, who shall deliver me
from the body of this death?* Is there any of them that
groan in this tabernacle [13] because they are *burdened with*

a corruptible body,[14] who would not give thanks to God? First he says: *Who shall deliver me from the body of this death?* Then, seeing that he has been *delivered from the body of this death* through communion with Him, he will cry out in all piety: Thanks be to *God through Christ Jesus, Our Lord!* [15] If this seems hard to anyone, then he has not *thirsted after the strong living God;* nor has he panted after God *as the hart panteth after the fountains of water;* nor has he said, *When shall I come and appear before the face of God?* Nor has he reflected within himself as did the prophet *whilst it was said to him daily, Where is thy God?* He poured out his soul within him, and reproached it for still being disquieted and troubled because of his weakness, saying: *I shall go over into the place of the wonderful tabernacle, even to the house of God, with the voice of exultation and praise resounding as of one feasting.*[16]

4. I would wish you, then, during the whole of the present trial [17] to remember the great reward prepared in heaven for those who are persecuted and mocked *for justice's sake* and the Son of man.[18] Be *glad and rejoice* and exult, as did the Apostles when they were *accounted worthy to suffer reproach for His name!* [19] And if it happens that your soul feels some sadness, let the Spirit of Christ in us [20] say to that soul that wishes, in so far as it can, to trouble Him also: *Why art thou sad, O soul? And why dost thou trouble me? Hope in God, for I will give praise to Him.*[21] O that our soul might not be troubled, but that even before the judgment seats, before the swords ready to behead us, our soul be preserved by the peace of God which *surpasseth all understanding,*[22] and be tranquil in the thought that they that leave the body live with the Lord of all things! [23]

But if we are not such that we can always preserve tranquillity, at least we should not allow our anxiety of soul to show itself and become obvious to unbelievers. In this way we can still justify ourselves before God, saying to Him: *My God, my soul is troubled within myself.*[24] Reason, too, invites us to remember the word spoken in Isaias: *Fear ye not the reproach of men and be not overcome by their blasphemies.*[25] God manifestly watches over the movement of the heavens and the stars and over all the animals and plants of all kinds that on the earth and in the sea through His divine art are brought to perfection in birth, development, nourishment, and increase. So it would clearly be absurd for us to close our eyes to this[26] and not to look to God, and to have regard rather for men and to fear them—men who will soon die and be delivered up to the punishment which they deserve.

5. God once said to Abraham, *Go forth out of thy country.*[27] Soon perhaps we may hear it said to us, "Go forth out of every country." It will be well for us to obey, so that soon we may see the heavens in which is to be had what is called "the kingdom of the heavens."

You will observe that life is filled with contests and contestants for many virtues. Thus it will appear that many even of those who are not on God's side[28] have fought for *temperance;* that others have died with *fortitude* in remaining faithful to their convictions for a common master. Men who are versed in the investigation of the sciences have been concerned about *prudence,* and men who proposed to live justly have given themselves to *justice.* And against every virtue is ranged either *the wisdom of the flesh* or most of the forces from outside. But on the side of piety there fights only *the chosen generation, the kingly priesthood, the holy nation, the purchased people.*[29]

When piety meets with opposition, all other men do not even pretend to show that they are ready to die for piety, and that they prefer death and piety to life and impiety. But whoever wishes to belong to *the chosen generation* obediently listens to God saying at all times to him—even when the atheists (although they may claim to be polytheists[30]) conspire against him: *Thou shalt not have strange Gods before me;*[31] and, *The name of strange gods you shall not remember* in your hearts, *neither shall it be heard out of your mouth.*[32] Therefore such men *believe with the heart unto justice, but with the mouth make confession unto salvation.*[33] They realize that they cannot be justified except they believe in God in this way and their heart be so disposed, and that they will not be saved unless their speech correspond to such disposition. They who think that to attain this final goal in Christ it is enough to *believe with the heart unto justice,* without *with the mouth making confession unto salvation,* deceive themselves. One might say that it is better to honour God with our lips and have our heart far from Him, than to honour Him in our heart,[34] and not confess Him with our mouth unto salvation.

PART II: WARNING AGAINST IDOLATRY AND APOSTASY

IDOLATRY

6. In the same way when God says: *Thou shalt not make to thyself idols nor the likeness of any thing,*[35] etc., apparently drawing a distinction between *Thou shalt not bow before them* and *Thou shalt not worship them,*[36] He warns a man inclined to idolatry not to practise it. But when a man who is not so inclined, but yet through cowardice, which he calls "accommodation," pretends to worship idols as the masses do, he does not, it is true, *worship* idols, but he does bow *before them.* And I would say that they who abjure Christianity in the courtroom or even before they are brought there, do not *worship* idols, but they do *bow* down *before* them; for they apply to inanimate and unheeding matter the name of the Lord God, namely "God." In like manner *the people that committed fornication with the daughters of Moab*[37] bowed down before idols, but did not worship them. At least, this is stated clearly: *They called them to the sacrifices to their idols, and the people ate of their sacrifices, and they bowed down to their idols and they were initiated to Beelphegor.*[38] Note that it is not said, "they worshipped their idols." Indeed, it was impossible that after so many signs and prodigies they should have allowed themselves to be persuaded in an instant by the women, with whom they committed fornication, that the idols were gods. It may be also that

they *bowed* down *before* the calf, of which there is mention made in Exodus,[39] without *worshipping* an object that they gazed at when it was in the process of construction.

We must believe then that the present trial is a test and scrutiny of our love for God: *For the Lord trieth you,* as is written in Deuteronomy, *that He may know whether you love the Lord your God with all your heart and all your soul.*[40] But in the trial, *follow the Lord your God, and fear Him, and keep His commandments* (and especially this one: *Thou shalt not have strange Gods before me*[41]) *and hear His voice. And to Him you shall cleave.*[42] He does indeed take you from these regions, but for that He draws you to what the Apostle calls *the increase of God*[43] in Him.

APOSTASY

7. If *every evil word is an abomination to the Lord thy God,*[44] how great an abomination must be the evil word of denial, the evil word of public recognition of another god, and the evil oath taken by the fortune[45] of men, a thing that does not endure! When this oath is proposed to us, we should remember Him who said: *But I say to you not to swear at all.*[46] If he that swears *by heaven* insults *the throne of God;* if he that swears *by the earth* blasphemes in making divine *the footstool of God;*[47] if he that swears by Jerusalem sins because it is *the city of the great king;*[48] and he that swears *by his head*[49] is blameworthy—then what kind of crime must be the oath taken by the fortune of a man? In such circumstances we should recall the words: *Every idle word that you shall speak, you shall render an account for it on the day of judgment.*[50]

And what word could be more idle than a denial rein-
forced by an oath?

It is quite likely that the Enemy will want to induce us
by every possible trick to bow down to *the sun and the
moon and all the host of heaven.*[51] But we shall reply that
the Word of God did not command us to do so. For in
no way may we bow down to the creature in the presence
of the Creator[52] who sustains all and anticipates their
prayer. Not even the sun himself would wish that any
friend of God[53] or anyone else, it would seem, should bow
down to him. He imitates Him who says, *Why callest
thou me good? None is good but one, that is God* the
Father.[54] He says, as it were, to him that would bow
down to him: "Why do you call me God? There is only
one true God: why do you bow down before me? *Thou
shalt bow down to the Lord thy God and Him only shalt
thou worship.*[55] I too am created. Why do you wish to
bow down to him who himself bows down? I too bow
down to God the Father and I worship Him; and obedient
to His commands, I am *made subject to vanity . . . by
reason of Him that made me subject in hope. . . . I shall
be delivered from the servitude of corruption,* (I who am
also clothed in a corruptible body) *into the liberty of the
glory of the children of God.*"[56]

8. We can be prepared to find some prophet even of
impiety—and perhaps not just one, but several—who will
tell us of a word of the Lord, which the Lord has not at all
commanded,[57] or of a *word of wisdom,*[58] which has nothing whatever to do with wisdom. His purpose is to slay
us by the word of his mouth. But as for ourselves, when
the sinner comes before us, let us say: *But I, as a deaf man,
heard not, and as a dumb man not opening his mouth.*

And I became as a man that heareth not.[59] It is indeed virtuous to be deaf to impious words, when we despair of correcting them that speak evil.

9. When men try to seduce us to apostasy, it is useful to reflect upon what God wishes to teach us when He says: *I am the Lord thy God, jealous.*[60] In my view, just as the bridegroom who wishes to make his bride live chastely so as to give herself entirely to him and beware of any relationship whatever with any man other than her husband, pretends, though he be wise, to be jealous—he uses this pretence as a kind of antidote for his bride—so the Lawgiver, especially when He reveals Himself as *the firstborn of every creature,*[61] says to His bride, the soul, that He is a jealous God. In this way He keeps His followers from any fornication with demons and pretended gods. And it is as God jealous in this sense that He says of them that have fornicated in any way with strange gods: *They have made me jealous of that which was not God; they have angered me with their idols. And I shall make them jealous of that which is not a people; I shall anger them with a foolish people. For a fire is kindled in my wrath; it shall burn even to the lowest hell.*[62]

10. If it is not in his own interest that the bridegroom, acting wisely and temperately, keeps his bride away from all defilement—at any rate, it will be for her sake. He sees the defilement and abomination that come on her, and employs every means to heal and win her back. He sees in her a being endowed with free will, and addresses himself to her with arguments that may have the effect of turning her from fornication. Does anyone believe that a soul could suffer greater corruption than to call upon a strange god and to refuse to bear witness to Him who is truly the

one and only God? In my opinion, just as he *who is joined to a harlot is one body*,[63] so he who bears witness to someone, especially in a time of persecution and trial of faith, unites and joins himself to him to whom he bears witness. And he who denies is by the denial, just as by a sharp sword, separated from him whom he denies. He experiences the separation in being cut off from him whom he has denied.

Know, then, that naturally and necessarily he who bears witness will have witness borne to him, and he that denies will be denied, as it is said: *Every one that shall bear witness to me before men, I will also bear witness to him before my Father who is in heaven.*[64] And He who is the Word itself and Truth itself may well say to him who bore witness to Him and to him who denied Him: "*With the same measure that you shall mete withal, it shall be measured to you again.*[65] You, then, who have measured with the measure of bearing witness and have filled up that measure, you will receive of me the measure of my bearing witness to you, *pressed down and shaken together and running over*, which will be *given into your bosom.*[66] But you who have measured with the measure of denial and have denied me, you likewise will receive, according to the measure of your denial, the measure of my denial of you."

PART III: ADMONITION TO PERSEVERE

BEARING WITNESS TO GOD

11. As to how the measure of bearing witness is filled up, or is not filled up but falls short, the following reflections may show. If during all the time of trial and test we *give no place to the devil* [67] in our hearts, when he would defile us with evil thoughts of denial, as indecision or some inducement draws us away from martyrdom and perfection; if in addition we do not defile ourselves with any word that is incompatible with bearing witness; if we endure all the taunts of our adversaries, their insults, mockery, obloquy, and their pretended pity when they treat us as fools and madmen and say that we are mere dupes; and if besides we do not permit ourselves to be seduced either by love for our children or their mother or any one of those regarded as dearest to us in life, nor to be lured away to their possession and this kind of life; but if turning from all of these we give ourselves entirely to God and to life with Him and near Him with a view to sharing union with His Only-Begotten Son and those who have a share in Him: [68] then we can say that we have filled up the measure of bearing witness. But if we are wanting in as little as one of these points, we have not filled up, but rather defiled, the measure of bearing witness, and have mixed with it some foreign element; and we shall therefore be in need of the same as they who have built on a foundation of wood or hay or stubble.[69]

THE FOLLOWING OF CHRIST

12.   This we must know also that we have received the
so-called covenants from God in virtue of agreements we
made when we accepted the Christian way of life.
Amongst these agreements which we made with God was
the observance of the entire pattern of living set out in the
Gospel, which says: *If any man will come after me, let him
deny himself and take up his cross and follow me. For he
that will save his life shall lose it: and he that shall lose his
life for my sake shall save it.* And often we have been
filled with enthusiasm when we heard these words: *For
what doth it profit a man if he gain the whole world and
suffer the loss of his own soul? Or what exchange shall a
man give for his soul? For the Son of man shall come in
the glory of His Father with His angels: and then will He
render to every man according to his works.*[70]

But not only Matthew, whose words we have quoted,
but also Luke and Mark tell us that we must deny ourselves, take up our cross, and follow Jesus. Listen, for
example, to what Luke says: *And He said to all: If any
man will come after me, let him deny himself and take up
his cross and follow me. For whosoever will save his life
shall lose it: and he that shall lose his life for my sake shall
save it. For what is a man advantaged if he gain the whole
world and lose himself and cast away himself?*[71] And
Mark: *And calling the multitude together with His disciples, He said to them: If any man will follow me, let him
deny himself and take up his cross and follow me. For
whosoever will save his life shall lose it; and whosoever
shall lose his life for the sake of the gospel shall save it.
For what shall it profit a man, if he gain the whole world,*

*and suffer the loss of his soul?   Or what shall a man give
in exchange for his soul?* [72]

It is a long time, then, since we contracted the obligation
to deny ourselves and say, *I live, now not I;* [73] and now let
it appear whether we have taken up our cross and follow
Jesus,—which is the case if *Christ liveth in us.* [74] If we wish
to save our soul so as to receive it back better than a soul,
let us lose it in martyrdom.   For if we lose it for Christ's
sake, laying it before Him in dying for Him, we shall
achieve for it its true salvation.   If we do the opposite, we
shall be told that it profits nothing to gain the whole material universe at the price of our own destruction or loss.
Once a man has lost his soul or forfeited it, even if he gain
the whole world, he cannot give that world *in exchange
for his soul* that is lost.   For that soul, *created to the image
of God,* [75] is more precious than all material things.   One
alone can redeem our soul if it is lost—He who purchased
us with His precious blood. [76]

13.   Isaias has some profound words on this when he
says: *I have given Egypt for thy ransom and Ethiopia and
Syene for thee.   Since then thou becamest precious in my
eyes.* [77] If you are eager to study in Christ the exact meaning of this and the other texts; if, in wishing to pass beyond
that knowledge which we have *through a glass* and *in a
dark manner*, you hasten after Him who summons you—
you will understand all as never before, *face to face,* [78] as
being friends of the heavenly Father and Teacher.   For
His friends see things as they are, and not *in a dark manner*
or through mere book knowledge of words and expressions, symbols and types.   They discover the nature of in-
telligibles and the beauty of truth.

If you believe that Paul *was caught up to the third*

heaven and that he *was caught up into paradise and heard secret words which it is not granted to man to utter,*[79] you must logically conclude that you yourselves will as a matter of course know secrets both more and greater than the ineffable words then revealed to Paul. For he descended from *the third heaven,* when he had heard them; but you, having heard them, will not descend. You will have *taken up your cross and followed* Jesus [80] in whom we *have a great high priest that hath passed into the heavens.*[81]

If you remain united with His followers, you, too, will pass into the heavens, passing beyond not only the earth and its mysteries but the heavens and all that concerns them. For in God as in a treasury are stored up wonders much greater than those mentioned, which cannot be grasped by a nature joined to a body until it has put off all that is of the body. I am convinced that God keeps stored in reserve in Himself far sublimer things than those that have been seen by sun, moon, and the chorus of stars and even the holy angels whom God has made *spirits* and *burning fire.*[82] He will reveal these wonders when every *creature . . . shall be delivered from the servitude* of the Enemy *into the liberty of the glory of the children of God.*[83]

THE MARTYR'S REWARD

14. And to these sublime things some outstanding martyr in the future, one of those who have a greater zeal for learning in Christ than many other martyrs, will ascend more quickly. You can see for yourself, my pious friend Ambrose, in contemplating closely a text in the Gospels, that probably no one of those who ever lived, or, at any rate, only a very few will receive that certain special and

greater fulness of beatitude. You, too, will be of this number if you come through the combat without faltering.
The text is as follows: *Peter once said to the Saviour: Be-*
hold, we have left all things and have followed Thee: what
therefore shall we have? And Jesus said to them (clearly,
to the apostles): *Amen, I say to you that you, who have*
followed me, in the regeneration when God shall sit on the
seat of His majesty, you also shall sit on twelve seats judg-
ing the twelve tribes of Israel. And every one that hath
left . . . brethren or sisters or parents or children or lands or
houses for my name's sake, shall receive many times more
and shall possess life everlasting.[84] In view of these words
I myself would like to possess all the earthly goods that
you possess or even more, and be a martyr to God in
Christ so as to receive *many times more*, or, as Mark says,[85]
a hundredfold more, which indeed is much more than the
little—even if it were multiplied by a hundred—that we
shall give up if we are called to martyrdom.

For this reward I would, if I were a martyr, wish to
leave behind children and lands and houses that I might,
in the presence of God the Father of Our Lord Jesus
Christ, *of whom all paternity in heaven and earth is*
named,[86] be called father of many more and more holy
children, or, to be precise, of a hundred times more children. If they are fathers of whom it was said to Abraham:
And thou shalt go to thy fathers in peace, living to a ripe
old age,[87] perhaps one might say (I do not know if it be
true): Perhaps these fathers are such in having once upon
a time borne witness and left their children behind them.
In exchange for these, they have become fathers of the
fathers of the patriarch Abraham and other patriarchs.
For it is obvious that martyrs who leave their children be-

hind them and bear witness, become fathers, not of children, but of fathers.

15.   Someone, *zealous,* as it were, *for the better gifts* [88] and considering fortunate the rich martyrs and the martyrs who are fathers and are rich in that they beget a hundred times more children and receive a hundred times more lands and houses, may not be able to understand how it can be fair that these should possess in the spiritual world much greater riches than martyrs who were poor in the goods of this life.   We should answer him that as they who have endured tortures and pain gave more illustrious evidence of virtue in martyrdom than those who have not endured such trials, so they that have cut and torn not only the bonds of love for life and body, but also these other great worldly bonds, have shown a great love for God and have truly taken up *the word of God* that is *living and effectual and more piercing than any two-edged sword.* [89] Having cut so great bonds, they have *made for themselves wings like those of an eagle,* and can *fly up to the house of him who is their Lord.* [90]   Just as they who have not gone through the trial of tortures and pain give pride of place to those who have proved their constancy on the rack, through diverse tortures and fire, so we too who are poor, even if we be martyrs, are urged by reason to yield first prize to you, if for the love of God in Christ [91] you trod underfoot reputation, deceitful and sought for by the masses, your great possessions, and the affection of a father for his children.

16.   Here note also an illustration of the sublime character of Scripture in promising a return many times over or a hundredfold—of brothers and children and parents and lands and houses: but with these no mention is made

of a wife. It is not said: "Every one that hath left brethren
or sisters or parents or children or lands or houses *or a wife*
for my name's sake, shall receive them many times over."
For in the resurrection of the dead they shall neither marry
nor be married, but shall be as the angels of God in
heaven.[92]

OUR PROMISES TO GOD

17. What Josue said to the people when he was settling
them in the holy land could equally well be said to us now
by Scripture: *Now therefore fear the Lord, and serve Him*
with a perfect and most sincere heart.[93] And when they
would seduce us to idolatry, it will tell us what to do, as
follows: *Put away the strange gods which your fathers*
served on the other side of the river and in Egypt, and
serve the Lord.[94]

At the beginning when you were about to be instructed,[95] you might well have been told: *But if it does*
not please you to serve the Lord, choose for yourselves
this day whom you would serve, whether the gods which
your fathers served on the other side of the river, or the
gods of the Amorrhites, in whose land you dwell.[96] And
the instructor told you: *But as for me and my house, we*
will serve the Lord, for He is holy.[97] Now, however, it is
out of place to speak to you in that way. For you have
declared: *God forbid we should leave the Lord and serve*
strange gods. The Lord our God is the God who brought
us and our fathers out of Egypt and preserved us in all the
way by which we journeyed.[98] In the promises you once
made concerning the worship of God, you gave this reply
to those who instructed you: *We too will serve the Lord,*
for He is our God.[99] If, then, the man who breaks his

agreements with men receives no further credit and is denied security, what are we to say of those who by their denial break the promises they have made to God, and return to Satan whom they renounced at their baptism? [100] Of such an act we must say what Heli said to his sons: *If a man sinning shall sin against another, men will intercede for him. But if a man shall sin against God, who shall intercede for him?* [101]

A SPECTACLE BEFORE ALL

18. A great multitude is assembled to watch you when you combat and are called to martyrdom. It is as if we said that thousands upon thousands gather to watch a contest in which contestants of outstanding reputation are engaged. When you will be engaged in the conflict you can say with Paul: *We are made a spectacle to the world and to angels and to men.*[102] The whole world, therefore, all the angels on the right and on the left, all men, both those on the side of God [103] and the others—all will hear us fighting the fight for Christianity. Either the angels in heaven will rejoice over us, and *the rivers shall clap their hands, the mountains shall rejoice together, and all the trees of the plain shall clap their branches* [104]—or—and God forbid that it should happen—the powers of the lower world will gloat over our crime and will be glad.

It will certainly not be out of place for us to see what according to the written word of Isaias will be said by the denizens of hell to them that are overcome and fall from a martyrdom rewarded with heaven. We shall then tremble even <more> at the impiousness of denial. What will be said to one who has denied his faith is, I think, something like this: *Hell below was in an uproar to meet thee at thy coming. All the giants who rule the earth were stirred up for thee. They roused from their thrones all the kings of the nations. All shall answer and say to thee. . . .*[105] And what will the powers that were overcome say to them that are overcome? They that are already taken by the devil to them that are taken in their denial? What indeed will they say? *Thou also art taken as we are. Thou art become one of us.*[106] And if a man who has a great and glorious hope in God, permits himself in God to be overcome by fear or sufferings with which he is threatened in court, he will hear this: *Thy pride, thy great confidence, is brought down to hell. Under thee shall they strew corruption, and worms shall be thy covering.*[107] And if a man has shone in the churches, resplendent often as the morning star in the glory of his good works before men,[108] and if afterwards, fighting the great fight, he has lost the crown of such high estate, he shall have to hear: *How Lucifer has fallen from heaven, Lucifer who did rise in the morning! How he has been dashed to the earth!*[109] And because through his denial he has become like the devil, this will also be said to him: *Thou wilt be cast out in the mountains as a rotten carcass with many dead that have been pierced by the sword and that go down to hell. As a garment soaked with blood will be impure, so shall thou be impure.*[110] How could he be pure if he has sullied himself with bloody murder, the abominable crime of apostasy, and immersed himself in so great an evil?

Let us now show that we have heeded the words, *He that loveth son or daughter more than me is not worthy of me.*[111] Let us take care that we never show hesitation about denial or bearing witness, that the words of Elias may not be addressed to us: *How long do you halt be-tween two sides? If the Lord be God, follow Him.*[112]

19. It is probable that we shall be insulted by our neighbours, and certain people we associate with will turn up their noses and shake their heads at us as though we were mad.[113] When this happens, let us say to God: *Thou hast made us a reproach to our neighbours, a scoff and derision to them that are around us. Thou hast made us a byword among the Gentiles, a shaking of the head among the people. All the day long my shame is before me, and the confusion of my face hath covered me, at the voice of him that reproacheth and detracteth me, at the face of the enemy and persecutor.*[114] But in the face of all this befalling us there is also bliss in addressing to God the confident words of the Prophet: *All these things have come upon us, yet we have not forgotten Thee, and we have not done wickedly in Thy covenant. And our heart hath not turned back.*[115]

20. Let us remember while we are in this life and reflecting on the ways that are not of this life, to say to God, *Thou hast turned aside our footsteps from Thy way.*[116] Now is the time to recall that this place of our humiliation is a place of affliction for the soul; and so we can pray, saying: *Thou hast humbled us in the place of affliction, and the shadow of death hath covered us.*[117] And we shall take courage and say: *If we have forgotten the name of our God, and if we have spread forth our hands to a strange god: shall not God search out these things?*[118]

21. Let us fight so as to bear our witness perfectly not only in public, but also in secret, so as to be able to declare with the Apostle: *For our glory is this: the testimony of our conscience, that in holiness and sincerity of God . . .*

we have conversed in this world.[119]   Let us add the words of the Prophet to those of the Apostle, *He knoweth the secrets of our hearts* [120]—and especially is this true when we are driven to death, and say to God what martyrs alone say to Him: *For Thy sake we are killed all the day long; we are counted as sheep for the slaughter.*[121]   And if ever the *wisdom of the flesh* [122] should make us fear the judges that threaten us with death, then let us say to them these words from Proverbs: *My son, honour the Lord and thou shalt be strong. Fear no man apart from Him.*[123]

PART IV: EXAMPLES OF MARTYRDOM

ELEAZAR

22. The following also serves our purpose. Solomon says in Ecclesiastes: *I praised all the dead rather than the living, as many as are living up to now.*[124] What dead person could be more deserving of praise than he who of his own choice elected to die for his religion? Such a one was Eleazar,[125] who, *choosing rather a most glorious death than a hateful life, went forward voluntarily to the torment.*[126] *Reasoning in a noble-minded manner worthy of his ninety years and the dignity of his old age and the distinction that had come to him in his grey hair, and his excellent upbringing from childhood, but more so of the ordinances of the holy law made by God,* he said: *It doth not become our age to dissemble: whereby many young persons might think that Eleazar, at the age of fourscore and ten years, was gone over to the life of the heathens; and so they, through my dissimulation and for a little respite of a brief life, should be deceived, and hereby I should bring a stain and a shame upon my old age. For though for the present time I should be delivered from the punishments of men, yet should I not escape the hand of the Almighty, neither alive nor dead. Wherefore by departing manfully out of this life, I shall show myself worthy of my old age; and I shall leave an example of fortitude to young men—with a ready mind and constancy to*

suffer an honourable death for the venerable and holy laws.[127]

When you are at the gates of death, or rather, of liberty, I beg of you, especially if you are subjected to torture—and certainly the designs of the opposition do not permit us to expect that you will not suffer—to say words such as these: *To the Lord who hath the holy knowledge, it is manifest that, whereas I might be delivered from death, I suffer grievous pains in my body because I am scourged; but in my soul I am well content to suffer these things because I fear Thee.*[128] Thus did Eleazar die, and it can be said of him that *he left not only to the young men, but also to most of his nation, his death for an example of noble character and a memorial of fortitude.*[129]

THE SEVEN BROTHERS

23. The seven brothers, whose story is told in the books of the Machabees,[130] who were *tortured with whips and scourges* [131] by Antiochus, and who remained constant in their religion, can also serve as an admirable example of heroic martyrdom to all who ask themselves if they can allow themselves to be outstripped by mere children. They not only endured tortures in their own persons, but showed also a virile tenacity of faith when they had to look on at the sufferings of their brothers. One of them who, as the Scriptures term him, was their spokesman, said to the tyrant: *What wouldst thou ask or learn of us? We are ready to die rather than transgress the laws of our fathers.*[132]

Need we describe all their sufferings—*the frying pans and brazen cauldrons made hot* [133] in which they were to be tortured after they had each been subjected to various torments? The one, for example, who is called their spokesman, first had his tongue cut out, and then was scalped in the Scythian fashion. This he endured as others endure the circumcision ordained by the divine law, for he believed that in enduring this he was also carrying out the word of God.[134] Antiochus, not satisfied with all this, gave orders *to chop off the extremities of his hands and feet, the rest of his brethren and his mother looking on.*[135] In this way he meant to punish his brothers and mother by what they were witnessing, and thought he could shake their determination by something presumably so horrible. Antiochus, not satisfied, *commanded him* whose entire body had been maimed by the tortures he had already inflicted upon him, but who was still breathing, *to be brought to the fire of the frying pans and cauldrons and to fry him.*[136] And when because of the savagery of the tyrant, vapour was given forth by the flesh of the most noble champion [137] of faith as he was being roasted, *the rest, together with the mother, exhorted one another to die manfully,*[138] consoling themselves with the thought that God saw all these things. The conviction that the eye of God [139] was watching over their sufferings was sufficient assurance for their constancy. And the Judge of the champions of faith comforted them, comforted Himself and, so to say, rejoiced with them for struggling against such great sufferings. If we find ourselves in like pains, it would be well for us to say what they said to one another: *The Lord God looks upon us and takes pleasure in the truth in us.*[140]

24.   The first having been proved in this way as *gold is proved in the furnace,*[141] *the second was brought to be made a mockingstock.*[142] The servants of the tyrant's

cruelty, *having pulled off the skin of his head with the hair*,[143] called upon the sufferer to change his mind and asked him if he would eat of the meats offered to idols *before he were punished throughout the whole body in every limb*.[144] When he refused to change his purpose, he was made to endure the whole series of tortures, but he maintained his constancy to his last breath. Without breaking down in the least or giving in to his sufferings, he said to the impious man: *Thou indeed, O most wicked man, destroyest us out of this present life; but the King of the world will raise us up, who die for His laws, in the resurrection of eternal life.*[145]

25. The third, too, counting the tortures as nothing and as it were treading them under his feet in his love of God, *when he was required, quickly put forth his tongue and courageously stretched out his hands, and said: For the laws of God I abandon these. I hope to receive them again* [146] from God in such condition as God certainly will return them to His loyal athletes.

In the same way the fourth was tortured and bore his sufferings, saying: *When we are made to die at human hands, it is better to look for hope from God, and to be raised up again by Him* [147] in *a resurrection* where the tyrant will not be found. For he *will rise not to life* but to mockery and everlasting shame.

And then Antiochus had the fifth tortured, who rebuked him, telling him to his face that he was only a mortal man, but without making any impression on his arrogance and his notion that a tyranny of a few days was great power. In the midst of his sufferings he also declared that *his people was not abandoned by God*, who would presently torment Antiochus *and his seed*.[148]

And after him the sixth, *being close to death*, said: *Be not deceived: we willingly suffer these things and give satisfaction for our sins so as to be cleansed in our pains.* Then he told the king that *he should not think that he would escape unpunished for having attempted to fight against God;* [149] for he indeed fights against God who fights them that are made divine by the Word.[150]

26. Finally Antiochus took the youngest aside, and seeing that he was the brother of them that had made nothing of their terrible sufferings and that he shared their resolution, he resorted to other methods. He thought that he could be won *by persuasion and promises on oath to make him a rich and a happy man, if he would turn from the laws of his fathers, <and> to take him for a friend and put him in charge of the king's affairs.* When in his first effort he made no impression on the young man who paid no attention to words which were incompatible with his resolution, he *summoned the mother and counselled her to give the boy advice for his safety.* But she, acting as though she would try to win over her son to his wishes, *mocked the tyrant* and gave her son an earnest exhortation to perseverance—so much so that he did not wait for the torture to be inflicted upon him: he anticipated it and challenged the executioners, saying: "Why do you hesitate and delay? We obey the law given by God. We may not obey a commandment that is contrary to the words of God." Like a king handing down a decision on subjects to be judged, he also gave judgment on the tyrant, condemning him rather than being condemned by him. And he told him that *for raising his hand against the children of heaven, he would not escape from the judgment of the almighty God who beholdeth all things.*[151]

27. Then one could see the mother of so many sons *bearing courageously* the sufferings and death of her sons, *for the hopes she had in God.*[152] For the dew of piety and breath of holiness did not allow the fire of a mother's feelings, which inflames many mothers in the presence of most grievous ills, to be kindled within her heart.

I think that in view of our present purpose it was most useful to give here this story from the Scriptures. Thus we can see what piety and the love of God, which is stronger than all other loves, can achieve against the most cruel sufferings and the severest tortures. This love of God does not tolerate the co-existence of human weakness, but drives it away as an enemy alien from the whole soul. And this weakness has become powerless in the case of one who can say, *The Lord is my strength and my praise,*[153] and *I can do all things in Him who strengtheneth me, Christ Jesus, Our Lord.*[154]

PART V: THE NECESSITY, ESSENCE, AND KINDS OF MARTYRDOM

THE CHALICE OF SALVATION

28. From this episode we can learn also what martyrdom is and the special confidence [155] before God which is conferred by it. The saint has a special sense of honour and wishes to give a recompense for the benefits conferred on him by God; and so he looks around to see if he can do anything for the Lord in return for all that he has received. He finds that for a man of good intentions there is nothing to counterbalance, as it were, these benefits of God—except a martyr's death. In Psalm 115 there is written this rhetorical question: *What shall I render to the Lord for all the things that He hath rendered to me?* And then follows the reply to him who asks what he can render to the Lord for all he has received: *I will take the chalice of salvation, and I will call upon the name of the Lord.*[156] The "chalice of salvation" is the usual term used for martyrdom, as we see from the Gospel. There the Lord answers them that wish for a higher honour in sitting on the right and on the left of Jesus in His kingdom, saying: *Can you drink the chalice that I shall drink?*[157] He calls martyrdom a chalice, as is evident again from the words: *Father, if it be possible, let this chalice pass from me. Nevertheless not as I will but as Thou wilt.*[158] And again we learn that he who drinks the chalice that Jesus drank will sit, reign, and judge beside the King of Kings.[159] Such, then, is the chalice of salvation: he who takes it will *call upon the*

name of the Lord, and whoever *shall call upon the name
of the Lord shall be saved.*[160]

LET THIS CHALICE PASS FROM ME

29. But perhaps because of the words: *Father, if it be
possible, let this chalice pass from me*,[161] someone who does
not understand the meaning of Scripture thoroughly, may
think that the Saviour was in a way even afraid at the time
of His passion. And if Jesus was afraid, a man may argue,
how can a man remain steadfast forever?

Let us first ask those who make such an assumption regarding the Saviour whether He was inferior to him who
said: *The Lord is my light and my saviour: whom shall I
fear? The Lord is the protector of my life: of whom shall I
be afraid? Whilst the wicked draw near against me to eat
my flesh, they that trouble me and my enemies have themselves been weakened and have fallen. If armies in camp
should stand together against me, my heart shall not fear.
If war should rise up against me, in this will I be confident.*[162] Most likely these words spoken by the prophet
apply to no one else but the Saviour, who because of the
light and salvation which have come to Him from the
Father fears nobody and who because of the powerful protection given Him by God is afraid of no man. The heart
of the Saviour never feared in any way when the whole
camp of Satan was drawn up against Him. His heart,
filled with holy knowledge, was confident in God when
war rose up against Him. It is therefore impossible that
the same man should say in fear: *Father, if it be possible,
let this chalice pass from me;*[163] and with fortitude: *If
armies in camp should stand together against me, my heart
shall not fear.*[164]

In order that we may not overlook anything in this text, I would direct your attention to the demonstrative used with the word "chalice" in each of the three Gospels. Matthew wrote that the Lord said: *Father, if it be possible, let "this" chalice pass from me;* [165] Luke: *Father, if Thou wilt, remove "this" chalice from me;* [166] and Mark: *Abba, Father, all things are possible to Thee: remove "this" chalice from me.* [167] Now since every martyrdom that results in death, whatever be the cause of the death involved, is called a chalice, note whether it can be asserted that He did not ask for exemption from martyrdom as such when He said, *Let "this" chalice pass from me*—otherwise He would have said: "Let *the* chalice pass from me"; but that probably He meant *this* kind of chalice. One should remember the possibility that the Saviour considered the different kinds, so to speak, of chalice and what is achieved through each one of them; understood in His most profound wisdom their differences; asked to be excused from martyrdom with this particular issue; asked in silence, on the other hand, for a form of martyrdom much severer, so that through this other chalice might be wrought a benefit more universal, one reaching to a greater number of men. But such was not the will of the Father, which, as compared with the will of the Son and with the judgment of the Saviour, orders and disposes all things with superior wisdom. [168]

Clearly *the chalice of salvation* mentioned in the Psalms is the death of martyrs. And that is why the sentence, *I will take the chalice of salvation, and will call upon the name of the Lord,* [169] is followed by, *Precious in the sight of the Lord is the death of His saints.* [170] Death, then, comes precious for us, if we are saints of God, and if we are not unworthy to die—not the ordinary, so to speak, and fruitless death in religion, but that very special death, death for the sake of Christianity, piety, and holiness.

THE BAPTISM OF BLOOD

30.   Let us remember also the sins that we have committed, and that except by baptism it is not possible to obtain remission of sins.[171]   But according to the laws of the Gospel one cannot be baptized twice in water and the spirit for the remission of sins.[172]   We are given, however, the baptism of martyrdom.[173]   Obviously it bears this name from the fact that to the text: *Can you drink of the chalice that I drink?* [174] there is subjoined, *or be baptized with the baptism wherewith I am baptized?* [175]   Elsewhere it is said: *And I have a baptism wherewith I am to be baptized. And how am I straitened until it be accomplished?* [176] Note also that the baptism of martyrdom, as received by our Saviour, atones for the world; so, too, when we receive it, it serves to atone for many.   Just as they who assisted at the altar according to the law of Moses seemed to procure for the Jews remission for sins by the blood of goats and oxen,[177] so the souls of believers that *are beheaded for the testimony of Jesus,*[178] do not assist in vain at the altar of heaven,[179] but procure for them that pray the remission of sins.   And likewise we learn that as the High Priest Jesus Christ offered Himself in sacrifice, so the priests, whose leader He is, also offer themselves in sacrifice; [180] for this reason one sees them at the altar as their proper place.   But while some of the priests were without blemish and offered victims without blemish and so performed the divine service, others had blemishes such as are listed by Moses in Leviticus,[181] and were kept away from the altar.

Who then is the priest without blemish who can offer a victim [182] without blemish, if not he who bears witness to the last and fulfills every requirement of the concept of martyrdom? We have already spoken of him above.[183]

31. We must not be surprised if this blessed state of the martyrs which will consist in profound peace and tranquillity and calm, has to be preceded by weather that seems menacing and, so to speak, wintry. It is in traversing the difficult and narrow course [184] in the winter's storm that all the blessed must first show how they have mastered their pilotage. Then will be realized the words of the Canticle of Canticles addressed to the bride who has come through the winter's blasts: *My beloved answereth*, it is said, *and speaks to me: Arise, come, my neighbour, my beautiful one, my dove. For, look, winter is now past, the rain is over and gone.*[185] And remember that you will hear the words, *the winter is now past*, only if you will struggle bravely and valiantly through the present winter's storm. It is only when *the winter is past* and *the rain is over and gone* that the flowers appear: *Planted in the house of the Lord*, they *shall flourish in the courts of the house of our God.*[186]

THE CHOICE: MARTYRDOM OR IDOLATRY

32. Again, we know that, since we have been persuaded by Jesus to abandon idols and polytheism which is really atheism, the Enemy cannot persuade us to accept idolatry; but he tries to force it upon us. And so with this in view he sets upon those who come within his power and makes either martyrs or idolaters of them who are brought to trial. Even now he keeps on repeating: *All this will I give thee, if falling down thou wilt adore me.*[187] Let us

take care, therefore, never to adore idols or obey demons: for the idols of the Gentiles are demons.[188]   How monstrous is it to give up the *sweet yoke* of Christ *and His light burden* [189] to submit oneself once more to the yoke of demons and to carry the burden of the gravest sins!   And that, too, after we had learned that *the heart* of them that adore idols *is ashes*, and that their *life is more base than clay;* [190] and after we had said: *How deceitful are the idols which our fathers acquired; and there is none among them that can send rain!* [191]

33.   It was not only Nabuchodonosor of long ago who *set up a statue of gold*, nor were Ananias, Azarias and Misael of his day the only persons whom he then threatened to *cast into the furnace of burning fire* [192] if they did not adore it.   No, now too, Nabuchodonosor speaks the same words to us—the true Hebrews, the Hebrews of the world to come.[193]   But we, that we may experience the heavenly dew that will quench all the fire about us and refresh the higher part of our souls, shall imitate those holy youths. Aman may want you, as he did Mardochai, to bend the knee to him.[194] But you must say: *I will not place the glory of men above the glory of* the *God* of Israel.   Let us destroy Bel by the word of God, and with Daniel let us slay the dragon,[195] that as we are brought before the jaws of the lions, we may suffer nothing from them, while they alone who have stirred up the present combat against us, will be consumed by the very lions that could not devour us.   Let us take to heart that in the recital of the great deeds of Job it is also written: *If I placed my hand upon my mouth and kissed it: let this also be counted against me as a very great iniquity.*[196]   It is likely indeed that we shall be commanded to place our hand upon our mouth and kiss it.

34. And this too let us note that the Saviour foretells martyrdom not in His discourses delivered to the multitude, but in those reserved for the Apostles. Thus, following the words, *These twelve Jesus sent, commanding them, saying: Go ye not into the way of the Gentiles* etc., there is added: *Beware of men. For they will deliver you up in councils and they will scourge you in their synagogues. And you shall be brought before governors and before kings for my sake, for a testimony to them and to the Gentiles. But when they shall deliver you up, take no thought how or what to speak; <for it shall be given you in that hour what to speak.> For it is not you that speak, but the Spirit of your Father that speaketh in you. The brother also shall deliver up the brother to death and the father the son, and the children shall rise up against their parents and shall put them to death. And you shall be hated by all men for my name's sake. But he that shall persevere unto the end, he shall be saved. And when they shall persecute you in this city, flee into another; and if they drive you out of that, flee into still another. Amen I say unto you, you shall not finish all the cities of Israel till the Son of man come.*[197]

And Luke writes similarly: *And when they shall bring you into the synagogues and to magistrates and powers, be not solicitous how you shall answer or what you shall say. For the Holy Spirit shall teach you in the same hour what you must say.*[198] And further on: *Lay it up therefore in your hearts, not to meditate before how you shall answer: For I will give you a mouth and wisdom, which all your adversaries shall not be able to resist and gainsay. And you shall be betrayed by your parents and brethren and kinsmen and friends, and some of you they will put to death.   And you shall be hated by all men for my name's sake.   But a hair of your head shall not perish.   In your endurance you shall possess your souls.*[199]   Mark, too, has something similar: *When they shall lead you and deliver you up, be not thoughtful nor rehearse beforehand <what you shall speak>; but whatsoever shall be given you in that hour, that speak ye.   For it is not you that speak, but the Holy Spirit.   And the brother shall betray his brother unto death, and the father his son; and children shall rise up against the parents and shall work their death.   And you shall be hated by all men for my name's sake.   But he that shall endure to the end, he shall be saved.*[200]

Again, the following words referring to martyrdom in Matthew are addressed exclusively to the Twelve.   We, too, must heed them, and in heeding them we shall be brothers to the Apostles that heard them, and shall be counted among the Apostles.   The words are as follows: *Fear ye not them that kill the body and are not able to kill the soul; but rather fear him that can destroy <both> soul and body in hell.*[201]   In what follows the Lord teaches us that no one comes to the combat of martyrdom without Divine Providence.   The text is: *Are not two sparrows sold for a farthing?   And not one of them shall fall on the ground without your Father who is in heaven.   But the very hairs of your head are all numbered.   Fear not therefore: better are you than many sparrows.   Everyone therefore that shall confess me before men, I will also confess him before my Father who is in heaven.   But he that shall deny me before men, I will also deny him before my Father who is in heaven.*[202]   The same is conveyed in Luke: *This I say to you, my friends: Be not afraid of them who kill the body and after that have no more that they can do.*

*But I will show you whom you shall fear. Fear ye Him
who, after He hath killed, hath power to cast into hell.
Yea, I say to you, fear Him. Are not five sparrows sold
for two farthings, and not one of them is forgotten before
God? Yea, the very hairs of your head are all numbered.
Fear not therefore: you are of more value than many sparrows. And I say to you: Whosoever shall confess me
before men, him shall the Son of man also confess before
the angels of God. But he that shall deny me before men
shall be denied before the angels of God.*[203] And elsewhere: *For he that shall be ashamed of me and of my
words, of him the Son of man shall be ashamed, when He
shall come in His majesty and that of His Father and of
the holy angels.*[204] And Mark writes in a similar vein, as
follows: *For he that shall be ashamed of me and of my
words, in this adulterous and sinful generation: the Son of
man also will be ashamed of him, when He shall come in
the glory of His Father with the holy angels.*[205]

They that kill us, therefore, kill only the life of the
body, as is clearly signified by the words, *fear ye not them
that kill the body*—expressed in the same terms by Matthew and Luke.[206] When they have slain the body, they
cannot, even if they wished it, slay the soul: *they have no
more that they can do.*[207] For how can the soul be slain
when it has been given life by the very fact of martyrdom?
The soul it is to which He who in Isaias encourages us to
martyrdom, in His turn bears witness with His Son where
it is written in *Isaias: Be ye witnesses to me and I also shall
be a witness to you and my Son whom I have chosen, saith
the Lord God.*[208]

Notice also that it is not to slaves but to His friends that
Jesus gives the following precept: *Be not afraid of them*

who kill the body and after that have no more that they can do.[209] Accordingly one has to *fear Him that can destroy both soul and body in hell.*[210] For He only, *after He hath killed, hath power to cast into hell.*[211] He casts into hell them that fear the slayers of the body, but do not *fear Him that can destroy both the soul and body in hell;* [212] *who, after He hath killed, hath power to cast into hell.*[213] And if in the case of another *the very hairs of his head are numbered,*[214] and that certainly in the case of those who are beheaded for the sake of Jesus, then let us confess the Son of God before men and the gods that are not gods. He who will have had witness borne to Him, will in return bear witness to us before God and His Father; and He Himself will bear witness in heaven to him who has borne witness to Him on earth.

APOSTATES WILL BE DENIED BY THE SON

35. Is there any man that will not quote, when he reflects upon all this, the words of the Apostle: *The sufferings of this time are not worthy to be compared with the glory to come that shall be revealed in us.*[215] Is not the bearing of testimony before the Father a far greater thing than bearing testimony before men? And in comparison with the testimony borne on earth by the martyrs to the Son of God, is not the testimony borne to them in heaven by Him of transcending significance? If a man thinks of denying before men, let him remember Him who said without any lie, *I will also deny him before my Father who is in heaven!* [216]

In view of what Matthew says, *I will also confess him before my Father who is in heaven,*[217] and Luke, *him shall the Son of man also confess before the angels of God,*[218] I suggest that the *first-born of every creature, the image of the invisible God,*[219] will bear testimony before the Father who is in heaven to him who bore testimony to Him; and that He who *was made of the seed of David according to the flesh,*[220] and who is therefore the *Son of man;*[221] who is born of woman, herself of the race of man, and is therefore again the *Son of man,* a term we apply to the humanity of Jesus—He will bear testimony before the angels of God to them that have borne testimony to Him. And, corresponding to this, witness is to be given regarding those who deny Him.

We should also remember that he who bears witness to the Son before men recommends so far as he can Christianity and the Father of this Christianity to those in whose presence he bears witness. And he to whom witness is borne by *the first-born of every creature*[222] and by *the Son of man,* is recommended by the testimony of *the Son of God* and *the Son of man* to the Father who is in heaven, and the angels of God. And if it is *not he who commendeth himself that is approved, but he whom the Lord commendeth,*[223] must we not believe that he is indeed approved who is judged worthy of recommendation before the Father who is in heaven, and before the angels of God? If he is approved—he and others like him—whom the Lord *has tried as gold in the furnace* by tortures and questionings, and whom He *has received as a victim of a holocaust,*[224] what are we to say of them who, tested in the furnace of temptation,[225] have denied Him? Them will He who denies him that deserves to be denied, deny and refuse to approve before the Father who is in heaven, and *before the angels of God.*

36. Nor must one's combat be concerned with merely

not denying: we must also sense no shame whatever at suffering what God's enemies consider to be shameful. This is particularly your duty, Ambrose, consecrated to God as you are. You have been honoured and well-received by numerous cities, but now you appear, as it were, in triumphal procession, *taking up the cross* of Jesus and *following Him* [226] as He goes before you to appear before magistrates and kings, that by making the journey with you He may *give you a mouth of wisdom.* [227] And He will do the same for you, Protoctetus, his companion in the conflict, and for you who are their fellow witnesses, who *fill up those things that are wanting of the sufferings of Christ.* [228] May He be with you, on your way to God's Paradise, to show you how to walk through the midst of *the Cherubim and the flaming sword turning every way and keeping the way of the tree of life.* [229] If these two guard the way to the tree of life, they do so that no one unworthy may pass by it and come to the tree of life. The flaming sword will, for example, keep back them that on the *foundation which is laid, which is Christ Jesus, have built wood or hay or stubble,* [230] and that wood which is most flammable and burns most fiercely, namely apostasy. The Cherubim will receive them that could not be overcome by the sword of fire, because they have built nothing which it could touch, and will bring them to *the tree of life* and to all that which God *had planted . . . from the beginning and brought forth of the ground.* [231] And since Jesus travels with you to Paradise, contemn the serpent that is overcome and trodden under the feet of Jesus and, through Him, under your feet also. For He *has given you power to tread upon serpents and scorpions and upon all the power of the Enemy, and nothing shall hurt you.* [232]

37. We must not, then, deny the Son of God or blush because of Him, His followers, or His words. Rather we should heed this: *He that shall deny me before men, I will also deny him before my Father who is in heaven;* [233] and again: *He that shall be ashamed of me and mine, of him the Son of man shall be ashamed, when He shall come in His majesty and that of His Father and of the holy angels;* [234] and again: *For he that shall be ashamed of me and of my words in this adulterous and sinful generation: the Son of man also will be ashamed of him, when He shall come in the glory of His Father with the holy angels.* [235]

Jesus having once *endured the cross, despising the shame,* [236] sits on that account *on the right hand* of God. [237] So, too, those who imitate Him, *despising the shame, will* sit and *reign* in heaven *with Him* [238] who *came to send peace*—not indeed *upon earth,* but in the souls of His disciples—and *to send the sword upon earth.* [239] Since *the Word of God is living and effectual and more piercing than any two-edged sword and reaching unto the division of the soul and the spirit, of the joints also and the marrow, and is a discerner of the thoughts and intents of the heart,* [240] He brings in recompense to our hearts especially now the prize of *peace which surpasseth all understanding,* [241] that which He left to His apostles. [242] But He has sent the sword between *the image of the earthly* and that *of the heavenly,* [243] so that, taking possession now of what is of heaven, He may later, when we no longer deserve to be divided in two, make us entirely of heaven.

He has come to bring not only the sword upon earth, but also fire. *And what will I,* He says, *but that it be kindled?* [244] May this fire therefore be kindled in you also. May it consume your every calculation that is

earthly and of the body.   May you now with heart and
soul submit to that baptism wherewith Jesus *was straitened
until it was accomplished.*[245]   And you, who have a wife
and children, brothers and sisters, remember the words: *If
any man come to me, and hate not his father and mother
and wife and children and brethren and sisters, he cannot
be my disciple.*[246]   And both of you should remember
these words: *If any man come to me, and hate not*—in
addition—*his own life also, he cannot be my disciple.*[247]
Hate your life, and in hating it you will *keep it unto life
eternal: He that hateth,* says Scripture, *his life in this world
keepeth it unto life eternal.*[248]   Hate your life, then, for the
sake of life eternal, convinced that Jesus is teaching us a
hatred that is for our good and welfare.   And in the same
manner as we should hate our own life in order to keep it
for life eternal, so too in regard to wife, children, brothers,
and sisters.   You who possess them must hate them so as
to do good to them that are hated.   It is precisely through
this hate that you will become a friend of God and so become free to become their benefactors.

38.   Remember at the same time Him who prayed in
spirit for the children of martyrs left behind for the sake
of the love of God, and said: *Take possession of the children of them that have been put to death.*[249]   Know only
that *not they that are children of the flesh, are the children
of God;*[250] and that just as it was said to them of the seed
of Abraham, *I know that you are the seed of Abraham,*[251]
and, *If you were the children of Abraham, you did the
works of Abraham,*[252] in the same way will it be said to
your children, "I know that you are the seed of Ambrose,"
and, "If you are the children of Ambrose, do the works of
Ambrose."   They will, doubtless, do them; but you will

help them more by thus meeting your death than if you remained with them. In this way you will love them more wisely and pray for them with greater understanding, if you learn that they are not merely your *seed* but also your *children.* Now keep this on your lips: *He that loveth son or daughter more than me is not worthy of me;* [253] and, *He that findeth his life shall lose it, and he that shall lose his life for me shall find it.* [254]

39. By your readiness to undergo martyrdom give expression to *the spirit of your Father that speaketh to them that are delivered up* for the sake of religion. [255] If you see that you are hated and abhorred and that you are regarded as impious, remember the words: *Therefore the world hateth you, because you are not of this world. If you had been of this world, the world would love its own.* [256] You have already endured for the sake of Christ many outrages and many dangers since the time when you began to believe. Persevere to the end and advance in perseverance; for *he that shall persevere unto the end, he shall be saved.* [257] Know that, according to Peter, *you shall greatly rejoice, if now you must be for a little time made sorrowful in divers temptations: that the trial of your faith—much more precious than gold which is perishable and tried by the fire—may be found unto praise and glory and honour at the appearing of Jesus Christ.* [258] Notice the use of the words "be made sorrowful" in the sense of "labour," as is seen in the passage, *In sorrow shalt thou bring forth children.* [259] A woman does not really bring forth children in *sorrow,* but in *labour.*

If the following words are helpful to the disciples of Christ, namely: *Love not the world, nor the things which are in the world. If any man love the world, the charity of the Father is not in him. For all that is in the world is the concupiscence of the flesh and the concupiscence of the eyes and the pride of life, which is not of the Father but is of the world. And the world passeth away and the concupiscence thereof,*[260]—do not love, then, that which passes away, but do the will of God and become worthy to become one with the Son, the Father, and the Holy Spirit, according to the prayer of the Saviour: . . . *as I and Thou are one, that they also may be one in us.*[261] How many days can he gain who *loves the world* or the *things which are in the world,*[262] but who destroys and loses his soul,[263] and carries about with him a conscience burdened with the greatest possible burden,[264] the calamity of denial? Let each of us remember how many times he has been in danger of the ordinary death, and let us ask ourselves if we were not perhaps preserved from it in order that we might baptize ourselves in our own blood and wash ourselves from every sin, and so take our place at the heavenly altar [265] along with our companions in the fight.

40. But if a man because he is too tenacious of life or too weak in the face of suffering, or because of the apparently convincing arguments of such as seek to induce us to accept the evil choice, has denied the one only God and His Christ, and borne testimony to demons [266] or goddesses of fortune,[267] then this man must realize that in doing this he is *setting,* as it were, *a table for the demon and offering libations* to Fortune, *forsaking the Lord* and *forgetting His holy mount.* He will incur the reproaches written in Isaias in these words: *You that have forsaken me, that forget my holy mount, that set a table for the demon and offer a libation to fortune, I will hand you over to the sword, you shall all fall by slaughter: because I called you and you did*

*not answer, I spoke and you did not hear. And you did
evil before my eyes and you have chosen the things that
displease me. Therefore thus saith the Lord Lord: Behold,
my servants shall eat, but you shall be hungry: behold, my
servants shall drink, but you shall be thirsty. Behold, my
servants shall rejoice, and you shall be confounded. Behold, my servants shall praise for joyfulness of heart, but
you shall cry for sorrow of heart and shall howl for grief
of spirit. For you shall leave my name for the satisfaction
of my elect. And the Lord shall slay you.*[268] But if, because we know what *the table of the Lord* is, we wish to
partake of it, let us attend to the words, *You cannot be
partakers of the table of the Lord and of the table of
demons.*[269] And if we wish, understanding the words, *I
will not drink from henceforth of this fruit of the vine
until that day when I shall drink it with you new in the
kingdom of heaven,*[270] to be found among them that drink
with Jesus, let us weigh well these words also, *You cannot
drink the chalice of the Lord and the chalice of demons.*[271]

John, the son of thunder,[272] says: *Who denieth the
Father and the Son: whosoever denieth the Son, the same
hath not the Father. He that confesseth the Son hath the
Father also.*[273] When a man hears this, will he not have to
fear that if he says he is not a Christian, he is denying the
Son, and that in denying Him he will not have the Father?
And is there anyone who will not eagerly confess himself
a Christian in word and deed, that he may have the Father
as well? For they who bear testimony have the Father.

41. If we have *passed from death to life* [274] in passing
from unbelief to Faith, let us not be surprised *if the world
hates us.*[275] No one who has not *passed from death to life,*
but still remains in death, can love them that have passed

from the gloomy dwelling of death, so to speak, to the dwellings *built up of living stones*[276] and flooded with *the light of life.* Jesus *hath laid down His life for us,* and let us, therefore, *lay down ours:*[277] I shall not say for Him, but for ourselves, and I should think for all them that will be edified by our martyrdom. The time has come for us Christians to glory in ourselves, for it is written: *Not only so; but we glory also in tribulations, knowing that tribulation worketh patience, and patience trial, and trial hope; and hope confoundeth not.*[278] Only let *the charity of God be poured forth in our hearts by the Holy Spirit.*[279] Let Paul say, *If—according to man—I fought with beasts at Ephesus;*[280] and let us, "If—according to man—we were slain in Germany."[281]

42. *As the sufferings of Christ abound, so also by Christ doth comfort abound.*[282] Let us then welcome eagerly the sufferings incurred for Christ; and let them abound in us, if we truly strive for the abundant consolation with which all they who weep[283] shall be consoled, though perhaps in unequal measure. For if consolation were given in equal measure to all, it would not be written: *As the sufferings of Christ abound in us, so also by Christ doth our comfort abound.* They who *are partakers of the sufferings,* will be partakers *of the consolation also,*[284] according to the measure of the sufferings which they share with Christ. This you learn also from him who says with entire confidence: For *we know that as you are partakers of the sufferings, so shall you be also of the consolation.*

God, moreover, says by the Prophet: *In an acceptable time I have heard thee, and in the day of salvation I have helped thee.*[285] What time could be more acceptable than when, because of our piety towards God in Christ, we

make our solemn entry in this world surrounded by a
guard and when we are led out, more like triumphant con-
querors than conquered? For martyrs in Christ *despoil*
with Him *the principalities and powers*[286] and triumph
with Him, by partaking in His sufferings and the great
deeds accomplished in His sufferings—among which is His
triumphing over principalities and powers, which you will
soon see conquered and overcome with shame. What
other day could be for us such a day of salvation as the day
of so glorious a departure from here below? I exhort you:
Give no offence in anything, that the priesthood and *diaconate be not blamed because of you; but in all things
exhibit yourselves as the ministers of God in much patience,*[287] saying: *And now what is my hope? Is it not the
Lord?*[288] In *tribulation*[289] be persuaded that *many are the
tribulations of the just.*[290] In our *necessities,*[291] let us ask
for what is necessary—happiness. In *distresses,*[292] let us
walk without halting upon the strait and narrow way, so
as to arrive at life.[293] And if it be required, let us show our
mettle *in stripes, in prisons, in seditions, in labours, in
watchings, in fastings.*[294] For behold, the Lord is present,
and *His reward is in His hand, to be given to each one according to his works.*[295]

43. Let us show now that we have wished for *knowledge*[296] by doing the works which are in agreement with
knowledge. Let all *chastity*, which comes from the avoid-
ance of any possible defilement from sin, be manifested in
us. We are the sons of a patient God; the brothers of a
patient Christ: let us show ourselves patient in all that befalls us. *He that is patient has great wisdom; but he that
is impatient is greatly foolish.*[297] If it is necessary *to exhibit
ourselves . . . by the armour of justice on the right hand*

and on the left, let us now, having exhibited ourselves by *honour* without becoming vain, also endure *dishonour.* If we have lived so as to deserve *good report* and have received it, let us now endure also *evil report* from the impious. And again, if we have been admired by lovers of truth as truthful, let us now laugh when it is said that we are *deceivers.* Because of the many dangers from which we have been delivered, many have said that we are *known* of God. Now let anyone say that we are *unknown* to Him, when perhaps we are *known* more. Hence, if we endure whatever happens, we are chastised but not *killed;* apparently we are *sorrowful,* but in reality we *rejoice.*

44. Paul says somewhere to them that have endured the first sufferings, exhorting them to maintain their initial perseverance in the dangers next to come on account of the Word: *Call to mind the former days, wherein, being illuminated, you endured a great fight of afflictions. And on the one hand indeed, by reproaches and tribulations, were made a gazingstock; and on the other, became companions of them that were used in such sort. For you both had compassion on me that was in bands and took with joy the being stripped of your own goods, knowing that you have a better and a lasting substance. Do not therefore lose your confidence which hath a great reward. For you have need of perseverance.*[298] So let us too *endure a great fight of afflictions, by reproaches and tribulations made a gazingstock,* yet *taking with joy the being stripped of our goods.* For we are convinced that we have *a better substance,* not earthly, nor even corporeal, but in some way invisible and incorporeal. For *we look not at the things which are seen,* knowing that *these are temporal, while those others are eternal.*[299]

PART VI: THE CRIMINAL CHARACTER OF IDOLATRY

THE CULT OF DEMONS

45. Some people give no thought to the question of demons: [300] that is to say, to the fact that these demons, in order to be able to exist in the heavy atmosphere that encircles the earth, must have the nourishment of exhalations and, consequently, are always on the lookout for the savour of burnt sacrifices, blood, and incense. Since they attach no importance to the matter of sacrifice, we would express ourselves also on this subject. If men who give sustenance to robbers, murderers, and barbarian enemies of the Great King [301] are punished as criminals against the state, how much more will they be punished justly who through offering sacrifice proffer sustenance to the minions of evil and thus hold them in the atmosphere of the earth! And this holds true especially if knowing the text, *He that sacrificeth to gods other than the Lord alone will be destroyed utterly,*[302] they nevertheless sacrifice to these authors of evil on earth. In my opinion, when there is question of crimes committed by these demons operating against men, they who sustain them by sacrificing to them will be held no less responsible than the demons themselves that do the crimes. For the demons and they that have kept them on earth, where they could not exist without the exhalations and nourishment considered vital to their bodies, work as one in doing evil to mankind.

THE IMPORTANCE OF NAMES

46. Others again assume that the names of things are entirely arbitrary and have no natural relation to the objects of which they are the names.[303] They think that it does not matter which you say: "I worship the first God, or Zeus, or Zēn";[304] and whether you assert: "I pay honour and veneration to the sun or Apollo, and the moon or Artemis, and the spirit of the earth or Demeter"—and so on according to what has been said by the wise men of the Greeks. We reply that on the question of names there is a special science which is both very profound and very subtle. A man versed in it will see that if these names were a matter of convention merely, the demons or whatever powers there are invisible to us, would not respond when addressed by such as mean to address them, but do so on the understanding that the names are but arbitrarily given. But in fact certain sounds, syllables, and names pronounced with a rough or smooth breathing, or with lengthening or shortening, bring to us them that are summoned—in virtue, doubtless, of some natural factor which we cannot discern. If this is so and names are not purely conventional, then we must call the first God by no other name but that which His Servant [305] and the Prophets and Our Lord and Saviour Himself used—for example, *Sabaoth, Adonai, Saddai;* or, again, the *God of Abraham, God of Isaac, God of Jacob. This is a name for ever*, says Scripture, *and this is a memorial unto all generations.*[306] It should not surprise us that the demons should apply their own nomenclature to the first God, so as to be adored as the first God; but with our Servant, the Prophets, and Christ who fulfilled the Law,[307] and His Apostles this is not customary.

It was necessary to add all this lest someone deceive us

by sophistry or in any way vitiate our judgment. We must give careful consideration to these matters so as not to offer our adversaries any opportunity of foisting their views on us.

PART VII: FINAL EXHORTATION

47.   A man continues to love this life, even though he is persuaded that the rational substance of the soul has some affinity to God.   Both substances are intelligible, invisible and, as the prevailing opinion demonstrates, incorporeal. Why, in effect, should He who created us have placed in us a desire to reverence Him and to be united with Him—a desire which continues to show some traces of the divine will even in those who are in error—if it were not possible, and indeed quite possible, for rational beings to satisfy this natural desire?

It is clear that as each of our members maintains a relationship towards its proper object, the eyes for things visible, the ears for things audible, in the same way the intelligence maintains a relationship towards things intelligible, and towards God who is above things intelligible. Why then do we hesitate and waver about putting off the impediment of the *corruptible body* that *is a load upon the soul, the earthly habitation pressing down the mind that museth upon many things?* [308]   Why not be delivered from our bonds and free ourselves from the storms that are born of flesh and blood?   We would then repose with Christ Jesus in the repose that comes with eternal bliss alone; [309] we would contemplate the all-pervading living Word in His entire essence, nourished by Him, and understanding the *manifold wisdom* [310] that is in Him; we would be marked with the seal of Him who is Truth itself; and our spirit would be illumined in the true and unfailing light [311] of knowledge for the contemplation of things which can be seen as they are, thanks to this light, by *eyes* that have been *enlightened by the commandment of the Lord.*[312]

48. We have for a long time now heard the words of Jesus. For a long time too we have been instructed in the Gospel and we have all built a house for ourselves. On what have we built it? *Upon a rock, digging and laying deep the foundations? Upon the sand, without a foundation?* [313] The answer will appear in the present trial. For a storm has arisen, bringing with it rain, floods, and winds or, as Luke has it, *a deluge.* When all this beats upon our house, it will either not be able to shake it or make it fall, *because it is founded upon a rock* which is Christ; or it will expose the weakness of the building which is bound to collapse on this ominous occasion.

May what we have built not share this fate! Woefully *great is the fall* that comes with apostasy, or, as Luke says of a house built without a foundation: *the ruin is great.* Let us pray, then, to be like *the wise man who built his house upon a rock.* Let the rain caused by *the spirits of wickedness in high places* come upon such a house; or the floods of *principalities and powers* inimical to us; or the fierce winds let loose by the *rulers of the world of this darkness;* [314] or the deluge of the infernal spirits. Let them hurl themselves against our house built upon the rock. Not only will our house not fall, but it will not even begin to be shaken. And so the evil spirits [315] will be made to suffer by us rather than achieve anything with us. And let each one of us say, as he strikes the enemy, *I so fight, not as one beating the air.*[316]

49. *The sower went forth to sow his seed.*[317] Let us show that our soul has received His seed, not as that *by*

the wayside, nor that *upon stony ground*, nor that *among thorns*, but as that *upon good ground.* We shall glory [318] as well as we can in the Lord, that the word of Jesus has not fallen *by the wayside*, nor *among thorns.* For *we have understood* what was said, and therefore *the Wicked One has not taken away that which was sown in our hearts.* Many will testify for us that the seed has not been sown *among thorns*, when they see that neither *the cares of this world*, nor *the deceitfulness of riches*, nor *the pleasures of life* have been able to choke up the word of God in our souls.

Finally, there remains that men should ask themselves if the word of God has fallen, so far as depends on us, *on stony ground* or *on good ground. Tribulation and persecution* have come to us *because of the word. A time of great trial* is upon us when he that has sown upon *stony ground* will be revealed, and they too that have not dug deeply and have not received Jesus in the depth of their souls. But he that *has understood the word bears fruit* and *keeps the word* until the end, *yielding a hundredfold in patience.*

We know how the Scriptures speak of them that *are scandalized* in the time of *tribulation and persecution*, after having apparently *received* the sacred teaching *with joy.* [319] They are scandalized, because they have no root, and believe only for a time. Matthew says: *He that received the seed upon stony ground is he that heareth the word and immediately receiveth it with joy. Yet hath he not root in himself, but is only for a time; and when there ariseth tribulation and persecution because of the word, he is presently scandalized.* [320] And Mark: *These are they that are sown on the stony ground: they who, when they have heard the word, immediately receive it with joy. And they have no root in themselves, but are only for a time; and then when tribulation and persecution ariseth for the word they are presently scandalized.*[321] And Luke: *They upon the rock are they who, when they hear, receive the word with joy; and these have no roots, for they believe for a while and in time of temptation they fall away.*[322] Concerning them that bear fruit well, the Scripture teaches us: *But he that received the seed upon good ground is he that heareth the word, and understandeth, and beareth fruit, and yieldeth the one an hundredfold, and another sixty, and another thirty;*[323] or: *And these are they who are sown upon the good ground, who hear the word, and receive it, and yield fruit: the one thirty, another sixty, and another a hundred;*[324] or again, *But that on the good ground are they who in a good and perfect heart, hearing the word, keep it and bring forth fruit in patience.*[325]

Since, then, to quote the Apostle, *you are God's husbandry, God's building*[326]—"husbandry" *upon good ground*, and "building" *upon a rock*—let us as *God's building* stand unshaken by the storm; and as *God's husbandry*, let us pay no heed to evil, *nor the tribulation and persecution* that arises *because of the word*, nor *the care of this world*, nor *the deceitfulness of riches*, nor *the pleasures of this life*.[327] But let us despise all these things and receive *the spirit of wisdom*[328] without care. Let us hasten to the riches that have no deceit whatever. Let us speed on to what we may call the pleasures of *the paradise of delight*,[329] reflecting in all our sufferings that *that which is at present momentary and light of our tribulation worketh for us above measure exceedingly an eternal weight of glory, while we look not at the things which are seen, but at the things which are not seen.*[330]

50.   Let us realize, too, that the story of Abel who was slain by the criminal and murderer Cain is applicable to all them whose blood has been unjustly shed.   Let us remember that the words, *The voice of thy brother's blood crieth to me from the earth*,[331] are also said of each one of the martyrs, the voice of whose blood cries to God from the earth.

It may be that as we have been purchased by *the precious blood* of Jesus [332] who has received *a name above all names*,[333] so some will be ransomed by the precious blood of martyrs; for the martyrs themselves are exalted higher than they would have been if they had been *justified* only and not also become *martyrs*.   And indeed with good reason has the death of martyrdom been given a name all of its own—"exaltation"—as is clear from the words, *If I be "exalted" from the earth, I will draw all things to myself.*[334] Let us, too, glorify God, exalting Him by our death; for the martyr does glorify God by his death, as we again know from John when he says: *And this He said, signifying by what death He should glorify God.*[325]

EPILOGUE

51.   These are my suggestions to you, made as best I could under the circumstances.   I hope they may prove useful to you in the present combat.   If, however, because now especially you are worthy to see more of the mysteries of God, you have a more profound and richer understanding, one more helpful to your present purpose, and so will disregard these my observations as being childish and trivial, I myself would wish for you that such be the

case. For you the point is that your goal should be accomplished, not that it should be accomplished through me. My wish is that it be accomplished through the greater sublimity and fuller understanding, transcending all human nature, of God's words and wisdom.[336]

NOTES

LIST OF ABBREVIATIONS

ACW Ancient Christian Writers (Westminster, Md.–London 1946-)
DACL Dictionnaire d'archéologie chrétienne et de liturgie (Paris 1924-)
DCB Dictionary of Christian Biography and Literature (London 1911)
DTC Dictionnaire de théologie catholique (Paris 1903-1950)
GCS Die griechischen christlichen Schriftsteller der ersten drei Jahrhunderte (Leipzig 1897-)
OCD Oxford Classical Dictionary (Oxford 1949)
PG J. P. Migne, Patrologia graeca
RE Realenzyklopädie der classischen Altertumswissenschaft (Stuttgart 1894-)
SCA The Catholic University of America Studies in Christian Antiquity (Washington 1941-)
TWNT Theologisches Wörterbuch zum Neuen Testament (Stuttgart 1933-)

INTRODUCTION

[1] Cf. Eusebius, *H.E.* 6.3.3; see J. Daniélou, *Origène* (Paris 1948) 24 f.

[2] Matt. 19.12; cf. Eusebius, *op. cit.* 6.8.1-3; Jerome, *Ep.* 84.8.

[3] A man of wealth and standing, originally from Alexandria, and reclaimed from Valentinianism by Origen, whom he furnished with a staff of copyists and shorthand writers (Eusebius, *op. cit.* 6.23.1 f.). In one way or another he provided the occasion for the writing not only of the treatise on *Prayer* and the *Exhortation to Martyrdom*, but also for the more important work, the *Contra Celsum*. The monumental *Commentary on the Gospel of St. John* is dedicated, and both works in this present volume are addressed to him.

⁴ Cf. Eusebius, *op. cit.* 6.3.3; see Daniélou, *op. cit.* 57 f., 62 f.

⁵ Cf. ch. 27; Daniélou, *op. cit.* 77.

⁶ Cf. Daniélou, *op. cit.* 75, 83.

⁷ See n. 104 to *Prayer.*

⁸ See below, n. 394 to *Prayer.*

⁹ Cf. below, n. 617 to *Prayer.*

¹⁰ Cf. below, nn. 454, 505, 529 to *Prayer.*

¹¹ Cf. *In Luc.* hom. 16; Daniélou, *op. cit.* 24, 41, and below, n. 262 on *Prayer.*

¹² C. Bigg, *The Christian Platonists of Alexandria* (Oxford 1913) 329.

¹³ Cf. the preface to his translation of Origen's *Homilies on Ezechiel.*

¹⁴ *Opera* (Basel 1558) 3.99.

¹⁵ Cf. Daniélou, *op. cit.* 15, 88 f., 99. For Origen's use of such terms as νοητός, ἡγεμονικόν, οὐσία, ἐνέργεια, etc., cf. the important works of W. Völker, *Das Volkommenheitsideal des Origenes* (Tübingen 1931), and A. Lieske, *Die Theologie der Logosmystik bei Origenes* (Münsterische Beiträge zur Theologie, Heft. 22, Münster i. W. 1938).

¹⁶ PG 1049–105; P. Koetschau, *Des Gregorios Thaumaturgos Dankrede an Origenes,* in: Sammlung ausgewählter Quellenschriften zur Kirchen- und Dogmengeschichte 9 (Freiburg i. Br. 1894).

¹⁷ For a complete and up-to-date bibliography, see J. Quasten, *Patrology* 2 (Utrecht and Westminster, Maryland 1953) 37–101. There is a good bibliography in the recent translation by H. Chadwick of the *Contra Celsum* (Cambridge 1953) XXXV–XL. G. W. Butterworth in his translation of the *De principiis, Origen on First Principles* (London 1936) XXXVII–XXXIX, lists some useful books in English. Add R. P. C. Hanson, *Origen's Doctrine of Tradition* (London 1954).

¹⁸ See Quasten, *op. cit.* 2.94–101.

¹⁹ DCB 4.124.

²⁰ *Opera* (Basel 1558) preface.

²¹ Cf. Quasten, *op. cit.* 2.66.

²² A Christian woman, possibly wife or sister of Ambrose. Nothing more is known of her.

²³ This part may have been used in the instruction for baptism; cf. Daniélou, *op. cit.* 13.

²⁴ Cf. Daniélou, *op. cit.* 45.

[25] For Origen's use of Scripture see especially H. de Lubac, *Histoire et esprit. L'intelligence de l'Écriture d'après Origène*, (Paris 1950). See also Quasten, *op. cit.* 2.92 f., and below, n. 205 to *Prayer*.

[26] Cf. G. F. Diercks, *Tertullianus: De oratione* (Bussum 1947) LXIX–XCVIII, and E. Evans, *Tertullian's Tract on The Prayer* (London 1953).

[27] E. G. Jay, *Origen's Treatise on Prayer* (London 1954) 3–44, has a useful discussion on prayer in the early Church. See also G. Walther, *Untersuchungen zur Geschichte der griechischen Vaterunserexegese* (Texte und Untersuchungen 40.3, Leipzig 1914), and F. H. Chase, *The Lord's Prayer in the Early Church* (Theological Studies 1.3, Cambridge 1891).

[28] See A. Klawek, *Das Gebet zu Jesus* (Neutestamentliche Abhandlungen 6.5, Münster i.W. 1921) 102 ff.; J. Lebreton, "La prière dans l'Église primitive," *Rech. de science rel.* 14 (1924) 5 ff., 97 ff.

[29] See J. Kroll, "Die christliche Hymnodik bis zu Klemens von Alexandria," *Programm der Akademie v. Braunsberg* (1921–22) 1–76; J. Quasten, "Carmen," *Reall. f. Antike und Christentum*, Lief. 14 (1954) 901–910.

[30] See F. J. Dölger, *Sol salutis* (2 ed. Münster i.W. 1925) 115 n. 2.

[31] See J. Jungmann, *Die Stellung Christi im liturgischen Gebet* (Liturgiegech. Forsch. 7–8, Münster i.W. 1925) 137–41; cf. the present treatise itself, 33.6.

[32] This priest of Caesarea is otherwise unknown to us.

[33] Such "protreptics" were written by Aristotle, Epicurus, Cleanthes, Posidonius, Cicero, Clement of Alexandria, and others. Cf. P. Wendland, *Anaximenes von Lampsakos* (Berlin 1905) 81 ff.; also O'Meara, ACW 12 (1950) 165 n. 150.

[34] Cf. 1 Cor. 1.6 and 2.1; also 2 Tim. 1.8.

[35] Where cf. 2.2, 14.2, 15.2, 19.1, etc., for μάρτυς, μαρτύριον = "martyr," "martyrdom." Cf. H. Strathmann, TWNT 4 (1942) s. v. μάρτυς, etc., 511 f. Among others, H. Delehaye, *Sanctus. Essai sur le culte des saints* (Subsidia hagiographica 17, 2 ed. Brussels 1933) 79, holds that μαρτυρεῖν in Clement of Rome, *1 Cor.* 5.4 and 7, already carries this special sense. In general, see H. v. Campenhausen, *Die Idee des Martyriums in der alten Kirche* (Göttingen 1936).

[36] Cf. Koetschau's app. crit. to the title.

[37] Cf. Chadwick, *op. cit.* XXX f.

TEXT

PRAYER

[1] Cf. Titus 3.5 f.

[2] Cf. Ps. 103.24.

[3] 1 Cor. 1.30.

[4] Wisd. 9.13–16.

[5] 2 Cor. 12.2, 4.

[6] Rom. 11.34; 1 Cor. 2.16.

[7] About three lines are missing here. It is conjectured that they were taken up with the citation of John 15.15: *I will not now call you servants: for the servant knoweth not what his lord doth. But I have called you friends: because all things, whatsoever I have heard of my Father, I have made known to you.* Cf. Koetschau *ad loc.*

[8] I have omitted the first τὸ θέλημα: either it or the following one seems to be redundant. At any rate by the omission of one of them the sense is improved.

[9] 1 Cor. 2.11.

[10] *Ibid.* 2.12 f.

[11] Cf. n. 3 to Intro.

[12] Cf. n. 22 to Intro.

[13] Gen. 18.11.

[14] About four lines are missing here. It is probable that they at least concluded with some reference to St. Paul and 2 Cor. 12.6 f. Cf. Koetschau *ad loc.*

[15] 2 Cor. 12.6 f.

[16] Rom. 8.26.

[17] Cf. Matt. 6.33 and the following note.

[18] Cf. John 3.12; Matt. 6.33; Luke 12.31. For sayings such as this, attributed to the Saviour but not found in the New Testament, cf. E. Jacquier, "Les sentences du Seigneur extracanoniques," *Rev. Bibl.* 15 (1918) 124; Jay, *op. cit.* 82 n. 4.

[19] Luke 6.28.

[20] Matt. 9.38; cf. Luke 10.2.

[21] Luke 22.40; cf. Matt. 26.41; Mark 14.38.

[22] Matt. 24.20; cf. Mark 13.18.

[23] Matt. 6.7.

[24] 1 Tim. 2.8–10.
[25] Matt. 5.23 f.
[26] Cf. Eph. 5.2.
[27] 1 Cor. 7.5.
[28] Mark 11.25.
[29] 1 Cor. 11.4 f.
[30] Rom. 8.26.
[31] *Ibid.* 8.26 f.
[32] Gal. 4.6.
[33] Cf. Wisd. 9.15.
[34] Ps. 43.25.
[35] Phil. 3.21.
[36] 2 Cor. 12.4.
[37] Rom. 8.37.
[38] There is wordplay here on ἐντυγχάνειν (intercede), ὑπερεντυγχάνειν, (intercede mightily), νικᾶν, (overcome), ὑπερνικᾶν (overcome gloriously).
[39] 1 Cor. 14.15.
[40] *Ibid.* 2.10.
[41] Luke 11.1. About two lines are missing here. Perhaps Matt. 3.5 f. was quoted.
[42] Matt. 3.5.
[43] *Ibid.* 11.9.
[44] Cf. 1 Kings 1.12 f.
[45] Osee 14.10.
[46] Cf. Rom. 8.29; Col. 1.15, 18; Heb. 1.6; etc.
[47] Cf. Gen. 27.41 ff.
[48] *Ibid.* 28.20–22. There are about two lines missing here.
[49] That is, "prayer" is used for "vow." Origen's use of εὐχή and προσευχή here are as follows:

εὐχή { (2) "prayer" (that is, vow)
        (1) prayer (as ordinarily understood) = (2) "invocation"
                                    (1) invocation (as ordinarily understood) } προσευχή

[50] About two lines are missing here.
[51] Exod. 8.8.
[52] *Ibid.* 8.9.
[53] *Ibid.* 8.17 ff. The σκνίψ or κνίψ (Slav. *sknipa*, gnat) is described as an insect found under the bark of trees and eaten by

the woodpecker. Cf. Aristotle, *Hist. anim.* 614b.1; *De sensu* 444b.12. It was a jumping insect and very troublesome to man and beast.

[54] *Ibid.* 8.28 (Sept.).

[55] *Ibid.* 8.29.

[56] *Ibid.* 8.30.

[57] *Ibid.* 9.27.

[58] *Ibid.* 9.33.

[59] *Ibid.* 10.17 f.

[60] Cf. § 1 of this chapter and n. 47.

[61] Lev. 27.1–3.

[62] Num. 6.1–3. The Nazarites, mentioned in the following, were persons specially consecrated to God. They bound themselves by vow to certain restrictions, e.g. to abstain from intoxicating liquors, not to cut their hair and to avoid contact with dead bodies.

[63] *Ibid.* 6.11 f. (Sept.).

[64] *Ibid.* 6.13.

[65] *Ibid.* 6.20 f.

[66] *Ibid.* 30.2–5.

[67] About two lines are missing. They are probably to be supplied from Prov. 7.14 and 19.13.

[68] Supplied from Prov. 20.25.

[69] Eccles. 5.4.

[70] Acts 21.23.

[71] Cf. above, 3.2 and n. 49.

[72] 1 Kings 1.9–11.

[73] That is, "vow." See the preceding chapter, § 4. The Douay version does read: she "*prayed*" to the Lord. . . . *And she "made a vow."*

[74] Judges 11.30 f.

[75] About two lines are missing. Koetschau (*ad loc.*) suggests that they referred to those who scoffed at all prayer as useless.

[76] The Epicureans and, possibly, the Aristotelians; cf. Daniélou, *op. cit.* 32, 86, 92 f.

[77] Cf. 2 Thess. 2.9.

[78] Cf. Clement of Alexandria, *Strom.* 7.7.41; Irenaeus, *Adv. haer.* 1.14.3; Theodoret, *Haer. fab. comp.* 1.10.11; Origen, *C. Cels.* 2.13.1.

[79] Matt. 6.8.

[80] Wisd. 11.25.

81 Ps. 57.4.

82 Gal. 1.15.

83 Rom. 9.11 f. (cf. Gen. 25.23).

84 Cf. Phil. 4.13.

85 Cf. Gen. 25.23.

86 Ps. 89.1 f. A lacuna of about one-and-one-half lines follows.

87 Cf. Eph. 1.3–5.

88 Cf. Rom. 8.29 f. (Phil. 3.21).

89 Cf. 4 Kings 22.11 ff., 18 f.; 23.3 ff.

90 Cf. 3 Kings 13.1 ff.

91 Cf. Ps. 108.7 f. (Acts 1.16, 20).

92 The addressee, Ambrose, had submitted these difficulties; cf. n. 3 to the Intro. For more information on Origen's views on predestination than is given in this text, cf. G. Bardy, *Origène* (Paris 1931) 47 ff.; Daniélou, *op. cit.* 86 ff., 104 ff., 277 ff.; R. Cadiou, *Introduction au système d'Origène* (Paris 1932) 105 ff.; Bigg, *op. cit.* 243 ff.; cf. below, n. 96.

93 ἐξ αὐτῶν, i.e. the plants referred to.

94 ἀφ' αὐτῶν.

95 δι' αὐτῶν: Koetschau's emendation of his own text as used in his translation.

96 For Origen's views on freedom of will, cf. below, 29.13; *De princ.* 3.1; Bigg, *op. cit.* 243, 274, 278; Bardy, *op. cit.* 47 ff.; above n. 92. The expression τὸ ἐφ' ἡμῖν is Stoic. For Stoic influence on Origen cf. Daniélou, *op. cit.* 94.

97 ὡς ἐπέχων περὶ παντὸς οὑτινοσοῦν. ἐποχή or suspension of judgment was necessarily practised by the followers of the New Academy, since it was their opinion that nothing can be perceived and that consequently one must not assent to anything.

98 A conflation of Rom. 1.20 and Matt. 25.34.

99 Cf. *C. Cels.* 4.70.

100 Eph. 3.20.

101 For the highly developed teaching of Origen on angels and demons see *De princ.* 1.8; 3.2. According to Origen, guardian angels are Christ's diligent co-workers in the saving of all mankind. Each one of us is attended by a good and a bad angel. Cf. Daniélou, *op. cit.* 222–242; the same, *Les anges et leur mission* (Chevetogne 1953) 93 ff.; E. T. Bettencourt, *Doctrina ascetica Origenis* (Rome 1945) 12–34, 126–43, *passim;* G. Bareille, "Angélologie d' après les Pères," DTC 1 (Paris 1909) 1216–19. Cf.

below, nn. 433 and 543, and n. 300 to the *Exhortation to Martyrdom*.

[102] Cf. 4 Kings 21–24; 22.2; 23.4–25.

[103] Cf. Matt. 27.5; Acts 1.18.

[104] This is the first hint in the present treatise of subordination of the Son to the Father in Origen's theology; cf. the Intro. 9 f.; also nn. 180, 241, 244, 248, 251, 253. Daniélou, *op. cit.* 249–58, has an excellent discussion on the subject. He says: "Sa notion du Logos est très haute et très profonde. Bien des traits pourront en être repris. Mais elle reste affectée d'un subordinationisme évident." Cf. also Bigg, *op. cit.* 207 ff., 227 ff.; Lieske, *op. cit.* 164 f., *passim;* G. L. Prestige, *God in Patristic Thought* (London 1936) 129 ff.; J. Scherer, *Entretien d'Origène avec Héraclide et les Évêques ses collègues* (Cairo 1949) 63.

[105] Ps. 108.1. In this psalm, following the traditional interpretation, Christ in the person of the psalmist imprecates His persecutors, especially the betrayer Judas (v. 8 is applied by Peter to Judas: Acts 1.20).

[106] Cf. Eph. 1.4.

[107] Cf. Gal. 1.15.

[108] Cf. Acts 7.57; 22.20.

[109] Cf. 1 Cor. 1.29.

[110] *Ibid.* 15.9.

[111] *Ibid.* 15.10.

[112] Cf. 2 Cor. 12.7.

[113] See above, 5.3.

[114] Ps. 148.3.

[115] Cf. *Deut.* 4.19 (Sept.).

[116] Origen believed that the sun, moon, and stars were living rational beings; cf. *De princ.* 1.7; *C. Cels.* 5.10 f.; Daniélou, *op. cit.* 216; also below, n. 56 to the *Exhortation*.

[117] Cf. Matt. 6.7; 1 Tim. 2.8.

[118] Cf. Matt. 6.12; Luke 11.4.

[119] Cf. Ps. 7.10.

[120] Cf. 1 Tim. 2.8; Matt. 6.12, 14, 18.21 f.; Mark 11.25 f.; Luke 11.4; etc.

[121] 1 Tim. 2.8.

[122] *Ibid.* 2.9 f.

[123] *Loc. cit.*

[124] Ps. 122.1.

[125] Ps. 24.1.

[126] 2 Cor. 3.18.

[127] Ps. 4.7. For ἀπορροὴ νοητοῦ τινος θειοτέρου cf. below, n. 383.

[128] Ps. 24.1.

[129]   πῶς οὐχὶ ἤδη ἀποτιθεμένη τὸ εἶναι ψυχὴ πνευματικὴ γίνεται; ψυχή implies relation with matter, while πνευματική implies relation with intelligence (spirit) only; cf. De princ. 2.8.

[130] A conflation of Jer. 7.22 f. and Zach. 7.10.

[131] Mark 11.25.

[132] Isa. 58.9.

[133] Cf. n. 92.

[134] Isa. 58.9.

[135] Job 2.10. (Sept.).

[136] Ibid. 1.22. (Sept.).

[137] Deut. 15.9.

[138] Jer. 23.24.

[139] Cf. John 1.26.

[140] Cf. Heb. 2.17; 3.1; 4.14 f.; 5.10; 6.20; 7.26; 8.1; 9.11; 10.10.

[141] Cf. John 14.16, 26; 15.26; 16.7.

[142] Luke 18.1 f.

[143] Ibid. 11.5 f.

[144] Ibid. 11.8.

[145] Matt. 7.7 f.; Luke 11.9 f.

[146] Rom. 8.15.

[147] Cf. John 6.33, 35, 41, 48, 51; Matt. 4.3; Luke 4.3.

[148] A conflation of Matt. 7.11 (Luke 11.13) and Exod. 16.4.

[149] Luke 15.7; cf. Matt. 18.13.

[150] Tob. 12.12.

[151] Ibid. 3.24 (Sept.).

[152] Ibid. 12.12 (Sept.).

[153] Ibid. 12.15 (Sept.).

[154] Ibid. 12.8 (Sept.).

[155] 2 Macc. 15.13.

[156] Ibid. 15.15.

[157] The high priest Onias, praised ibid. 15.12.

[158] Ibid. 15.14.

[159] 1 Cor. 13.12.

[160] Cf. Matt. 5.43 ff.; Luke 6.35; 10.27.

[161] 1 Cor. 12.26.

[162] 2 Cor. 11.28 f.

[163] Cf. Matt. 25.35–40.

[164] Cf. ibid. 4.11.

[165] Cf. Luke 22.27.

[166] Cf. Isa. 27.12; John 10.16, 11.52; Acts 2.21; Rom. 10.12 f.

[167] Cf. Apoc. 1.20; 2.1, 8, 12, 18; 3.1, 7, 14.

[168] John 1.51; Osee 10.12 (Sept.).

[169] Cf. Matt. 10.30; Luke 12.7.

[170] Cf. *ibid.* 18.10.

[171] Cf. 1 Cor. 14.15.

[172] 1 Thess. 5.17 (cf. Luke 18.1).

[173] Cf. Ps. 63.4 ff.; Prov. 5.22.

[174] Cf. Dan. 6.13. For the thought of life as continuous prayer see also Clement of Alexandria, *Strom.* 7.12.7.1; again, Origen, *In Matt.* 16.22. See Daniélou, *op. cit.* 47, who calls attention to the distinction of "actual" and "virtual" prayer.—In the following Origen gives the second (morning) and third (evening) prayers before the first (at midnight); cf. Ps. 54.18.

[175] Acts 10.9–11.

[176] Ps. 5.4 f.

[177] *Ibid.* 140.2.

[178] *Ibid.* 118.62.

[179] Cf. Acts 16.25.

[180] Cf. n. 104.

[181] Mark 1.35.

[182] Luke 11.1.

[183] *Ibid.* 6.12.

[184] John 17.1.

[185] *Ibid.* 11.42.

[186] Cf. Jer. 15.1; Ps. 98.6.

[187] Cf. 1 Kings 1.9 ff.

[188] Cf. 4 Kings 20.1 ff.; Isa. 38.1 ff.; Matt. 1.9 f.; cf. Origen, *C. Cels.* 8.46.

[189] Cf. Esth. 3.5 ff.; 4.16 f.; 9.26 ff. (institution of the feast of Purim).

[190] Cf. Judith 13.4 ff.

[191] Cf. Dan. 3.24, 50 (Sept.).

[192] Cf. *ibid.* 6.18 ff.

[193] Cf. Jonas 2.3 ff.

[194] Ps. 19.8.

[195] *Ibid.* 32.17.

[196] Cf. P. de Lagarde, *Onomastica sacra* (Göttingen 1887) 7.18; 169.84; 193.13.

[197] Cf. Dan. 3.49 f., 94.

[198] Cf. 1 Cor. 6.15; cf. Dan. 6.22.

[199] Ps. 57.7 f.

[200] Cf. Jonas 2.1 f.

[201] Isa. 25.8 (Sept.).

[202] Cf. Rom. 8.2.

[203] Cf. 2 Cor. 10.3.

[204] Cf. Rom. 8.13.

[205] That is, of Sacred Scripture. Cf. Bigg, *op. cit.* 174 f.: "Scripture has in general three senses—the literal, the moral, and the spiritual (in the note he adds: "For the spiritual sense O. uses more than a score of different terms. . . . Some have thought that he made a triple division of the spiritual into allegoric, tropologic, and anagogic, or a double into allegoric and anagogic. . . . [The three senses] answer to body, soul, and spirit. . . .ἀναγωγή is a technical Platonic phrase for 'the road up'; Plotinus, *Enn.* 1.3.1."). Not that every passage is susceptible of all three modes of interpretation—many texts have no literal sense at all. Some, like the Decalogue, have a moral signification, of such a kind that it is needless to seek farther. The distinction between the two higher senses is not always very clearly drawn, as there are regions where the one shades off into the other by very fine gradations. But there is an abundance of passages where they are so sharply defined as to show us exactly what O. meant. Thus the grain of mustard is first the actual seed, then faith, then the Kingdom of Heaven." Cf. Daniélou, *op. cit.* 164 ff.; de Lubac, *op. cit.* 139–94: "Le sens spirituel"; Quasten, *op. cit.* 2.92 f.

[206] Cf. above, nn. 187, 188.

[207] Cf. above, nn. 189, 190.

[208] Cf. Deut. 4.20; Jer. 11.4.

[209] Cf. Dan. 3.50: The angel *made the midst of the furnace like the blowing of a wind bringing dew.*

[210] Ps. 73.19.

[211] *Ibid.* 90.13.

[212] Luke 10.19.

[213] Cf. n. 192.

[214] Job 3.8 (Sept.): "it" = the night Job was conceived, "day" = the day he was born.

[215] Jonas 2.1.

[216] Cf. Gal. 5.22.

[217] Cf. Jonas 4.2.

[218] Cf. Rom. 11.22.

[219] 1 Kings 12.16 f.

[220] *Ibid.* 12.18.

[221] John 4.35 f.

[222] Cf. 3 Kings 17 and 18; James 5.17 f.; Luke 4.25.

[223] Cf. above, 2.2 and nn. 17, 18.

[224] Cf. Mark 4.24; Luke 6.38.

[225] 1 Tim. 2.1. The terms are δεήσεις (supplications), προσευχαί (prayers), ἐντεύξεις (intercessions), and εὐχαριστίαι (thanksgivings). Cf. above n. 49 for προσευχή meaning "invocation." Cf. Origen, *In Ps.* 28.2.

[226] Luke 1.13.

[227] Exod. 32.11.

[228] Deut. 9.18.

[229] Esth. 13.8 f.

[230] *Ibid.* 14.3.

[231] Dan. 3.25.

[232] Tob. 3.1 f. (Sept.).

[233] 1 Kings 1.10 f. The verb "obelize" designates the use of the mark ÷ (or ⁻). Origen himself employed it in his celebrated *Hexapla* to indicate in his recension of the Septuagint what words or passages were not found in the Hebrew text (see Origen, *In Matt.* 15.14).

[234] Hab. 3.1 f. (Sept.).

[235] Jonas 2.2 ff.

[236] Rom. 8.26 f. See above, 2.3.

[237] Jos. 10.12 (Sept.).

[238] Judges 16.30 (Sept.).

[239] Matt. 11.25; cf. Luke 10.21.

[240] Cf. Matt. 16.19; 18.18.

[241] Cf. above, n. 104.

[242] Acts 7.60.

[243] Matt. 17.14; cf. Luke 9.38.

[244] Cf. above, n. 104.

[245] Luke 11.1.

[246] Matt. 6.9.

[247] *Comm. in Ioann.* 10.37 (21).

[248] The terms used—ἕτερος . . . κατ᾽ οὐσίαν καὶ ὑποκείμενον— occur also in the text referred to in the preceding note. Cf. above, n. 104, for literature on Origen's subordinationism. For the present passage note Prestige, *op. cit.* xxvii.

[249] Cf. Heb. 7.20 f.

250 Ps. 109.4 (Heb. 7.21).

251 See above, nn. 104 and 248.

252 John 16.23 f.

253 τὸ προσκυνεῖν. The term is used of prostration before gods or their images and especially of the oriental fashion of prostrating oneself before kings. It is used also in Christian texts of the highest worship paid to God. Examples in the N. T. of the term: for worship of God: Matt. 4.10, John 4.21, 23 (the Father), 1 Cor. 14.25; of Christ: Matt. 2.2, 8.2, John 9.38, etc. Satan asks Christ to worship him thus: Matt. 4.9, Luke 4.7. The soldiers mock Christ with the προσκύνησις: Mark 15.19. Origen employs the term of Christ—but only inasmuch as Christ is in, and is One with, the Father, who is the proper object of προσκύνησις; cf. *C. Cels.* 1.51: ὁ ὑπὸ χριστιανῶν προσκυνούμενος . . . γεγένηται ᾽Ιησοῦς —cf. Chadwick, *op. cit.* 328.3. See J. Horst, *Proskynein. Zur Anbetung im Urchristentum nach ihrer religionsgeschichtlicher Eigenart* (1932). Cf. also n. 104 above.

254 Deut. 32.43 (Sept.) as quoted in Heb. 1.6. For the Church as Jerusalem, the future "City of God," see Ps. 86.3–5; for this and other passages, J. C. Plumpe, *Mater Ecclesia* (SCA 5, Washington 1943) 1–3.

255 Isa. 49.22 f. (Sept.).

256 Mark 10.18; cf. Luke 18.19 (Matt. 19.17); "the Father" is not found in any of these texts.

257 Cf. Heb. 8.3.

258 Cf. 1 John 2.1.

259 Heb. 4.15.

260 Cf. Rom. 8.14 f., 19, 23; Gal. 4.5 f.; 1 Peter 1.3.

261 Ps. 21.23.

262 Apparently an indication of the anxiety of Origen to keep in line with the main body of Christians. Cf. H. v. Balthasar, "Le Mysterion d'Origène," *Rech. de sc. rel.* 26 (1936) 547.

263 ἰδιωτικὴν ἁμαρτίαν.

264 Matt. 22.32; Mark 12.27; Luke 20.38.

265 Cf. Rom. 8.15; Gal. 4.1, 3, 6 f.; Clement of Alexandria, *Eclog.* 19.1.

266 Cf. 1 John 4.18; Heb. 2.15.

267 Rom. 8.27.

268 Cf. above, 2.2 and nn. 17, 18.

269 Cf. Rom. 12.6 and 1 Cor. 12.1, 4, 7, 11.

270 Cf. 1 Kings 1.19 f.; nn. 187–191.

271 Cf. 4 Kings 20.18; Isa. 39.7.

272 Cf. Esth. 6 and 7.

273 Cf. Judith 13.

274 Gen. 27.28.

275 Cf. Dan. 3.49 f.

276 Cf. *ibid.* 6.22.

277 Cf. Jonas 2.1 f., 11; Job 3.8; also Origen, *In Ioann.* 1.17 (95).

278 Following Koetschau in the reading οὐδ' ὅλως adopted by him in his translation.

279 Cf. Heb. 6.4.

280 1 Cor. 1.5.

281 Cf. Plotinus, *Enn.* 1.6.5.54 ff. (Henry and Schwyzer). Daniélou, *op. cit.* 85 ff., has an excellent discussion on Origen's relations with earlier and contemporary philosophers.

282 Cf. John 3.29.

283 Isa. 40.6–8.

284 Cf. John 1.12 f.

285 Cf. Heb. 12.28.

286 Cf. Luke 2.13.

287 Cf. Col. 1.16; Eph. 1.21.

288 Cf. Plotinus, *Enn.* 1.6.7.36.

289 Matt. 6.8.

290 Cf. Eph. 4.7.

291 Matt. 6.9–13.

292 Luke 11.2–4.

293 Matt. 5.1 f.

294 Cf. *ibid.* 5.3 ff.

295 Luke 11.1.

296 Cf. Chapters 8 and 9.

297 Matt. 6.5–9; cf. below, n. 323.

298 John 5.44.

299 Matt. 6.2, 5.

300 *Locc. citt.*

301 Luke 16.25.

302 Matt. 6.5.

303 Gal. 6.8.

304 Matt. 6.2, 5.

305 *Ibid.* 7.13.

306 *Ibid.* 6.5. Reading οὐκ' ἄλλως (ἢ ὁ) with Koetschau (translation).

307 Ps. 81.7. Reading εὐσεβεῖν with Koetschau (translation).

[307a] 2 Tim. 3.4.

[308] Matt. 7.14.

[309] Eph. 5.27.

[310] Cf. Deut. 23.1–8.

[311] Cf. Luke 7.5, 9; Matt. 8.10.

[312] Cf. Deut. 16.16. Above, the wordplay "likes" – "loves" = φιλεῖ – ἀγαπᾷ. Origen uses it elsewhere, e.g. *In Ier.* hom. 15.3; *Comm. in Lam. Ier.* fr. 11.

[313] Cf. Deut. *ibid.* and Isa. 61.2.

[314] Deut. *ibid.*

[315] Matt. 6.5.

[316] *Ibid.* 6.6.

[317] Col. 2.3; cf. 1 Tim. 6.18 f.

[318] Cf. John 1.14, 18; 3.16, 18; 1 John 4.9.

[319] John 14.23.

[320] Cf. Matt. 6.6; Eph. 2.22; *Ep. Barn.* 16.8 (J. A. Kleist, ACW 6.61).

[321] Matt. 6.7.

[322] Cf. Matt. *ibid.* and Isa. 66.1.

[323] πολυλογεῖν means to "speak much." βαττολογεῖν, occurring only once in the Bible—Matt. 6.7 (and there it is spelled βατταλογεῖν) — is a word of uncertain etymology (formed perhaps on the analogy of βατταρίζειν, to "stutter," "stammer") meaning to "babble," "chatter," etc. The non-Christian thinks that by continued repetition and multiplication of names for the divinity he can call attention to himself and weary the divinity into granting his petition: cf. G. Delling, TWNT 1 (1933) 597 f., s. v. See also Gregory of Nyssa, *De or. Dom.* serm. 1: ACW 18 (1954) 26–28.

[324] 1 Cor. 2.6.

[325] Cf. Matt. 6.7—Origen's notion of the oneness or singleness of the good and the multiplicity of moral evil is exemplified with particular clarity in *In Ezech.* hom. 9.1 (trans. by Jerome): "Ubi peccata sunt, ibi et multitudo, ibi schismata, ibi haereses, ibi dissensiones; ubi autem virtus, ibi singularitas, ibi unio, ex quo omnium credentium erat cor unum et anima una." See also *De princ.* 2.9.2 ff. On the profounder concepts of this subject—the pre-existential unity of all things in the contemplation of God, of its loss and ultimate restoration through the Word (Λόγος), cf. Lieske, *op. cit.* 98, 132.

[326] Cf. Ps. 57.5: *Their madness is according to the likeness of a*

serpent, like the deaf asp that stoppeth her ears. For the sentence following, see Matt. 6.8.

³²⁷ Chase, *op. cit.* 22 ff., believes that the longer (*Our Father who art in heaven*) and the shorter (*Father*) forms were both current in the Apostolic age, but that the former was "specially endeared to the Disciples," and was "the original Greek form of the first clause of the Prayer." On the other hand, the use of the shorter form *may* be implied by Our Lord's words in the Garden of Gethsemane (*Father . . . not what I will, but what thou wilt:* Mark 14.36), and by St. Paul (*God hath sent the spirit of his Son into your hearts, crying: Abba, Father:* Gal. 4.6; *the spirit of adoption of sons*, whereby we cry: Abba [Father]: Rom. 8.15). Cf. also A. Jones, in *A Catholic Commentary on the Holy Scripture*, 686g, and R. Ginns, *ibid.*, 757c.

³²⁸ Cf. *Comm. in Ioann.* 14.1.

³²⁹ Deut. 32.18.

³³⁰ *Ibid.* 32.6.

³³¹ *Ibid.* 32.20.

³³² Isa. 1.2.

³³³ Mal. 1.6.

³³⁴ Gal. 4.1 f.

³³⁵ *Ibid.* 4.4.

³³⁶ Rom. 8.15.

³³⁷ John 1.12.

³³⁸ 1 John 3.9.

³³⁹ 1 Cor. 12.3.

³⁴⁰ 1 John 3.9.

³⁴¹ Rom. 8.16 f.

³⁴² *Ibid.* 10.10.

³⁴³ Cf. Gal. 4.19.

³⁴⁴ Col. 1.15.

³⁴⁵ *Ibid.* 3.10.

³⁴⁶ Matt. 5.45.

³⁴⁷ 1 Cor. 15.49.

³⁴⁸ Cf. Phil. 3.21.

³⁴⁹ Cf. *loc. cit.* and Rom. 12.2.

³⁵⁰ 1 John 3.8 f.

³⁵¹ Cf. Gal. 4.19.

³⁵² 1 John 3.8.

³⁵³ Above, ch. 12.

³⁵⁴ 1 Thess. 5.17.

[355] Cf. Phil. 3.20.

[356] 1 Cor. 15.49.

[357] John 13.1, 3.

[358] *Ibid.* 14.28.

[359] *Ibid.* 16.5.

[360] *Ibid.* 14.23.

[361] Cf. Phil. 2.7 f.

[362] John 13.1.

[363] Cf. Phil. 2.7; Col. 1.19; 2.9; Eph. 1.23.

[364] John 16.5.

[365] *Ibid.* 20.17.

[366] This is a good example of Origen's characteristic emphasis on the intellectual or spiritual as opposed to (but not to the exclusion of) the corporeal. Cf. Daniélou, *op. cit.* 52: "Sa tendance spiritualisante le porterait à déprécier l'importance de l'aspect visible."

[367] Gen. 3.8.

[368] Cf. Luke 13.25.

[369] Jer. 23.24.

[370] Cf. Matt. 5.34 f.; Isa. 66.1.

[371] Gen. 3.9.

[372] Origen's 17 homilies on Genesis survive only in the Latin translation, with additions, by Rufinus: GCS 29 (1920). Of the 13 books of his commentary, which is referred to here, only sparse fragments remain: PG 12.45–92.

[373] The quotation is not from Deuteronomy, but from 2 Cor. 6.16, which refers back to Lev. 26.12. Koetschau thinks that the text may be correct, but that Origen's reference is inaccurate.

[374] Heb. 10.35 followed by Gen. 4.16 (Sept.).

[375] 1 Cor. 15.49.

[376] Cf. Phil. 2.15; Apoc. 1.20.

[377] Ps. 122.1.

[378] Eccles. 5.1 (Sept.).

[379] Phil. 3.21.

[380] Reading with Koetschau τῆς instead of καί.

[381] Cf. Heb. 1.8; Matt. 5.34 f.

[382] Cf. 1 Par. 29.11.

[383] The expressions, ἀπορροὴ τῆς θεότητος here and in 24.4, and ἀπορροῆς νοητοῦ τινος θειοτέρου in 9.2, have a Platonic overtone; cf. Plato, *Phaedr.* 251B.

[384] Matt. 6.9; Luke 11.2.

385 Cf. *Exhortation to Martyrdom* § 46.

386 Cf. Acts 13.9.

387 Cf. Gen. 17.5.

388 Cf. Mark 3.16; John 1.42.

389 Cf. Acts 9.4 f.; 13.9.

390 Cf. Exod. 3.14.

391 *Ibid.* 20.7.

392 Deut. 32.2 f. (Sept.).

393 Ps. 44.18.

394 An indication of Origen's acceptance of the Platonic theory of recollection (ἀνάμνησις) and his view on the pre-existence of the soul, in which primordial state it was a pure spirit endowed with vision of God. Sin obscured this vision, but not entirely for all: certain reminiscences remain—knowledge, of whose primal source the soul is not aware. Cf. Origen, *De princ.* 2.8.3 f.; Lieske, *op. cit.* 116–32; Quasten, *op. cit.* 2.91 f.; J. Lebreton, "Les degrés de la connaissance religieuse d'après Origène," *Rech. de sc. rel.* 12 (1922) 265–96.

395 Ps. 33.4.

396 1 Cor. 1.10, followed by Ps. 29.2.

397 Ps. 30.19. The translators referred to are those of the Septuagint.

398 Ps. 108.11 f. (Sept.). The Vulgate (Douay) has the wish-form.

399 Tatian, a Syrian apologist of the second century and the author of the *Oratio ad Graecos* and the *Diatessaron*, founded the rigourist sect of the Encratites and apparently died outside of the fold. Cf. A. Puech, *Histoire de la littérature grecque chrétienne* (Paris 1928) 2.171 ff.; Quasten, *op. cit.* 1.220 ff. Origen discusses this point in *C. Cels.* 6.51 also; cf. Chadwick, *op. cit.* 368 n. 1.

400 Gen. 1.3.

401 *Ibid.* 1.11, 9, 20, 24.

402 Luke 17.20 f.

403 Deut. 30.14; cf. Rom. 10.8.

404 Cf. Matt. 13.23; Mark 4.20; Luke 8.15.

405 John 14.23; cf. above, 23.1.

406 Cf. John 1.1, 14; 1 Cor. 1.30.

407 John 12.31; 14.30; 16.11. Cf. Ignatius of Antioch, *Ephes.* 19.1.

408 Gal. 1.4.

[409] Rom. 6.12.

[410] Cf. 1 Cor. 12.8.

[411] Cf. *ibid.* 13.9–12.

[412] Phil. 3.13.

[413] 1 Cor. 15.24–28.

[414] 1 Thess. 5.17.

[415] 2 Cor. 6.14 f.

[416] Reading Βελίαρ. Cf. Koetschau *ad loc.*

[417] Rom. 6.12.

[418] Gal. 5.19.

[419] Cf. Col. 3.5.

[420] Cf. John 15.8, 16; Gal. 5.22.

[421] Cf. Gen. 3.8; 2 Cor. 6.16.

[422] Cf. Matt. 26.64; Mark 14.62; Luke 22.69.

[423] Cf. Ps. 109.1; Isa. 66.1; Mark 12.36; Luke 20.43; Heb. 10.13; Acts 7.49.

[424] 1 Cor. 15.24.

[425] Cf. *ibid.* 15.26.

[426] A conflation of Osee 13.14 and 1 Cor. 15.55.

[427] Cf. 1 Cor. 15.53 f.

[428] Cf. Matt. 19.28.

[429] Luke 11.3.

[430] Cf. 1 Cor. 15.49.

[431] Cf. Matt. 7.21 and 25.34.

[432] Chase, *op. cit.* 40, quotes the *Catechismus Romanus* (4.10.3) put forth by the Council of Trent, which enjoins the interpretation given here by Origen.

[433] Eph. 6.12. Cf. Bettencourt, *op. cit.* 65 and n. 17; see also above, n. 101 and n. 300 to the *Exhortation to Martyrdom.*

[434] Cf. Isa. 34.5.

[435] Cf. *ibid.* 66.1; Acts 7.49.

[436] Cf. John 4.34; 6.38; 17.4.

[437] Cf. 1 Cor. 6.17.

[438] Matt. 28.18.

[439] Cf. John 1.9.

[440] Matt. 13.40.

[441] Cf. 1 Peter 3.22; John 1.1, 14; 14.6; 17.17.

[442] Col. 1.15.

[443] Cf. Eph. 4.24; Col. 3.10.

[444] Cf. Phil. 2.8.

[445] Cf. John 1.14, 18; 3.16, 18; 1 John 4.9.

[446] Cf. Phil. 3.20 and Matt. 6.20 f.

[447] Cf. 1 Cor. 15.49.

[448] Cf. John 3.31; 8.23; 18.36; etc.

[449] Cf. Eph. 6.12; cf. above, n. 433.

[450] Cf. 1 Cor. 15.49.

[451] Job 40.14 (19: Sept.).

[452] Luke 10.18.

[453] Cf. Gen. 3.19.

[454] A possible reference to ἀποκατάστασις. See Intro. 6f. and below, nn. 505, 529.

[455] Cf. John 6.64 followed by 1 Cor. 6.9 f.; 15.50.

[456] Matt. 6.11 and Luke 11.3.

[457] Cf. above 2.2 and n. 18.

[458] John 6.26.

[459] *Ibid.* 6.27.

[460] *Ibid.* 6.28 f.

[461] Ps. 106.20.

[462] John 6.32 f.

[463] Cf. Gen. 1.26 f. and Col. 3.9 f.

[464] Cf. John 1.1, 14; 14.6; 17.17; Luke 11.49; 1 Cor. 1.24, 30; cf. Daniélou, *op. cit.* 74 ff: in general, Origen's eucharistic theology is orthodox; but he tends to depreciate a little communion with the Word in the Eucharist in favour of communion with the Word in Scripture.

[465] John 6.32.

[466] *Ibid.* 6.34 f.

[467] *Ibid.* 6.51 f.; *flesh "which I will give"* is a frequent variant reading.

[468] Cf. Deut. 9.9; Origen, *Comm. in Ioann.* 10.17.

[469] John 6.52.

[470] *Ibid.* 6.54–57.

[471] *Ibid.* 1.14.

[472] *Ibid.* 6.59.

[473] 1 Cor. 3.1, 3, 2.

[474] Heb. 5.12–14.

[475] Rom. 14.2.

[476] Cf. Matt. 4.4 (Deut. 8.3).

[477] Prov. 15.17 (Sept.).

[478] Cf. 2 Cor. 10.5; Matt. 5.17.

[479] Cf. Amos 8.11; Rom. 14.8.

[480] Origen's observation on the rarity of the celebrated word

ἐπιούσιος has been completely sustained through the centuries: in addition to its use in the report by Matthew (6.11) and Luke (11.3) of The Lord's Prayer, scholars have been able to point to only one other, and that only probable, occurrence of the word (in a papyrus listing certain expenses, published in 1925). Of course, the word is found frequently in patristic discussions of the present fourth petition of the Our Father: cf. Chase, *op. cit.* 42–58. See also Jay, *op. cit.* 220–23. For an excellent survey of the various interpretations of the word and the vast literature devoted to it, see W. Foerster, TWNT 2 (1935) s. v., 587–95. For interpretations in the works of the Fathers published in the series so far, see ACW 5.112–15: Augustine, *The Lord's Sermon on the Mount* 2.7; ACW 18.12, 63–70: Gregory of Nyssa, *The Lord's Prayer* serm. 3.

[481] Origen points out two other extremely infrequent verbs occurring first in the Septuagint: the two verbs ἐνωτίζεσθαι (Gen. 4.23, Ps. 5.2, Job 33.1, where cf. the imperative form ἐνωτίζου) and ἀκουτίζειν (Ps. 50.10, Eccles. 45.5, but the imperative ἀκουτίσθητι does not occur). Liddell-Scott lists no instance of either verb occurring in profane literature.

[482] Exod. 19.5.: ἔσεσθέ μοι λαὸς περιούσιος ἀπὸ πάντων τῶν ἐθνῶν. Neither the Douay, *you shall be my peculiar possession above all people*, nor the Revised Version, *ye shall be a peculiar treasure unto me from among all peoples*, helps much towards the elucidation of the precise meaning of περιούσιος. The term is also found *ibid.* 23.22, in Deut. 7.6, 14.2, and 26.18 (cf. Titus 2.14).—It will be found, I think, that *substance* is throughout this section the least troublesome rendering for οὐσία. For the technicalities of matter and form see, for example, A. E. Taylor, *Aristotle* (London 1943) 65–79, and F. Copleston, *A History of Philosophy* (London 1946) 310 ff., or any standard introduction to Greek or Scholastic philosophy. As to Origen's derivation of both words from οὐσία, this has been advocated also by some modern scholars; but to-day the etymology is sought more often in a combination of the preposition (for ἐπιούσιος) ἐπί + the participle of εἶναι; or, more generally, in ἐπί + ἰέναι in the participial form. The latter was also considered by Origen—see below 27.3. Cf. Foerster, *loc. cit.*; A. Jones, in *A Catholic Commentary on Holy Scripture* 686h.

[483] For example, the Platonists; cf. Plato, *Tim.* 34C.

484 For example, the Atomists, Epicureans, and Stoics; cf. Aristotle's account of Demetrius' views—fr. 208.

485 τόνος, a Stoic term meaning *tension* or *force*. Cf. Plutarch, *De Stoic. repugn.* 43 p. 1054AB.

486 John 6.51.

487 Cf. Heb. 5.12 ff.; Rom. 14.2.

488 Cf. 4 Kings 4.40. See also Origen, *Comm. in Ioann.* 13.33.

489 Cf. Gen. 2.9; 3.22; John 5.24.

490 Prov. 3.18 (Sept.).

491 Ps. 77.25.

492 Cf. Exod. 16.15; Ps. 77.24.

493 Cf. Heb. 1.14.

494 Cf. Gen. 18.2–6.

495 Apoc. 3.20. Cf. Origen, *In Ezech.* hom. 14.3.

496 Cf. Ps. 103.15; 1 Thess. 3.13; James 5.8.

497 Cf. Ps. 73.14; Apoc. 12.3–17; 13.2, 4, 11; 16.13; 20.2.

498 Matt. 3.7; Luke 3.7.

499 Ps. 73.13 f.

500 Cf. 2 Thess. 2.3 f.; 1 Tim. 5.14; cf. *In Ezech.* hom. 6.4.

501 Cf. Acts 10.1, 11 f., 24, 27; 11.5 f.

502 *Ibid.* 10.14 f., 11.7 f.

503 *Ibid.* 10.28, 15; 11.9.

504 Cf. Origen, *C. Cels.* 4.93; 5.49.

505 Cf. Matt. 13.47. Here Origen is again, apparently, referring to ἀποκατάστασις; cf. Intro. 6 f. and nn. 454 and 529.

506 Cf. John 1.1.

507 That is, ἐπιούσιος means "of the coming day." Chase, *op. cit.* 44–53, argues at length in favour of this interpretation. Cf. above, n. 480.

508 Origen means that the second meaning of ἐπιούσιος, "*of the coming day*," when used with either *this day* or *each day* (especially as he understands *day*, namely, as equivalent to *age*) would cause tautology. Cf. the following note.

509 It is clear from the sequel that by αἰών (*age*) Origen means a period of time which recurs—something cyclic. "This day" means, then, *the whole of the present age*, and "each day," *all ages*. Cf. Origen, *Comm. in Ioann.* 32.32. See H. Sasse, TWNT 1 (1933) s. v.: 197–209.

510 Gen. 19.37.

511 *Ibid.* 19.38.

512 Matt. 28.15.

[513] Ps. 94.8.

[514] Cf. Jos. 22.29 (Sept.).

[515] Ps. 89.4.

[516] Heb. 13.8. For the following, cf. also the lucid parallel in Origen, *Comm. in Matt.* 15.31.

[517] Heb. 10.1. In his homilies on Numbers (5.1) Origen says that Moses understood all these festal mysteries, but that he did not disclose them.

[518] Cf. Exod. 12.2–18.

[519] Osee 14.10.

[520] James 2.23.

[521] Cf. Deut. 16.9 ff.

[522] Cf. Lev. 16.29 ff.; 23.24, 27 f.

[523] Cf. Exod. 21.2.

[524] Cf. Lev. 25.4 ff.; Deut. 15.1 ff.

[525] Cf. Lev. 25.8 ff.; 27.17 ff.

[526] Rom. 11.33.

[527] Heb. 9.26.

[528] Eph. 2.7.

[529] Cf. Matt. 12.32; Mark 3.29; Luke 12.10. Cf. *Comm. in Ioann.* 19.14; *Comm. in Matt.* 15.31; *C. Cels.* 5.16; *De princ.* 2.3.5. See Daniélou, *op. cit.* 279 ff. for a discussion of this and the following sections. On ἀποκατάστασις see also H. C. Graef. ACW 18 (1954) 6, 189 f. See Intro. 6 f. and above, nn. 454, 505.

[530] Deut. 16.16.

[531] Eph. 3.20.

[532] 1 Cor. 2.9.

[533] *Ibid.* 3.22.

[534] Rom. 13.7 f.

[535] Cf. 1 Peter 1.3, 23.

[536] Cf. Eph. 2.10.

[537] Mark 12.30; Luke 10.27; Matt. 22.37 (Deut. 6.5).

[538] 1 Kings 2.25 (Sept.).

[539] Cf. Acts 20.28; 1 Peter 1.18 f.; Apoc. 5.9.

[540] Eph. 4.30.

[541] Cf. John 15.8, 16.

[542] Cf. *Ibid.* 6.64.

[543] Matt. 18.10; cf. above, no. 101.

[544] 1 Cor. 4.9.

[545] On the relative gravity of the obligations of the clergy, see Origen, *In Ier.* hom. 11.3; 14.4; *In Ezech.* hom. 5.4.

546 1 Cor. 7.3, 5.
547 Col. 2.14.
548 A conflation of Rom. 14.10 and 2 Cor. 5.10.
549 Prov. 22.26 f. (Sept.).
550 Cf. Matt. 18.23–35.
551 Cf. Ps. 72.8.
552 A conflation of Matt. 5.25, 18.33–35, 25.26.
553 Luke 17.3 f.
554 Prov. 15.32 (Sept.).
555 *Isa.* 51.21; 28.1, 7.
556 *Loc. cit.*
557 Matt. 6.12.
558 Luke 11.4.
559 Cf. Matt. 7.16, 20; Luke 6.44.
560 Cf. 1 Cor. 2.14 f.; Rom. 8.14; Gal. 5.18.
561 John 20.22 f.
562 Cf. Lev. 7.37; Ps. 39.7; etc.
563 Cf. Heb. 4.14.
564 Cf. 1 Kings 2.22 ff.
565 *Ibid.* 2.25 (Sept.).
566 1 John 5.16.
567 Job 1.5 (Sept.).
568 On this important section, regarding the remission of sin through a duly constituted minister, the dispositions required of the penitent, etc., cf. also Origen, *Comm. in Matt.* 13.30; *In Lev.* hom. 15.2. See Daniélou, *op. cit.* 80 ff.; P. Galtier, "Les péchés incurables d'Origène," *Gregorianum* (1929) 209, and *L'Église et la remission des péchés aux premiers siècles* (Paris 1932) 184–213.
569 Luke 11.4.
570 Cf. Gal. 5.17; James 4.1; 1 Peter 2.11.
571 Cf. Rom. 8.7.
572 Job 7.1.
573 Ps. 17.30.
574 1 Cor. 10.13.
575 Cf. Eph. 6.12; Gal. 5.17; James 4.1; 1 Peter 2.11.
576 Lev. 17.11 (Sept.).
577 τὸ ἡγεμονικὸν ὃ καλεῖται καρδία.
578 Cf. Eph. 6.12 and Ps. 90.13.
579 Eph. 6.12.
580 Reading Ἰουδίθ as against Ἰουδαία.
581 Judith 8.26 f. (Sept.).

582 Ps. 33.20.

583 Acts 14.21.

584 2 Cor. 11.23–25.

585 *Ibid.* 4.8 f.

586 1 Cor. 4.11–13.

587 Ps. 25.2.

588 Cf. Prov. 30.9.

589 1 Cor. 1.5.

590 2 Cor. 12.7.

591 2 Par. 32.25 f.

592 Ps. 36.14.

593 Prov. 13.8 (Sept.).

594 Luke 16.22 ff.

595 Eph. 5.3.

596 Col. 1.5.

597 1 Cor. 3.17.

598 Prov. 4.23.

599 Cf. Luke 9.26; Phil. 3.19.

600 Matt. 6.2.

601 John 5.44.

602 Cf. above, 29.1 f. (Job 7.1).

603 Cant. 2.9 (Sept.). Origen takes the word δίκτυα in its original and common meaning of "nets" (for hunting or fishing). The Vulgate reads *per cancellos* = "through the lattices" (= "trellis") of the Douay translation.

604 *Ibid.* 2.10.

605 Ps. 1.2.

606 Prov. 10.31.

607 Cf. Origen, *C. Cels.* 8.16.

608 Cf. John 1.14, 18.

609 Matt. 26.41; Mark 14.38; Luke 22.40.

610 *Locc. citt.*

611 Matt. 7.18.

612 Rom. 1.22–24, 27 f. In v. 28, "disgraceful" (Knox for μὴ καθήκοντα) = Douay "not convenient" for Vulgate *quae non coveniunt.*

613 *Ibid.* 1.26 ff.

614 That is, the followers of Marcion of Sinope, a Gnostic of the second century, who founded a sect (Marcionites) which became widespread in the Orient and survived till the early Middle Ages. Marcion rejected all of the Old Testament, the

Gospels of Matthew, Mark, and John, the pastoral letters, and the Epistle to the Hebrews. He "purged" the Gospel of Luke and St. Paul's letters, and so arrived at his guides of the faith, termed by him the *Gospel* and the *Apostle*. Regarding Marcion's dualistic theology, his distinction between "the 'good' Father of Our Lord and the God of the Law," see Irenaeus, *Adv. haer.* 1.27.2; Hippolytus, *Ref. haer.* 7.17; Tertullian, *Adv. Marc.* 1.2, *passim*. We are indebted to Irenaeus, *op. cit.* 3.3.4, for the celebrated account of a meeting between Bishop Polycarp of Smyrna and Marcion: "Do you recognize me?" asked Marcion. Polycarp replied, "I recognize you as the first-born of Satan." Cf. also Irenaeus, *op. cit.* 3.40.2; Origen, *De princ.* 2.4.5; *Comm. in Ioann.* 1.14; *In Ierem.* hom. 9.1; and the excellent summary and literature by Quasten, *op. cit.* 1.268–72.

[615] Cf. *De princ.* praef. 5; 1.8.3; 3.13 f.; 3.6.7.

[616] Num. 11.4–6, 10, 18–20.

[617] There is here and in what follows an unmistakable instance of Origen's teaching of metempsychosis-apocatastasis of the human soul (see above, Intro. 6 f., and nn. 454, 505, 529). Man's free will makes it possible for him to oppose God and to sin, to repent and to return to Him. When he has departed from this life, his soul may relapse and reform again and again, until after a succession or cycle of existences, extending perhaps over many centuries or aeons, it finally conforms completely and eternally to God's will and plan of salvation. The condemnation of this doctrine by the Fifth Oecumenical Council of Constantinople (553) has already been referred to in the Introduction. Cf. Daniélou, *op. cit.* ch. 5: "Eschatologie."

[618] Rom. 1.23 f.

[619] *Ibid.* 1.27.

[620] Cf. Isa. 4.4; Mal. 3.2; 1 Cor. 3.13. For the φρόνιμον πῦρ see also Clement of Alexandria, *Protr.* 53.3; *Paed.* 3.8.44.2; *Strom.* 7.6.34.4; *Eclog.* 25.4; Origen, *In Ezech.* hom. 1.3; Minucius Felix, *Oct.* 35.3. These passages are studied for Clement's and Origen's teaching on purgatory by G. Anrich, "Klemens und Origenes als Begründer der Lehre vom Fegfeuer," *Theologische Abhandlungen: Festgabe für H. J. Holtzmann* (Tübingen 1902) 95–120; T. Spacil, "La dottrina del purgatorio in Clemente Alessandrino ed in Origene," *Bessarione* (1919) 131–45.

[621] Cf. Matt. 5.25 f.

[622] Cf. Isa. 6.10.

[623] *Ibid.* 4.4 (Sept.).
[624] Mal. 3.2 (Sept.).
[625] Rom. 1.28.
[626] Exod. 9.27.
[627] Prov. 1.17 (Sept.).
[628] Ps. 65.11.
[629] Cf. Matt. 10.29; Luke 12.6.
[630] Rom. 1.24, 26, 28.
[631] Deut. 8.2.
[632] Job 40.8 (Sept.).
[633] Deut. 8.3, 15, 2 (Sept.).
[634] Gen. 3.1–6.
[635] *Ibid.* 4.8.
[636] Acts 15.8.
[637] Gen. 4.5.
[638] *Ibid.* 9.20 f.
[639] Cf. *ibid.* 27.41.
[640] Cf. Heb. 12.15 f.; Deut. 29.17 (18).
[641] Cf. Gen. 39.7 ff.
[642] Rom. 8.28.
[643] Cf. above, n. 92.

[644] For the question of the precise force of ἀπό and the gender of τοῦ πονηροῦ, cf. Chase, *op. cit.* 77–167.

[645] Ps. 33.20 (Sept.).

[646] 2 Cor. 4.8. In the following Origen's distinction between being "afflicted" and "distressed" concerns the verbs θλίβεσθαι and στενοχωρεῖσθαι: for the meaning of the former, also with attention to the considerable range of concepts in Hebrew which it renders, cf. H. Schlier, TWNT 3 (1938) s. v. 139–48.

[647] Ps. 4.2.

[648] Job 1.9–11. Note "curse": literally, "bless," used here as elsewhere in the prologue to the book of Job (see also Ps. 10.3) euphemistically: cf. H. W. Beyer, TWNT 2 (1935) s. v. εὐλογεῖν, B 6–p. 756.

[649] *Ibid.* 2.9 f.
[650] *Ibid.* 2.4 f.
[651] *Ibid.* 2.10.
[652] Matt. 4.1–11; Mark 1.12 f.; Luke 4.1–13.
[653] Cf. 2 Cor. 6.9; Eph. 6.16.
[654] Osee 7.6.
[655] Eph. 6.16.

[656] John 4.14; 7.38.

[657] 1 Cor. 2.13, 15; 14.37; Gal. 6.1. At the conclusion of Origen's disquisition on The Lord's Prayer it may be observed that he makes no reference to the use of a doxology such as *For Thine is the kingdom, the power and the glory for ever,* found in some versions of St. Matthew's text; cf. Chase, *op. cit.* 168 ff.

[658] Cf. Chapters 2 and 9.

[659] 1 Tim. 2.8.

[660] *Loc. cit.*

[661] Ps. 140.2.

[662] 1 Tim. 2.8.

[663] Wisd. 16.28. *Prevent the sun . . .,* that is, "bless Thee before sunrise." Prayer should be made facing the East—see below, ch. 32.

[664] Cf. Matt. 6.14 f.; Mark 11.25.

[665] Such posture of the body during prayer is well-known from classical antiquity—cf., for example, Homer, *Il.* 8.346 f.; Aristotle, *De mundo* 6. Patristic testimonies for standing as the normal position taken by the early Christians during prayer, are very numerous: cf. *Apost. Const.* 2.57.14; Tertullian, *Apol.* 30; Cyprian, *De dom. orat.* 31 (quando autem *stamus ad orationem . . .*); etc. See J. C. Plumpe, ACW 5.198 n. 29. For illustration, Daniélou, *op. cit.* 44, aptly refers to the *Orantes* represented in the paintings of the Catacombs.

[666] Eph. 3.14 f. Tertullian, who, as is suggested by Daniélou, *op. cit.* 45, may have been used as a source by Origen, also mentions (*De or.* 23) kneeling as a posture to be taken during penitential prayer, for example, on days of fasting. He further recommends it for prayers of adoration such as the morning prayer. Adoration on bent knees is also included by Origen in the Scripture texts quoted by him at the close of the present paragraph. Tertullian, *loc. cit.,* indicates further that kneeling at prayer was not practised on Sundays and during the Paschal season—a practice still adhered to in the recitation of the Angelus and the *Regina Caeli.* Cf. H. Leclercq, "Genuflection," DACL 6.1 (1924) 1017–21.

[667] Phil. 2.10.

[668] Cf. Plato, *Tim.* 33B; Aristotle, *Analyt. post.* 1.13.

[669] Cf. Galenus, *De anat. admin.* 6.9.

[670] Phil. 2.10.

[671] Isa. 45.24.

[672] Mal. 1.11 and 1 Tim. 2.8.

[673] Cf. Matt. 6.6.—In the present section Daniélou, *op. cit.* 45, sees evidence of the existence in the time of Origen of oratories in private homes. There is early witness of a Christian Hipparchus saying prayers seven times daily before an image of the Cross painted on the east wall (cf. below, n. 685) of a room in his house: see E. Peterson, "La croce e la preghiera verso l'oriente," *Ephem. liturg.* 59 (1945) 52 ff.—quoted by Daniélou, *op. cit.* 43.

[674] Cf. 1 Cor. 7.6, 5.

[675] Ps. 33.8.

[676] Gen. 48.16.

[677] On men's guardian angels see above, 6.4 and 28.3, with nn. 101 and 543. On Origen's teaching of the communion of saints cf. Lieske, *op. cit.* 33, 35 f., 41, 79, 84 f., 211, *passim.*

[678] Tob. 12.12.

[679] 1 Cor. 1.10; 5.4.

[680] *Ibid.*

[681] Isa. 1.12, 15.

[682] Ps. 25.4 f.

[683] Cf. Luke 8.18.

[684] Cf. Matt. 21.18 f.; Mark 11.13 f., 20 f.

[685] The practice of orientation, of facing the east during worship and prayer, was quite common among the ancients—the Egyptians, Persians (cf. Tertullian, *Apol.* 16.11), and others. Among many passages attesting the practice among the early Christians, see also Clement of Alexandria, *Strom.* 7.7.43–46; Origen, *In Num.* hom. 5.1; Tertullian, *Ad nat.* 1.13; Basil, *De Spir. Sancto* 27.66; Augustine, *De serm. Dom. in monte* 2.5.18; etc. "Ancient Christianity retained the custom of facing the east during prayer, but gave a new, Christian significance to the practice. The terrestrial Paradise lay to the east (Gen. 2.8: κατ' ἀνατολάς) and the celestial Paradise of the blessed was believed to be in the east since Christ's Ascension had taken place 'to the east' (Ps. 67.34); so, too, the final 'coming of the Son of man' was placed in the east (cf. Matt. 24.27)" (Plumpe, ACW 5.198 n. 29). On the subject see the monumental work by F. J. Dölger, *Sol Salutis: Gebet und Gesang im christlichen Altertum, mit besonderer Rücksicht auf die Ostung in Gebet und Liturgie* (Liturgiegesch. Forsch. 5.5, 2. ed., Münster i. W. 1925); E. Peterson, *art. cit.* 52 ff.; Daniélou, *op. cit.* 42 f.; H. Leclercq, "Orientation," DACL 12.2 (1936) 2665–69; etc.

686 Cf. John 1.9.

687 In ch. 31.1 Origen promised to treat here also of "the time most suitable and desirable for prayer." He does not do so. He has actually dealt with the matter earlier (12.2).

688 These four essential parts (τόποι) are: δοξολογία (praise, glorification of God), εὐχαριστία (thanksgiving), ἐξομολόγησις (confession of sin), and αἴτησις (petition).

689 Ps. 103.1–7 (Sept.).

690 2 Kings 7.18–22.

691 Ps. 38.9.

692 Ibid. 37.6 f.

693 Ibid. 27.3.

694 Rom. 16.27; cf. Heb. 13.21; Gal. 1.5; 2 Tim. 4.18.

695 Phil. 3.13.

EXHORTATION TO MARTYRDOM

[1] For the title see the Intro. 10 f. and nn. 33–36.

[2] Cf. Isa. 28.9–11 (Sept.). As quoted, these verses, serving as a caption or motto, are difficult to correlate: in the first part Origen apparently took together the end of v. 9 (note the pl. participle) and the beginning of v. 9 (note the sing. imperative) which are really parts of separate sentences. Of v. 11 only the initial phrases are given. The device serves to offer certain catchwords as it were of thoughts with which he introduces his treatise.—For θλῖψις, "tribulation," see n. 646 to the preceding treatise.

[3] For the addressees see nn. 3 and 32 to the Intro.

[4] Cf. 1 Cor. 3.1 and Luke 2.52. We are reminded here of Philo's division of men into two classes, the non-moral (including the carnal) and the moral. The moral are again subdivided into the babes (infants) and the perfect (advanced). Cf. Philo, *De migr. Abr.* 1.440–46; Bigg, *op. cit.* 46 n. 3.

[5] Heb. 5.12.

[6] ἀθληταί, an early Christian term made popular by St. Paul (1 Cor. 2.24, Eph. 6.12, Phil. 3.14, etc.), to describe the life of struggle and trial required of a Christian who wishes to gain heaven. For its favoured application to martyrs see e.g. St. Basil's panegyrics on the martyrs, *passim.* Cf. the articles ἀγών, etc., and ἀθλέω, etc., by E. Stauffer, in TWNT 1 (1930) 135–40 and 166 f.; also E. L. Hummel, *The Concept of Martyrdom according to St. Cyprian of Carthage* (SCA 9, Washington 1946) 79–87; further literature by R. T. Meyer, ACW 10.121 n. 179.

[7] Rom. 8.18.

[8] Cf. 2 Cor. 4.17 (Knox).

[9] Cf. 2 Tim. 2.5 ("struggled" =ἀθλήσασι—see above, n. 6).

[10] Cf. 2 Cor. 4.7; Matt. 22.37.

[11] Phil. 3.21.

[12] Rom. 7.24.

[13] 2 Cor. 5.4.

[14] Wisd. 9.15.

[15] Rom. 7.25.

[16] Cf. Ps. 41.3, 2, 3, 4, 5, 6, 5 (Sept.).

17 The persecution of Maximin Thrax who became Emperor in 235 A.D. Eusebius, *H.E.* 6.28, tells us that it was aimed at the heads of the Church.

18 Cf. Matt. 5.10–12 and Luke 6.23.

19 Acts 5.41.

20 ὁ ἐν ἡμῖν Χριστοῦ νοῦς.

21 Ps. 41.6 (Sept.).

22 Cf. Phil. 4.7.

23 Cf. 2 Cor. 5.8.

24 Ps. 41.7.

25 Isa. 51.7.

26 Cf. *ibid.* 6.10; Matt. 13.15; Acts 28.27.

27 Gen. 12.1.

28 Cf. Deut. 32.9; Col. 1.12.

29 Cf. Rom. 8.6; 1 Peter 2.9.

30 Polytheism tended in practice to become atheism; cf. *Mart. Polycarpi* 9.

31 Exod. 20.3.

32 *Ibid.* 23.13.

33 Rom. 10.10.

34 Cf. Isa. 29.13; Matt. 15.8. In a time of persecution oral profession of Christianity was obviously a very important test of sincerity in belief.

35 Exod. 20.4.

36 *Ibid.* 20.5: οὐ προσκυνήσεις (bow down, make obeisance) αὐτοῖς καὶ τοῦ· οὐδὲ μὴ λατρεύσῃς (worship) αὐτοῖς. Origen does not mean to imply that προσκύνησις might be offered to idols, but not λατρεία. In point of fact προσκύνησις can only figuratively, according to him, be offered even to Christ; cf. *Prayer* 15.3 and n. 253. Hence, bowing down before idols through the cowardice of accommodation cannot be excused, no matter what reservations one may make in the interior of one's soul.

37 Num. 25.1.

38 *Ibid.* 25.2 f.

39 Cf. Exod. 32.8.

40 Deut. 13.3 (Sept.).

41 Exod. 20.3.

42 Deut. 13.4.

43 Cf. Col. 2.19.

44 A conflation of Matt. 12.36, Exod. 20.5, and Prov. 15.26.

45 For the cult of the Latin *Fortuna* and the Greek *Tyche*, cf.

OCD s. vv. Fortuna was the special guide and protectress of the Roman emperors: cf. W. F. Otto, in RE 17 (1912) 36 ff. and 1164 ff. A very interesting account of the important discovery made at the great temple of *Fortuna* at Praeneste since the bombing of the site in June 1944 is given in the London *Times* of March 28th, 1951. Cf. F. Fasolo—G. Gullini, *Il Santuario della Fortuna Primigenia a Palestrina* (Rome 1953). Even a casual reading of Caesar's *Civil War* will convince one of the outstanding significance of that great, but much underrated, cult in Republican and Imperial Rome. When Christians were asked to take an oath by the *Fortune* of the Emperor (cf., e.g., *Mart. Polycarpi* 8.2, 10.6), they were faced with a very searching test. Cf. Origen, *C. Cels.* 8.65.

[46] Matt. 5.34.

[47] Cf. *ibid.* 5.34 f.; Isa. 66.1.

[48] Matt. 5.35; cf. Ps. 47.3.

[49] Cf. Matt. 5.36.

[50] *Ibid.* 12.36.

[51] Deut. 17.3.

[52] Cf. Rom. 1.25.

[53] Cf. Deut. 32.9; Col. 1.12.

[54] Mark 10.18; cf. Luke 18.19; Matt. 19.17.

[55] Matt. 4.10; Luke 4.8; cf. Deut. 6.13, 10.20.

[56] Rom. 8.20 f.; cf. n. 116 on *Prayer*. From this personification of, and remonstration by, the sun, it suggests itself that Origen regarded it as a living, rational being. That such was his thought on the sun, moon, and stars, is demonstrated particularly in his *De principiis* (1.7; cf. *C. Cels.* 5.10 f.); cf. Daniélou, *op. cit.* 216; also the old, but still invaluable, biography of Origen by E. R. Redepenning, *Origenes. Eine Darstellung seines Lebens und seiner Lehre* (Bonn 1846) 2.349, 355, 448. It may also be said that the Christian scholars of Alexandria, among them Origen, for that reason were more tolerant of the pagan sun worship than of idolatry concerned with inanimate objects.

[57] Cf. Deut. 18.20, 22.

[58] Cf. 1 Cor. 12.8.

[59] Ps. 37.14 f.

[60] Exod. 20.5.

[61] Col. 1.15. For Origen's concept of the soul as the bride of the Λόγος Christ, see especially his *Commentary on the Canticle*

of Canticles, passim. Cf. Lieske, *op. cit.* 61 ff., 147 ff.; Quasten, *Patrology* 2.98–100.

[62] Deut. 32.21 f. (Sept.). With the ancient Christian authors "fornication" is the classical term for sins against the faith—apostasy and heresy. Such sins are harlotry and attack the virginity of Christ's bride, the soul, or, more often, the Church. For Origen, cf. Bettencourt, *op. cit.* 105; also S. Tromp, "Ecclesia Sponsa Virgo Mater," *Gregorianum* 18 (1937) 20; J. C. Plumpe, *Mater Ecclesia* (SCA 5, Washington 1943) 25 ff., 40, 82, etc.

[63] 1 Cor. 6.16.

[64] Matt. 10.32.

[65] Luke 6.38; Matt. 7.2; Mark 4.24.

[66] Luke 6.38.

[67] Cf. Eph. 4.27.

[68] Cf. John 3.16; Heb. 3.14.

[69] Cf. 1 Cor. 3.12.

[70] Matt. 16.24 f.

[71] Luke 9.23–25.

[72] Mark 8.34–37.

[73] Cf. Gal. 2.20.

[74] *Loc. cit.*

[75] Cf. Gen. 1.27.

[76] Cf. 1 Peter 1.19.

[77] Isa. 43.3 f. (Sept.).

[78] Cf. 1 Cor. 13.12.

[79] 2 Cor. 12.2, 4.

[80] Cf. Matt. 16.24; Mark 8.34; Luke 9.23.

[81] Heb. 4.14.

[82] Cf. Ps. 103.4; Heb. 1.7; cf. above, n. 56.

[83] Rom. 8.21.

[84] Matt. 19.27–29.

[85] Mark 10.30.

[86] Eph. 3.15.

[87] Gen. 15.15.

[88] 1 Cor. 12.31.

[89] Heb. 4.12.

[90] Prov. 23.5 (Sept.).

[91] Cf. Rom. 8.39.

[92] Matt. 22.30; Mark 12.25.

[93] Jos. 24.14.

[94] *Loc. cit.*

[95] In the following section Origen is obviously recollecting his experience at the celebrated catechetical school at Alexandria; cf. Daniélou, *op. cit.* 25–28, 66–68. On catechesis and catechumenate, see J. P. Christopher, ACW 2.93 f. nn. 4, 7.

[96] Jos. 24.15 (Sept.).

[97] *Loc. cit.*

[98] *Ibid.* 24.16 f. (Sept.).

[99] *Ibid.* 24.18. Regarding the interrogation of the candidate for baptism on his motives for wishing to become a Christian, see the *Traditio apostolica* (ca. 220 A.D.) 40—available in T. Schermann, *Die allgemeine Kirchenordnung des zweiten Jahrhunderts* (Paderborn 1914) 54 f.

[100] The reception of baptism was prefaced by a renunciation of Satan. In performing this solemn act, the catechumen faced the west, the region of the devil and his cohorts of evil angels. He then turned toward the east, the land of salvation (cf. above, n. 685 to *Prayer*), to be baptized. For a clear illustration of this rite, cf. St. Ambrose, *De myst.* 2.7.

[101] 1 Kings 2.25.

[102] 1 Cor. 4.9.

[103] Cf. Deut. 32.9; Col. 1.12.

[104] A conflation of Ps. 97.8 and Isa. 55.12 (Sept.).

[105] Isa. 14.9 f. (Sept.).

[106] *Ibid.* 14.10 (Sept.).

[107] *Ibid.* 14.11 (Sept.).

[108] Cf. *ibid.* 14.12 and Matt. 5.16.

[109] Isa. 14.12 (Sept.).

[110] *Ibid.* 14.19 f. (Sept.).

[111] Matt. 10.37.

[112] 3 Kings 18.21.

[113] Cf. Ps. 21.8; 43.14 f.; Matt. 27.39.

[114] Ps. 43.14–17.

[115] *Ibid.* 43.18 f.

[116] *Ibid.* 43.19.

[117] *Ibid.* 43.20.

[118] *Ibid.* 43.21 f.

[119] 2 Cor. 1.12.

[120] Ps. 43.22.

[121] *Ibid.* 43.23; Rom. 8.36.

[122] Cf. Rom. 8.6 f.

[123] Prov. 7.1 (Sept.).

[124] Eccles. 4.2 (Sept.).

[125] G. Bardy, *Origène: De la prière: Exhortation au martyre*, 234 n. (a), points out that the stories of Eleazar and the Machabees became one of the stock themes of hagiography, used, for example, by St. John Chrysostom, St. Gregory Nazianzen, St. Ambrose, and St. Augustine. Cf. Intro. 12.

[126] 2 Mac. 6.19 (Sept.).

[127] *Ibid.* 6.23–28 (Sept.).

[128] *Ibid.* 6.30 (Sept.).

[129] *Ibid.* 6.31 (Sept.).

[130] *Ibid.* 7.1 ff. (Sept.).

[131] *Ibid.* 7.1.

[132] *Ibid.* 7.2.

[133] *Ibid.* 7.3.

[134] Cf. Col. 1.25.

[135] 2 Mac. 7.3 f.

[136] *Ibid.* 7.5.

[137] Cf. above, n. 6.

[138] 2 Mac. 7.5.

[139] *Ibid.* 7.6.

[140] *Loc. cit.*

[141] Wisd. 3.6; cf. Prov. 17.3.

[142] 2 Mac. 7.7.

[143] *Loc. cit.*

[144] *Loc. cit.*

[145] *Ibid.* 7.9.

[146] *Ibid.* 7.10 f.

[147] *Ibid.* 7.14.

[148] *Ibid.* 7.15–17.

[149] *Ibid.* 7.18 f.

[150] Cf. 2 Peter 1.4; Acts 5.39.

[151] 2 Mac. 7.24–35 (Sept.).

[152] *Ibid.* 7.20.

[153] Ps. 117.14.

[154] A conflation of Phil. 4.13 and 1 Tim. 1.12.

[155] παρρησία: in classical Greek the word denotes "freedom of speech," which goes with political freedom. In the spiritual domain, Adam and Eve had παρρησία before their fall, the Apostles had it when they preached the Gospel, and so, too, the Christians if they lived the message of the Gospel. It was also a very special prerogative of the martyrs—cf. the informative note by H. C. Graef, ACW 18.183 n. 26.

[156] Ps. 115.12, 13. Cf. Origen, *Comm. in Matt.* 16.6.

[157] Matt. 20.22; Mark 10.38.

[158] Matt. 26.39; cf. Mark 14.36.

[159] Here Origen is repeating the then accepted view that martyrs were not judged by God, but rather sat in judgment with Him; cf. Hippolytus, *In Dan.* 2.37; Tertullian, *De res. carn.* 43; Cyprian, *Ad Fort.* 13; Eusebius, *H. E.* 6.42.5 (quoting Dionysius of Alexandria); etc. Cf. J. P. Kirsch, *The Doctrine of the Communion of Saints in the Ancient Church* (London 1910) 82.

[160] Joel 2.32; cf. Acts 2.21; Rom. 10.13.

[161] Matt. 26.39.

[162] Ps. 26.1–3.

[163] Matt. 26.39.

[164] Ps. 26.3.

[165] Matt. 26.39.

[166] Luke 22.42.

[167] Mark 14.36.

[168] Cf. above, n. 104 on *Prayer*.

[169] Ps. 115.4 (13).

[170] *Ibid.* 115.6 (15).

[171] οὐκ ἔστιν ἄφεσιν ἁμαρτημάτων χωρὶς βαπτίσματος λαβεῖν: cf. Acts 2.38. The teaching here is that the blood baptism of martyrs obtains remission for the sins of others, in the same way as the death of the Saviour purified all; cf. n. 568 on *Prayer*.

[172] Cf. Matt. 3.11; Mark 1.8; Luke 3.16; John 1.33.

[173] Also called "baptism of blood" or "second baptism." It is the one exception to the prescript of baptism with water: see *Pass. SS. Perp. et Fel.* 18.3, 21.2; Tertullian, *De bapt.* 16. It is richer in graces conferred and is administered by the angels: see Cyprian of Carthage, *Ep.* 55.17, 20; 58.3; 73; *De unit. eccl.* 14; *Exh. mart.* 58.3; etc. Cf. J. E. Sherman, *The Nature of Martyrdom* (Paterson, N. J., 1942) 42 f.; E. Hummel, *The Concept of Martyrdom according to St. Cyprian of Carthage* (SCA 9, Washington 1946) 108–166; Quasten, *op. cit.* 1.182; 2.71, 279, 379.

[174] Mark 10.38.

[175] *Loc. cit.*

[176] Luke 12.50. Cf. Cyprian, *Ep.* 73.

[177] Cf. Lev. 16.3 ff.; Ps. 49.13; Heb. 9.13, 10.4.

[178] Apoc. 20.4; cf. 6.9.

[179] 1 Cor. 9.13.

[180] Cf. Heb. 5.1, 7.27, 8.3, 10.12.

[181] Lev. 21.17–21.

¹⁸² Cf. Heb. 9.14, 7.26.
¹⁸³ Cf. § 11.
¹⁸⁴ Cf. Matt. 7.14.
¹⁸⁵ Cant. 2.10 f. (Sept.).
¹⁸⁶ Ps. 91.14.
¹⁸⁷ Matt. 4.9.
¹⁸⁸ Cf. 1 Par. 16.26; Ps. 95.5; 1 Cor. 10.20. See below, n. 300.
¹⁸⁹ Cf. Matt. 11.30. The wordplay τὸν χρηστὸν Χριστοῦ ζυγόν defies translation.
¹⁹⁰ Wisd. 15.10.
¹⁹¹ A conflation of Jer. 16.19 and 14.22 (Sept.).
¹⁹² Cf. Dan. 3.1 ff. and 3.14 ff.
¹⁹³ "of the world to come," περατικοῖς—lit., "coming from abroad," "foreign"; cf. Heb. 11.13 ff.
¹⁹⁴ Cf. Dan. 3.50; Esth. 3.1–5.
¹⁹⁵ Cf. Dan. 14.2 ff.
¹⁹⁶ Job 31.27 f. (Sept.). To place one's hand upon one's mouth and kiss it meant to deny God: cf. 3 Kings 19.8, where this act indicates worship of Baal.
¹⁹⁷ Matt. 10.5, 17–23.
¹⁹⁸ Luke 12.11 f.
¹⁹⁹ *Ibid.* 21.14–19.
²⁰⁰ Mark 13.11 ff.
²⁰¹ Matt. 10.28.
²⁰² *Ibid.* 10.29–33.
²⁰³ Luke 12.4–9.
²⁰⁴ *Ibid.* 9.26.
²⁰⁵ Mark 8.38.
²⁰⁶ Matt. 10.28; Luke 12.4.
²⁰⁷ Cf. Luke 12.4.
²⁰⁸ Isa. 43.10 (Sept.).
²⁰⁹ Luke 12.4.
²¹⁰ Matt. 10.28.
²¹¹ Luke 12.5.
²¹² Matt. 10.28.
²¹³ Luke 12.5.
²¹⁴ Matt. 10.30; "of another," that is, than the Apostles.
²¹⁵ Rom. 8.18.
²¹⁶ Matt. 10.33.
²¹⁷ *Ibid.* 10.32.
²¹⁸ Luke 12.8.
²¹⁹ Col. 1.15; cf. 2 Cor. 4.4.

[220] Rom. 1.3.
[221] Cf. John 5.27; Matt. 1.20.
[222] Col. 1.15.
[223] 2 Cor. 10.18.
[224] Wisd. 3.6.
[225] Cf. Dan. 3.6; Matt. 13.42, 50.
[226] Cf. Matt. 10.38, 16.24; Mark 8.34; Luke 9.23.
[227] Luke 21.15.
[228] Col. 1.24.
[229] Gen. 3.24.
[230] 1 Cor. 3.11 f.
[231] Gen. 2.8 f.
[232] Luke 10.19.
[233] Matt. 10.33.
[234] Luke 9.26.
[235] Mark 8.38.
[236] Cf. Heb. 12.2.
[237] Cf. *ibid.* 8.1.
[238] Cf. 2 Tim. 2.12.
[239] Cf. Matt. 10.34.
[240] Heb. 4.12.
[241] Phil. 4.7.
[242] Cf. John 14.27.
[243] Cf. 1 Cor. 15.49.
[244] Cf. Matt. 10.34; Luke 12.49.
[245] Cf. Luke 12.50.
[246] *Ibid.* 14.26.
[247] *Loc. cit.*
[248] John 12.25.
[249] Ps. 78.11.
[250] Cf. Rom. 9.8.
[251] John 8.37.
[252] *Ibid.* 8.39.
[253] Matt. 10.37.
[254] *Ibid.* 10.39.
[255] *Ibid.* 10.20 f.
[256] Cf. John 15.19.
[257] Matt. 10.22.
[258] 1 Peter 1.6 f.
[259] Gen. 3.16.
[260] 1 John 2.15–17.
[261] Cf. John 17.21 f.

[262] Cf. 1 John 2.15.
[263] Cf. Matt. 16.26; Mark 8.36; Luke 9.25.
[264] Cf. Ps. 37.5.
[265] Cf. Apoc. 6.9.
[266] Cf. below, n. 300.
[267] Cf. above, n. 45.
[268] Isa. 65.11–15.
[269] 1 Cor. 10.21.
[270] Matt. 26.29.
[271] 1 Cor. 10.21.
[272] Mark 3.17.
[273] Cf. 1 John 2.22 f., where the first relative clause is preceded by *This is Antichrist*. Origen quotes the same text in the same manner in *Comm. in Ioann.* 19.1.
[274] John 5.24.
[275] Cf. *ibid.* 15.18.
[276] Cf. 1 Peter 2.5 (Eph. 2.20–22) and John 8.12.
[277] 1 John 3.16.
[278] Rom. 5.3–5.
[279] *Ibid.* 5.5.
[280] 1 Cor. 15.32.
[281] Maximin was proclaimed emperor at Mainz in 235 A.D. He remained in Germany till winter of that year, and doubtless the trial of some Christians was referred to him there. A. Harnack, *Geschichte der altchristlichen Literatur*, 2: *Die Chronologie* (Leipzig 1904) 56, thought that a copyist's error is involved.
[282] 2 Cor. 1.5.
[283] Cf. Matt. 5.5.
[284] 2 Cor. 1.7.
[285] Isa. 49.8; 2 Cor. 6.2.
[286] Cf. Col. 2.15.
[287] 2 Cor. 6.3 f. The "priesthood" is mentioned with reference to Protoctetus; the "diaconate," referring to Ambrose. Regarding the latter office, Origen quite strikingly—and certainly permissibly—quotes the passage from Second Corinthians, where St. Paul uses the term διαχονία in its original sense of "service," "ministry."
[288] Ps. 38.8. Here, by adding the interrogation from Psalms, ". . . *what is my hope* (ὑπομονή)?" the author is able to take up with good effect the concluding word of the text quoted from St.

Paul, *"patience"* (ὑπομονή). It is quite impossible to render with a single noun in English the Greek word which can signify "patient waiting," "patience" and also the motive of such "waiting" —"expectation," "hope," etc.

[289] Continuing 2 Cor. 6.4.

[290] Ps. 33.20.

[291] Again continuing 2 Cor. 6.4.

[292] Continuing the same.

[293] Cf. Matt. 7.14.

[294] 2 Cor. 6.5.

[295] Cf. Isa. 40.10, 62.11; Ps. 61.13; Prov. 24.12; Apoc. 2.23, 22.12. See also Clement of Rome, *Cor.* 34.3; Clement of Alexandria, *Strom.* 4.22. 135.3.

[296] In this section Origen continues his "exhortation" on the basis of key words taken from the 6th chapter of 2 Corinthians (6–10).

[297] Cf. Prov. 14.29.

[298] Heb. 10.32–36.

[299] Cf. 2 Cor. 4.18.

[300] Here we are given some of Origen's views about demons; cf. also *C. Cels.* 7.5. The term "demon" (δαίμων, δαιμόνιον) is used from the time of Plato onwards to indicate beings intermediate between gods and men. In the Bible it stands for a fallen angel or unclean spirit. Origen evidently shared with many of his contemporaries the idea that these demons were maintained in the world by the sacrifices offered to them by their devotees. Cf. Bettencourt, *op. cit.*, index s. v. "daemones"; G. Bardy, 'Origène et la magie,' *Rech. de sc. rel.* 18 (1928) 129–131; Daniélou, *op. cit.* 219 ff.; E. Schneweis, *Angels and Demons according to Lactantius* (SCA 3, Washington 1944); M. P. Nilsson, *Geschichte der griechischen Religion* (Munich 1941) 201–206; E. Mangenot, 'Démon,' *DTC* 4.1 (1911) 321–409; W. Foerster, "δαίμων," *TWNT* 2 (1935) 1–21. See also nn. 101 and 433 to *Prayer*.

[301] The term was applied at various times to the Persian and Parthian kings, to Alexander the Great, and the Roman emperors. For Christ as the Great King, cf. Origen, *C. Cels.* 8.76.

[302] Exod. 22.20.

[303] The discussion as to whether names and things are naturally (φύσει) or only conventionally (θέσει) connected was famous in antiquity. The Stoics, for example, held the former, the Peripatetics, the latter view. Cf. Cicero, *Tusc. Disp.* 1.62, ed. T. W.

Dougan (Cambridge 1905) 78 f.   For Origen's view cf. Bardy, *art. cit.* 133 ff.

[304] The form Zēn for the sky-god, Zeus, is frequently found in Greek tragedy; cf. Liddell-Scott-Jones s. v.

[305] Moses—cf. Num. 12.7; Heb. 3.5.   See also Origen, *C. Cels.* 2.53, 7.41; *In Ierem.* hom. 12.12; *Comm. in Ioann.* fr. 70; also Clement of Alexandria, *Paed.* 1.70.60.1; etc.

[306] Exod. 3.15.

[307] Cf. Matt. 5.17; Rom. 10.4.

[308] Wisd. 9.15.

[309] Cf. Wisd. 4.7; Matt. 11.29.

[310] Cf. Eph. 3.10 f.

[311] Cf. John 1.9; 1 John 2.8; 2 Cor. 4.6.

[312] Cf. Ps. 18.9; Eph. 1.18.

[313] For this and what follows cf. Matt. 7.24–27; Luke 6.48 f.

[314] Cf. Eph. 6.12.

[315] τὰ ἐνεργοῦντα: for ἐνεργέω as a verb used in the New Testament to designate the workings of both divine and demoniac "energy," cf. K. W. Clark, "The meaning of ἐνεργέω and κατεργέω in the NT," *Jour. of Bibl. Stud.* 54 (1935) 95–101; G. Bertram, TWNT 2 (1935) s. v. 649–51.

[316] 1 Cor. 9.26.

[317] For this section cf. Matt. 13.3 ff.; Mark 4.3 ff.; Luke 8.5 ff.

[318] Cf. Jer. 9.23 f.; 1 Cor. 1.31; 2 Cor. 10.17.

[319] Cf. Matt. 13.21.

[320] *Ibid.* 13.20 f.

[321] Mark 4.16 f.

[322] Luke 8.13.

[323] Matt. 13.23.

[324] Mark 4.20.

[325] Luke 8.15.

[326] 1 Cor. 3.9.

[327] Cf. Matt. 13.22; Mark 4.19; Luke 8.14.

[328] Cf. Eph. 1.17; Isa. 11.2; Wisd. 7.7.

[329] Cf. Gen. 3.23.

[330] 2 Cor. 4.17 f.

[331] Gen. 4.10.

[332] Cf. 1 Peter 1.19; Apoc. 5.9.

[333] Cf. Phil. 2.9.

[334] John 12.32.

[335] *Ibid.* 21.19—words addressed by Our Lord to St. Peter.

[336] Cf. Phil. 4.7.

INDEX

INDEX

Aaron, 22 f.

Abba, Father, 19, 74, 170, 214

Abel, 126, 195

Abraham, 81, 100, 114, 144, 155, 181, 189

Abram, 81

"accommodation," pretending to worship, 146, 230

actor(s), 70, 108

Acts of the Apostles, 25, 47, 114; of the Martyrs, 12

Adam, 78 f., 234

Adonai, 189

adoption of sons, the Father's, 29, 42, 59 f., 73 f.

adultery, 112

Adversary, 27, 42, 49 f., 101, 127 f. See devil

Advocate, Christ, 59

affliction, 127

αἴτησις, petition, 228

Alexander the Great, 239

Alexandria, 3, 5, 199, 231, 233

Aman, 49, 62, 173

Ambrose, St., 9, 234
    De myst. 2.7: 233

Ambrose, friend and patron of Origen, 4, 8, 10, 16, 139, 141, 154, 179, 181, 200, 205, 238

Ammon, 26

Ammonite(s), 69, 102

Amon, 34

Amorrhite(s), 56, 157

Ananias, 49, 62, 173

Anathema, 74 f.

angel(s), 34, 43 f., 59, 64, 80, 90, 99 f., 108, 134 f., 138, 152, 154, 157 f., 176 ff., 180, 205; nourished on the wisdom of God, 99; pray with us, 43, 45

f.; guardian, 34, 134 f., 205, 227

Anna, 21, 25 f., 48, 51, 55, 61

Anrich, G., 224

Antiochus, 163–166

apocatastasis, ἀποκατάστασις, 6, 218, 220 f., 224

Apollo, 189

apostasy, 12, 146 ff., 159, 179, 192; attacks virginity of Christ's bride, 232

Apostle(s), 35, 45, 53, 56, 73, 81, 86, 103–106, 108, 111 f., 114 f., 118, 120, 122, 132 f., 142 f., 147, 155, 160 f., 174 f., 177, 180, 189, 194; Acts of the, 25, 47, 114

Apost. Const. 2.57.14: 226

Arabia, 4 f.

archangels, 64

Aristotle, 201, 220
    Analyt. post. 1.13: 226; *De mundo* 6: 226; *De sensu* 444b.12: 204; *Hist. anim.* 614b.1: 204

Artemis, 189

atheism, atheists, 27, 145, 172, 230

Atomists, 220

Augustine, St., 7, 234
    De serm. Dom. in monte 2.5.18: 227; 2.7: 219

Azarias, 49, 55, 173

Azymes, feast of, 103

Baal, 236

Babylonians, 49

Balthasar, H. v., 211

baptism, 27, 158, 181, 200, 233, 235; necessary for remission

243

martyr(s), 35, 161, 168, 172, 177, 181, 186, 201, 234; glorify God by death, 195; reward of, 154 ff.; said to sit in judgment with God, 168, 235

martyrdom, 3 f., 11 f., 141, 151, 153–156, 158, 162 f., 168–172, 174 ff., 182, 185; foretold by the Saviour, 174; the chalice of salvation, 168 ff.; gives life to the soul, 176; death of termed "exaltation," 195; baptism of, 171; see martyr

μαρτύριον, μάρτυς, μαρτυρέω, *martyrium*, 10 f., 141, 201

Mart. Polycarpi, 11; 8.2: 231; 9: 230; 10.6: 231

Master, Christ, 92

Matthew, St., 8, 65 ff., 72, 81, 88 f., 96, 102, 111, 139, 152, 170, 175 ff., 193

Maximin Thrax, 238; persecution of, 10 f., 230

Melchisedech, 58

Mesopotamia, 22, 114

metempsychosis, 6, 224

Meyboom, H. U., 13

Meyer, R. T., 229

Migne, J. P., 199

millenium, 102

Minucius Felix, *Oct.* 35.3: 224

Misael, 49, 173

Moab(ites), 69, 102, 146

moods, imperative and optative, in translations of Scripture, 83 f.

moon, 35 f., 56, 103, 148, 154, 189; considered by Origen a rational being, 206, 231; said to have certain freedom of

will, 35 f.; God's holy new, 104

Moses, 21–24, 29, 48 f., 54, 94, 96, 101, 121, 171, 221

movement, of inanimate things, animals, rational beings, 30 ff.

mysteries, 34, 154, 195, 221; of worship, 82; of marriage, 18; mystical analogies, 63

Nabuchodonosor, 49, 62, 173

names, the importance of, 189 f.

Nathan, 138

Nazarite(s), 24, 204

Neo-Platonism, 7

Nicephorus Callistus, 10

Nilsson, M. P., 239

Ninive, 49, 52

Noe, 126

Numbers, 24, 26

Onias, 207

Only-Begotten, 90; Son, 70, 118, 151; Word, 75

Ophni, 112

orientation, at prayer, 136 f., 227

Origen, life and work, 3–7; birth, baptism, 3; occupation as teacher, 3 f.; ordination, 5; relations with Neo-Platonism, 7; helped toward definition of Church doctrine, 7; his doctrinal errors attacked and condemned, 6; desire and preparation for martyrdom, 3 f.; suffered in persecution of Decius, 6; not known to be a martyr, 5; ancient sources of information on life of, 7

Comm. in Ioann. 1.14: 224;

ANCIENT CHRISTIAN WRITERS

The Works of the Fathers in Translation

Edited by

J. QUASTEN, S. T. D., and J. C. PLUMPE, Ph. D.